KV-621-279

# CONTENTS

# CONTENTS

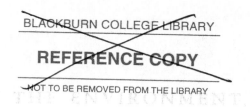
# EMPLOYMENT AND SUSTAINABLE DEVELOPMENT

In recent years the environment has become an increasingly important issue in many sectors of society, from business and industry to community and government. This volume offers an original analysis of the progress being made in a number of European countries towards sustainable development and the impact this is having on the jobs market and the career structure of those employed for their environmental skills and expertise.

It examines institutionalised environmental policies, including the impact of the European Environment Agency and European Community environmental directives, as well as global conventions and agreements on biodiversity and sustainable development. The book reviews the areas of expertise, training and education required across Europe to meet these environmental challenges and examines the resultant job opportunities in the private and public sectors.

With contributions from across Europe and wide-ranging analysis and empirical case studies, *The Environment, Employment and Sustainable Development* is an important work for students, researchers and practitioners with an interest in environmental studies, business and economics.

**Monica Hale** is Director of the London Environment Centre at London Guildhall University. She is the Vice-President of the Institute of Ecology and Environmental Management and has published widely on environmental issues. Her recent books include *Ecology in Education* (CUP, 1993) and *Environmental Education for Biodiversity and Sustainable Development*.

**Mike Lachowicz** is an Associate of the London Environment Centre. He is a freelance trainer in environmental management and an Associate Member of the Institute of Environmental Management.

# THE ENVIRONMENT,

TLEDGE

London and New York

First published 1998
by Routledge
11 New Fetter Lane, London EC4P 4EE

Simultaneously published in the USA and Canada
by Routledge
29 West 35th Street, New York, NY 10001

Typeset in Garamond by Florencetype Ltd, Stoodleigh, Devon
Printed and bound in Great Britain by
Clays Ltd, St Ives PLC

*British Library Cataloguing in Publication Data*
A catalogue record for this book is available from the British Library

*Library of Congress Cataloguing in Publication Data*
A catalogue record for this book has been requested

ISBN 0–415–18029–5 (hbk)
ISBN 0–415–18030–9 (pbk)

# CONTENTS

# FIGURES

# TABLES

# CONTRIBUTORS

**Antoni Alarcón**, Collegio Oficial de Biologos, Bailen 20 Se 1a, 08010 Barcelona, Spain

**Nora Cantini**, Academie Internationale de l'Environment, Chemin de Conches 4, 1231 Conches, Geneva, Switzerland.

**Hilary Course**, Consultant, 16 Rylston Way, Saffron Waldon, Essex, CB11 3BS, UK.

**Rita Raum Degrève**, Managing Director, Interdisciplinary Environmental Studies, EURECO, Rue St Ulric, 13–15, 2651, Luxembourg.

**Michelle Dobré** IFEN, 8 Allée, Domremy, 45560 St Denis en Val, France.

**Bernard Giovannini**, formerly Director, European Academy of the Environment, 4 Chemin de Conches, 1231 Conches, Geneva, Switzerland.

**Monica Hale**, Director, London Environment Centre, London Guildhall University, 100 Minories, London EC3N 1JY, UK.

**Hilary Hillier**, Head of Environmental Protection, Statistics Division, Department of the Environment, Room A118, Romney House, 43 Marsham Street, London SW1P 3PY, UK.

**Kay Hunt**, Department of the Environment, Room A, Romney House, 43 Marsham Street, London SW1P 3PY, UK.

**Nick Jagger**, Research Fellow, Institute for Employment Studies, Mantell Building, University of Sussex, Brighton BN1 9RF, UK.

**Thierry Lavoux**, IFEN, 8 Allée Domremy, 45560 St Denis en Val, France.

**Peter Maarleveld**, Secretary, Interdisciplinary Committee for Environmental Sciences, Association of Universities in the Netherlands, PO Box 19270, 3501 DG Utrecht, Netherlands.

**Alice McLure**, Room 634, Training, Infrastructure, Education and Employment Branch, Department of Employment, Moorfoot, Sheffield S1 4PQ, UK.

**Odile Mear-Harvey**, Consultant, 40 Avenue de Fré, 1180 Uccle, Brussels, Belgium.

**James Medhurst**, ECOTEC, Priestly House, 28–34 Albert Street, Birmingham B4 7UD, UK.

**Jørn Pedersen**, Head of European Foundation for the Improvement of Living and Working Conditions, Longlinstown House, Shankhill, Co. Dublin, Ireland.

**Steve Pullan**, Department of Marine Science and Coastal Management, Faculty of Agriculture and Biological Sciences, Ridley Building, The University, Newcastle upon Tyne NE1 7RU, UK.

**Romy Shovelton**, Wikima Consulting, 23 Leamington House Villas, London W11 1HS, UK.

**Raymond Van Ermen**, Executive Director, European Environmental Bureau, 26 rue de la Victoire, 1060 Bruxelles, Belgium.

**Eirene Williams**, Seale-Hayne College, University of Plymouth, Department of Food and Land Use, Newton Abbot, Devon TQ12 6NQ, UK.

**Karim Zein**, European Environmental Management Association, c/o General Waters, Boulevard de Grancy 39, 1006 Lausanne, Switzerland.

# FOREWORD

## The environment as a business issue

*Klaus Kohlhase*

The environment has a very high priority in BP and this is not surprising. Many of our operations, our refineries, our chemical plants, our tankers and our products have the potential to cause damaging effects on the environment.

The way we deal with environmental issues has a major impact on our performance, our reputation and our efficiency.

BP is a performance-oriented company, whose goal is continuous improvement, which applies equally to the environment as to the business. This is an obligation to all our stakeholders. Continuous improvement to the environment and to the business are closely linked.

We are applying expertise and resources to ensuring the health of the workforce, reducing the possibility of industrial accidents, minimising the impact on the environment and responding to consumer demands for green products.

BP is achieving this by fully integrating Health, Safety and Environment into the business management process and making it part of everyday business decisions.

The oil and chemicals industries have been accused of being protective and secretive industries. This may have been so in the past, but things are changing. BP is committed to an open dialogue with the public on environmental matters. For several years we have been publishing our environmental performance, our views and position in our environmental report, *New Horizons*.

BP welcomes this publication. Industry needs competent professionals to help deal with the many and ever increasing environmental issues and challenges. Professional scientists help us to understand the complexities of global climate change; professional engineers can build and operate the most efficient waste water treatment plants; and professional environmental managers can help our business management to develop the most effective environmental management systems.

In addition to developing competent environmental professionals, industry needs to educate its own business line management and raise their awareness and understanding of the importance of the environmental challenge. This is a major task which is often underestimated by industry. More attention needs to be focused on environmental awareness and the training of business management.

There is also a trend in industry where business line managers are spending part of their career as environmental managers. As much as environmental professionals have to understand the business, business managers need to become familiar with the environmental aspects. I myself spent twenty-seven years of my professional life in business line management until I became BP's Senior Health, Safety and Environmental Executive Officer four years ago.

Industry needs competent environmental professionals and business managers who have a high level of environmental understanding. Business managers can no longer delegate the environment to the professionals – they themselves are responsible and accountable for their company's environmental performance.

It is the role of industry and business to generate the wealth necessary for achieving high environmental standards. Industry is responsible for operating cleanly and efficiently to minimise environmental impacts. Government in turn must provide the legislative framework and the market context which allows industry to maintain its profitability and its international competitiveness. It is the balance which we have to strike between ecological requirements and business needs.

A key success factor during the transition to a more sustainable future will be for Europe to remain competitive. Only healthy and competitive industry will provide employment and jobs and a clean environment across the European economies.

Sustainable development is a shared responsibility and will require good and effective partnerships and co-operation between industry, governments, environmental organisations and academia.

Klause Kohlhase
Head Environmental Adviser
The British Petroleum Company, UK

# PREFACE

## Environmental employment and sustainable development

*Monica Hale*

During the late 1980s and early 1990s the number of job advertisements incorporating the word 'environment' suddenly increased. Posts ranging from environmental policy officers to environmental engineers and others with environment implicit in their name such as 'Local Agenda 21 Officers' are now commonplace.

If sustainable development, heralded at the Earth Summit in Rio de Janeiro in 1992 as the universal answer to global environmental problems, is to be realised in national and local policies and actions, then all sectors (government, business, industry, community, etc.) require appropriately qualified and experienced personnel to implement the required actions.

Over the past few years the environmental careers market has been transformed from what was often regarded as an amateur, predominantly voluntary body employment sector, to a highly professionalised area of specialist expertise. The demand for expert advice and assistance to business and industry and local and central government in environmental policy formulation, environmental management and conservation has grown rapidly. In addition, industry specific environmental expertise and knowledge are increasingly required in existing professional, industry and business areas.

The further application of statutory regulations as well as voluntary codes of practice to both the public and private sectors, in areas such as pollution control and sustainable resource management, has meant that personnel with the appropriate environmental skills are needed to find practical work-based solutions to these new environmental demands.

In addition to the new legislative requirements, the commercial logic of 'going green' has also been more widely recognised. This can result in lower costs from increased energy efficiency, recycling initiatives and careful purchasing policies. Investment in state-of-the-art environmental technology and sound management practices also result in tangible efficiency and cost benefits, as well as providing image-improving publicity.

Career opportunities have expanded as a result of the increased importance and relevance of environmental issues to all sectors of economic activity. In the late 1980s and early 1990s the demand for environmental consultants was more or less outstripping supply. It has been said that the growth in the environmental consultancy sector has proved to be a reliable barometer of environmental activities in the community as a whole.

In 1992 it was estimated that there were approaching 500,000 people employed in the environment industry in the United Kingdom and that there was evidence that this number was increasing (ENDS 1992). However, in the most recent market assessment it was found that while the demand for environmental consultants is likely to rise, this will not be at the rate forecast two years ago. At that stage, based on the steady rate of growth up to then, it was expected that the sector would be earning £1 billion by the year 2000, but now the projection has been revised downwards to about £700–850 million (ENDS 1995).

Throughout Europe the nature of environmental jobs, the potential of the environmental careers market, and the professionalisation of this area of expertise are all changing and developing. The papers in this volume are drawn from a number of European countries where experiences are similar in some respects and quite different in others. On the basis of evidence presented and commented upon in this volume we may be allowed to speculate as to what can be expected in this employment sector in the future.

There is inadequate accessible and relevant information about the environmental career opportunities available in the UK and in Europe. This is also true of environmental qualifications required to supplement and complement other business and industry qualifications. Insufficient guidance exists on whether postgraduate qualifications are necessary, and if so which ones, and whether these are recognised across Europe.

The London Environment Centre's 'Careers in the Environment' initiative which commenced in 1993 to investigate the situation in the UK has now been developed to examine and review progress, and to identify the differences in the evolution of the environmental profession across Europe. Some of the key issues concerning environmental employment and sustainable development are addressed in this volume. However, as with any investigative work of this nature, a number of questions are raised which engender further discussion and identify areas where further research and action are urgently needed.

The chapters in this book are based on the contributions made and the outcomes of discussions at the 'Careers in the Environment across Europe' conference held in London in May 1995.

# REFERENCES

Environmental Data Services Ltd (ENDS) (1992) *Environmental Consultancy in Britain: A Market Analysis*, ENDS, UK.

Environmental Data Services Ltd (ENDS) (1995) *Directory of Environmental Consultants*, fourth edition, ENDS, UK.

# ACKNOWLEDGEMENTS

Grateful thanks are expressed to the European Commission, DGV, for their support of the 'Careers in the Environment across Europe' initiative. In addition, thanks are also extended to BP Oil, Marks and Spencer plc and the National Rivers Authority, without whose support this initiative would not have been possible. The continued interest and support of these organisations is greatly appreciated.

Advice on the issues which should be addressed when examining the development of environmental employment was received from the Institute of Ecology and Environmental Management (IEEM), and the European Federation of Environment Professionals (EFEP), in particular the former EFEP co-ordinator, Martin Cahn.

The support and encouragement of London Guildhall University, in particular, Dr D. R. Hopkin, Vice Provost of London Guildhall University, was invaluable. Grateful thanks are also extended to Robert Hale for his editorial and DTP assistance.

# 1

# THE ROLE OF THE EUROPEAN ENVIRONMENT AGENCY IN ENSURING STANDARDISATION OF ENVIRONMENTAL INFORMATION ACROSS EUROPE

*Hilary Hillier*

## BACKGROUND

The European Environment Agency (EEA) was established by the Council of the European Union under Regulation 1210/90 and it is independent of the Commission.

The EEA began work on 30 October 1993, the day after it was agreed to site the Agency in Copenhagen, and it was officially launched in Copenhagen on 31 October 1994.

The Agency is open to countries which are not members of the European Union, and representatives from both Norway and Iceland (as members of the European Economic Area) already fully participate in the Management Board and other Agency institutions.

## MISSION

The main goals of the EEA are to:

- Produce objective, reliable and comparable information for those who frame, implement and develop European environmental policy and for the wider European public.
- Co-ordinate the European Information and Observation Network (EIONET) and publish a report on the state of Europe's environment every three years.

- Liaise with other relevant national, regional and global environmental programmes and institutes.

The priority areas of work identified in the Regulation are:

- Air quality and atmospheric emissions;
- Water quality, pollutants and water resources;
- The state of the soil, of fauna, flora and biotopes;
- Land use and natural resources;
- Waste management;
- Noise emissions;
- Hazardous chemical substances;
- Coastal protection.

## Management Board

The Management Board is the Agency's main decision-making body and consists of one representative from each Member State, two from the Commission and two scientists nominated by the European Parliament. The Board is also supported on scientific matters by a Scientific Committee. It will advise the Director on technical matters such as staff recruitment and will also provide scientific expertise and advice on progress with European Topic Centres set up to work on major projects under contract to the EEA.

## Executive Director

The Board has appointed an Executive Director (Sr Domingo Jimenez-Beltran of Spain). He is responsible for the preparation and execution of decisions and programmes adopted by the Management Board; for the day-to-day administration of the Agency; for the preparation of state of the environment reports; and for all staff matters. He is also responsible for all financial matters and is fully accountable to the Management Board.

## Budget and staffing

The EEA's budget for 1994 was 9.5 million Ecu. For 1995 it was 11 million Ecu and for 1996 it was 15 million Ecu. Under its organigram (Figure 1.1) the Agency was set to have 23 professional staff, 11 administrative staff and 8 national experts by the end of 1995. It will also have at any one time up to 9 consultants on short-term contracts.

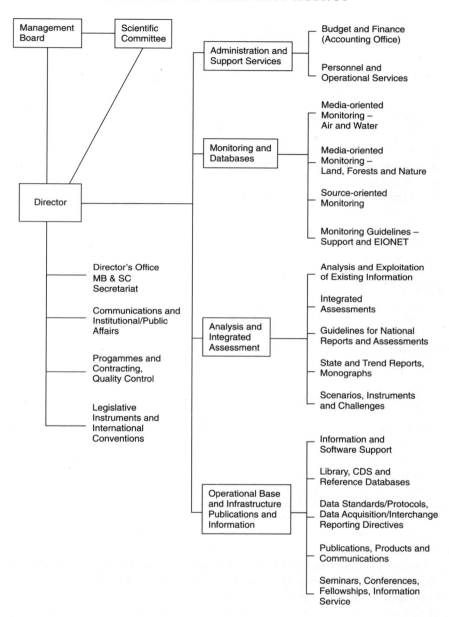

*Figure 1.1*   EEA organigram

# EUROPEAN INFORMATION AND OBSERVATION NETWORK (EIONET)

From the size of the Agency's staff and its budget it can be seen that it is not intended to set up new monitoring and information-collecting across the whole of Europe. Instead, the role of the Agency is primarily one of co-ordinating, setting standards and reporting environmental information, using established networks and expert organisations in Member States. This it will do via the EIONET, an EU-wide network for collecting and disseminating environmental information. The main elements of EIONET are:

- National Focal Points (NFP) in each Member State to serve as a co-ordinator between their national network and the EEA;
- Main Component Elements (MCE) – organisations in national networks which are regular collectors and suppliers of environmental information at the national level and/or possess relevant knowledge of environmental science, monitoring or modelling;
- National Reference Centres (NRC) – organisations which are also MCEs and are nominated by NFPs to play a role in technical co-ordination within their countries and co-operate with the EEA on specific themes;
- European Topic Centres (ETC) – centres of expertise which work under contract to the Agency to undertake tasks identified in the multi-annual work programme.

Other organisations, such as EUROSTAT and the Joint Research Centre (JRC), are not formally part of EIONET under the Regulation, but are linked to it to ensure there is no duplication of work between the respective bodies.

# UK NATIONAL INFORMATION NETWORK

The National Focal Point for the UK is situated within the Department of the Environment. The UK national information network consists of around 95 organisations, the majority of which are data suppliers already producing environmental data for the Department. The remainder are organisations with a proven expertise in environmental research in specific areas. There are 32 MCEs in the UK network, including the Countryside Commission, the Countryside Council for Wales, English Nature, Geological Survey for Northern Ireland, the RSPB and Scottish Natural Heritage. There are 17 NRCs (which are also MCEs) including the Institute for Terrestrial Ecology, British Geological Survey, Institute of Hydrology, Joint Nature Conservation Committee, National Rivers Authority and NETCEN.

## WORK PROGRAMME

The Management Board has agreed the first multi-annual work programme for the period to 1999. It has agreed that priority be given to improving data quality and comparability, to trans-frontier issues, to addressing needs at the European level and to the links between natural science and socio-economic conditions.

The ten programme areas of the multi-annual work programme are:

1 Dissemination and pooling of existing information and know-how;
2 Periodical reports on the state of the environment;
3 Guidelines for reports, assessments and data processing of special interest at the European level;
4 Media-oriented monitoring;
5 Source-oriented monitoring;
6 Integrated environmental assessment;
7 Scenarios for environmental improvement;
8 Instruments and challenges for environmental policy development and implementation;
9 Capacity building in the functions of the EEA and EIONET;
10 Exchange and dissemination of information through publications, seminars, conferences and education.

## EUROPEAN TOPIC CENTRES

European Topic Centres have been selected by the Management Board to work in the areas of air quality, air emissions, inland water quality, nature conservation and marine/coastal matters. The Inland Water Topic Centre is led by the Water Research Centre (WRC), Medmenham, and UK organisations are playing an active role in the other four ETCs. These are led by RIVM, The Netherlands (air quality); Umweltbundesamt, Berlin (air emissions); National Museum of Natural History, Paris (nature conservation); and Marine Environmental Research Centre, Italy (marine/coastal). It is expected that further Topic Centres will be set up on land cover and on cataloguing of data sources. Following these, it is planned that Topic Centres will be established covering soil, wastes, integrated assessment and forest conditions.

## DISSEMINATION OF INFORMATION

The EEA is required to produce an annual report detailing its activities over the previous year. This is sent to the European Parliament, the Council, the

Commission and all Member States. The Regulation also specified that the Agency produce a state of the environment report every three years.

The Agency assumed responsibility for publishing the pan-European Report on the State of the Environment (the Dobris Assessment). The EEA also issues a regular newsletter to Member States reporting recent developments within the Agency. The UK National Focal Point issues a newsletter to provide information on the work of the Agency to all members of the national network and other interested organisations.

## FUTURE ROLE OF THE AGENCY

Under the Regulation setting up the Agency, its role is to be reviewed by the Commission within two years of its commencing operation. Future roles envisaged for the Agency might include a role in implementation and enforcement of EU environmental legislation, setting standards in relation to eco-labelling of products and eco-auditing of companies, and advising on environmental impact assessment.

## STAFFING REQUIREMENTS OF THE AGENCY

The Agency will require staff with a range of skills and experience: environmental scientists will of course be necessary, as will statisticians and economists. Above all, however, the role of the Agency is to oversee and co-ordinate work done elsewhere – in Topic Centres and in Member States. Managerial skills will therefore be important – including personnel management, information management and project management. Interpersonal skills – influencing and negotiating – will also be very important. Finally, since the Agency is going to be operating with other countries across the whole of Europe, a working knowledge of at least one other language (probably French) is a highly desirable, if not essential, requirement.

# 2

# THE ENVIRONMENT AND INDUSTRY

## Legislation and voluntary standards schemes and their potential effects on environmental employment

*Rita Raum Degrève*

## SUMMARY

The EU Fifth Environmental Programme 'Towards Sustainability' aims to create a new interplay between the main groups of actors (authorities, enterprises, public) and industry through the use of an extended and integrated range of instruments that should allow for the integration of the requirements for competitiveness and the environment.

A successful strategy for integration needs to be based on the dual approach of high environmental standards combined with incentives to improve performance continually according to economic and environmental standards.

Initial reactions against measures taken by public authorities to reduce the environmental impact of industries tended to concentrate on the immediate costs compared with the less tangible benefits and a partial view of the situation possibly resulting in losses in competitiveness. Nevertheless, implementation of clean and low waste processes, products and services has progressively emerged as a key factor of industrial competitiveness. The environmental dimension has to be integrated in a progressive, responsible and constructive manner.

Therefore, the management of human resources must respond to the challenge of turning environmental concern into competitive advantage by bringing together the necessary skills to manage the integration process successfully.

# INTRODUCTION

According to the Treaty on European Union it is stipulated that environmental protection must be integrated into the definition and implementation of other policies. Industry is asked to take an important role in the promotion of the harmonious and balanced development of economic activities, which will lead to sustainable and non-inflationary growth respecting the environment. Industry will make a key contribution to the improved and continued welfare of EU citizens.

Conversely, however, industry is the main cause of environmental degradation as virtually all industries use natural resources for their processes/products and are responsible for various types of pollution emission. Perpetuation of this situation is not viable on either economic or environmental grounds.

The European Union framework is well placed to manage the co-ordination of industrial and environmental integration. It can serve to influence Member States and promote the integrity of Community achievements, notably the internal market.

## EU POLICY – FIFTH PROGRAMME: 'TOWARDS SUSTAINABILITY'

Industry has therefore been selected for priority attention under the EU Fifth Environmental Programme 'Towards Sustainability'. This aims to create a new interplay between the main groups of actors (authorities, enterprises, public) and industry through the use of an extended and integrated range of instruments to allow integration of competitiveness and the environment.

### Environmental regulations

In order directly to control the potential for industrial activities to harm the natural environment, a common strand of policy has been the development of environmental legislation that tended previously to be divided in sectors (water/wastes/air) with the emphasis on a 'command and control' approach. Increasingly, environmental legislation needs to be more comprehensive and based on integrated pollution control in order to avoid converting one form of emission into another, and to achieve more far-reaching improvements than are possible under individual regulatory requirements.

Regulatory approaches, however, cannot control all the environmental effects of industry. The reasons for this include the sheer cost of policing the regulatory framework to ensure compliance, and the fact that much environmental damage derives from second-order activities which are not so amenable to regulatory control; packaging and product life cycles are classic examples.

However, the regulatory approach will continue to be a basic tool for environmental management. Emphasis is to be placed on its implementation and the enforcement of existing instruments so that they can be effective.

## Voluntary initiatives

Voluntary initiatives range from the general, such as public education to promote greater awareness of environmental problems and encourage behaviours to reduce environmental effects, to specific programmes intended to provide information and give consumers confidence in the environmental claims made by industry. These latter include eco-labelling and eco-audit schemes. By providing all the relevant information on the environmental impact of industry, these initiatives are intended to enable the general public and the social partners to become more actively involved in industrial policy and to take up their environmental responsibilities as consumers and citizens.

In the past few years some federations and professional organisations have made efforts to increase their members' awareness of environmental aspects. Programmes, codes of conduct and guiding principles have been prepared to encourage and help companies systematically integrate environmental management into their policies. Environmental audits are preferred tools within this context. As well as verification of compliance with the existing regulations, companies need to evaluate the effectiveness of their internal organisation and management and identify the potential for improvements in environmental performance. At the same time they must optimise the capital expenditure and operating costs necessary to protect the environment. The Responsible Care Programme of the chemical industry is one example.

## Economic and fiscal measures ('polluter pays principle')

Economic and fiscal measures serve to ensure that the market price of pollution more accurately reflects society's costs and that this price is incorporated into business production costs. However, taxation of unleaded fuel is presently the only example of such economic or fiscal measures at the EC level. Currently the Commission's proposals with respect to the use of fiscal measures to limit $CO_2$ emission are under discussion.

Given the financial weight of such measures and their positive environmental impact, some intervention at Community level may be necessary in the future to ensure that national schemes are designed in a transparent and comparable way without the distortion of competition.

## Cross-relations between these instruments

As the Fifth Programme 'Towards Sustainability' emphasises, a successful strategy should be based on the dual approach of high environmental standards combined with positive measures to improve performance to raise both economic and environmental standards. Some regulatory instruments have a significant economic dimension. For instance, environmental liability, on which the Commission has issued a Green Paper, would produce a clear economic incentive for improved management and control of environmental impacts generated by industrial activities.

Voluntary agreements are in practice closely linked to the legislation to which they are a complementary instrument, being more adaptable to specific industrial conditions and leaving it to industry to implement the appropriate measures and transferring the responsibility of follow-up. In such circumstances, industry can take advantage of more flexibility to decide on the means and resources to dedicate to this, which will to lead to optimal cost effectiveness. At the same time, predictability of environmental regulations is guaranteed to them. Given that no formal sanction is imposed, the incentive to comply comes from the fact that authority could take regulatory measures and that non-compliance has a potentially disastrous effect on the public image of industry. Attention should also be given to improving the transparency and the participation of NGOs to such agreements, especially by allowing them to have better access to information.

In order to spread best environmental management practice and to encourage industries to fully and systematically apply standards, criteria and objectives providing a high level of protection, EU authorities have taken into account the results of voluntary initiatives and have adopted regulations establishing voluntary schemes, such as eco-auditing (EEC Regulation 1836/93) and eco-labelling (EEC Regulation 880/92).

## INDUSTRIAL COMPETITIVENESS

Initial reactions against measures taken by public authorities to reduce the environmental impact of industries tended to concentrate on the immediate costs of improving environmental performance compared with the less tangible benefits of being environmentally friendly. It was also thought that real losses in competitiveness might result.

A more positive view has progressively emerged. Companies meeting the highest environmental requirements increase their ability to trade freely and this produces gains in positive image which support industry's integration in society. It also induces a positive purchasing attitude on the part of consumers. Introduction of clean technologies corresponds generally with lean production processes and leads to significant improvements in the organisation and management of production systems.

A recent study concerning the relationship between the protection of the environment and the competitiveness of the German economy concluded that the costs of complying with stringent environmental policy are not a handicap for industry but rather a positive factor in competitiveness. Using several examples the study shows that many of the new clean and low waste technologies economise on the consumption of raw materials, water and energy to such an extent that cost savings can more than offset the initial higher investment costs and thereby reduce unit production costs. Environmental considerations not only contribute to cost reduction but also to an increase in output.

The market volume for German environmental protection technologies, goods and services, as well as their export rate, is increasing steadily. Germany has profited in this way from its 'early home demand' — severe regulation requirements led towards an advantage in technology (first-mover advantages).

## HUMAN RESOURCES

Under the pressure of environmental integration, companies engaged in industrial activities are assuming more complex responsibilities. Besides the identification of risk and damage to the environment and consequent control or limitation thereof, industries are forced to enhance their public image and strengthen their legal security by implementing a policy of public information geared towards projecting greater transparency about their performance and their intentions regarding the protection of the environment, consumers and the population.

Therefore, the development of environmental policies and the increasing requirements for better environmental management practices in both industry and regulatory agencies require the acquisition of new skills and competencies by an increasing number of managers and operatives.

### Employment

It cannot be denied that the environmental industry, with its multitude of geographical markets and sectors, presents a plethora of opportunities and has positive effects on employment. In the German example, the number of employees in the environmental sector is likely to increase from 500,000 in 1988 to more than 1,000,000 after 2000.

### Training needs

The expansion of environmental training (vocational and academic) is essential if environmental policies are to be effectively implemented. Moreover, as it is anticipated that existing technologies will continue to provide the main basis both for achieving environmental goals and improving competitiveness over the short and medium terms, training provisions must ensure efficient dissemination of good practices.

11

In order to ensure the speedy take-up of clean technologies, particular emphasis will be placed on the acquisition of necessary skills by the EU workforce through developing suitable qualifications for and ensuring that training schemes are implemented with regard to the installation, maintenance and operation of manufacturing systems incorporating clean technology and good organisational techniques.

Trans-European programmes have developed some provisions both at a vocational level (ESF-funded courses) and at a higher technical level (COMETT, Eurotechnet). These are of particular interest because of the potential to facilitate trans-national transfer of good practice.

## SMALL- AND MEDIUM-SIZED ENTERPRISES (SMES)

When formulating programmes for the integration of industrial and environmental policies, special consideration has to be given to the position of SMEs as, unlike large industries, they do not possess the range of managerial and technical skills required or the financial resources that are necessary to respond to the demands of new industrial policies.

SMEs are particularly unaware of their need for specific training and they are unlikely to find an appropriate organisation for the provision and delivery of environmental training. Many smaller companies find it difficult to assess the future business opportunities of taking a more environmental approach.

## CONCLUSION

The management of human resources must respond to the challenge of turning environmental concern into competitive advantage by bringing together the necessary skills to manage the integration process successfully.

The completion of the internal market is expected to cause an upsurge in economic activity and concomitant energy, transport and other demands. Nevertheless, it provides a unique opportunity for the Community to change the emphasis of its policies from regulation and control to a perspective which views a high quality environment as a key contributor to the Community's position in world trade, and the Community as a leader in the rapidly growing field of clean and low waste processes, products and services.

# 3

# NGO PERSPECTIVES ON ENVIRONMENTAL EMPLOYMENT

*Raymond Van Ermen*

Environmental non-government organisations (NGOs) have played a key role in developing awareness of environmental problems in both public and private sectors. This has led directly to the development of an employment market in the environment and sustainable development sector, notwithstanding the fact that NGOs are an employment sector themselves.

What follows is a brief account of some of the NGOs' perspectives at the European level concerning environmental employment.

The European Environment Bureau (EEB), a federation of environmental NGOs, represents NGOs on several EU advisory bodies. For instance, an EEB representative chairs the European Eco-Label Forum which is submitting comments to the Commission on the eco-labelling of products. Similarly, the EEB is commenting on the EC Eco-Management and Audit Scheme (EMAS) regulations. The EEB is also participating in the so-called Article 19 experts, meetings, which are meetings of representatives of all Member States and interested sectors. Thus we have a good picture of the evolution of environmental policies and developments in the field and in relation to the implications for employment in the environmental sector.

First, there is the question of quality. With regard to the implementation of the EMAS regulation a problem arises in the quality of the training which needs to be guaranteed throughout the EU. Such quality certification should also include the quality of teaching. The EMAS system is devised so that eventually it will be possible to qualify as an EMAS verifier in one country and work in another.

The second issue is a fair share. Certain markets for environmental contracts, such as the one for eco-audits, may give a number of companies the desire to monopolise the European market. It is not surprising that environmental NGOs are not in favour of this. High quality performance must be ensured and therefore it is important that new forms of partnership should be developed between professionals from several countries. For instance, regarding the EMAS regulations, it would not be acceptable if all EMAS verifiers came from a single country. This means that new forms of networking, twinning arrangements, etc. have to be designed.

Third, there is a need to avoid the unnecessary confusion which currently pertains. One of the sources of this confusion is that consulting companies are not, and cannot take on, the role of NGOs. The reverse is equally true. There are too many 'advisory committees', particularly at European Commission level, where there is no clear distinction between representatives from the sectors concerned with sustainable development (such as employers' federations, trade unions, NGOs, etc.) and various consultants who offer their services.

When the Commission wishes to hear the views of these sectors, or ask them to negotiations, these consultants are offering their services to the Commission as well as to the private sector and should therefore not be allowed to participate. An unfortunate situation has now arisen whereby the Commission has all too frequently engaged such consultants so that the Commission may hear what it wants to hear and not what the rest of society may have to say. Consultants should be registered as such with the EU. In the coming years more and more rules will be applied. We need consultants without doubt – even NGOs use their services – but there needs to be clarification concerning each sector's role.

Fourth, local development is an important factor. Work carried out by the Commission's Forward Studies Unit, as well as by the Organisation for Economic Co-operation and Development (OECD), shows the importance of local development actions to ensure the revival of employment. The drawing up of sustainable development plans, particularly of Local Agenda 21 strategies, requires great sensitivity to participatory democracy. Mechanisms, means and deadlines to help citizens take part in the process are essential. Few professionals are prepared for this and have fully grasped their importance.

A fifth point is the need to launch a major campaign for redirecting public funding. Unemployment is high among a number of professions. These people are offering their services to NGOs. Many of these professionals are civil engineers, chemical engineers, etc. A considerable number of such people are being trained as eco-counsellors to solve their employment difficulties. The situation Europe faces is difficult. Some commentators give the impression that there is a goldmine of opportunity for jobs in the environment. Similar things were being said in 1973 in an earlier recession. Twenty years later a lot still remains to be done, which shows the extent of the challenge ahead of us. It is not enough to be good professionals; we also need to enlarge the market, especially for young people.

This is the objective of the European Partners for the Environment – an association that has representatives from trans-national corporations, public authorities and NGOs such as the EEB and the European Trades Unions Confederation. There are a series of modules on topics such as EMAS, transport, etc. The European Partners work together as representatives of different sectors to design new strategies to promote jobs in the various field of employment. One of the most important issues is the redirection of public funds towards the job-creating sectors. The principle of 'double dividend' developed in the EU White Paper on 'Growth, Competitiveness and Employment' is important in this respect but this is not a tangible criterion by which the Commission can decide where to spend its money. The 'double dividend' means that priority funding should be given to projects securing sustainable development on the one hand and employment on the other. Even the Trans-European Infrastructures Project, which has been adopted, has applied the 'double dividend' principle.

The EEB requires assistance to propose modifications in the EU budget along the above-mentioned lines. The EU budget criteria need to be changed and so should the allocation criteria for public funds.

In summary, the three key factors in creating more jobs in the environmental field are as follows:

1   The first element is the tax reform issue. In all Member States, in one way or another, with or without European Union co-ordination, this issue will be a major one. Tax reform is a central issue to reduce charges on existing jobs and to facilitate the development of new areas of work. There will be no dramatic increase in jobs in the environmental sector if this question is not addressed.

2   The second element is that there is a need for experts to design integrated plans. The aim of sustainable development plans promised by heads of state of the governments participating in the 1992 Rio Earth Summit will succeed only if economic and environmental factors are integrated into development plans. Four countries have indicated that they do have a national sustainability plan, one of which is the UK. The criteria used in these four documents vary. A lot is done, in the UK for instance, at the local level but there are still major gaps in terms of people having the skills to deal with the necessary multi-disciplinary approach to issues and environmental problems. This is a key element to ensuring such plans become a reality.

3   The third element is that there is a need to launch new social contracts for sustainable development. Different sectors need to be brought together and new programmes, such as the Marshall Plan for Germany at the end of the Second World War, need to be designed to meet the basic economic and environmental needs both within Europe and outside Europe. For example, housing is an excellent illustration of an urgent need that exists, but where there is insufficient response to solve this problem.

At a recent EEB seminar on 'Health and the Environment', distinguished representatives from the UK and elsewhere explained the relationship between poor health and the environment with particular reference to the poor quality housing sector in areas requiring urban renewal and where incomes are low. This situation is common throughout Europe and elsewhere in the world. There are billions of people all over the world waiting to have clean water, decent housing and efficient energy. This presents enormous opportunities. There is fantastic potential for new development and new growth in Europe but much still remains to be done. Efforts must be directed towards convincing public authorities and public opinion to raise these issues to the top of the political agenda. We only have to look to the last polls and elections in Europe to see that the environment is not currently one of the top priorities.

# 4

# EMPLOYMENT IMPLICATIONS OF ENVIRONMENTAL ACTION

*Romy Shovelton*

## INTRODUCTION

The 'jobs vs the environment' debate continues to attract attention. Contradictory views abound: from those in the north-west of the US who feel that environmental action is a disaster for jobs, to environmental analysts and others who see enormous employment opportunities in environmental protection and management.

In 1993 the European Commission (Directorate General V, Employment, Industrial Relations and Social Affairs), charged with the urgent task of pursuing an effective employment agenda while continuing to support environmental progress, commissioned an investigation into the 'jobs and the environment' debate (Wikima Consulting 1993). Forecasts of 23 million unemployed in the European Union within three years were looming. The Fifth Environmental Action Programme called for wide-ranging tougher environmental action. The issues and the opportunities for jobs linked to the environmental agenda needed to be understood.

The objective of the 1993 report was to identify information showing the actual employment effects of environmental action. The conclusion of the study was almost unanimous – that much work needed to be done to take the debate beyond existing speculation and parochial reaction. Many agreed that it was time to alter the balance between the thick layer of beliefs and values at the foundation of the debate, and the thin veneer of hard evidence.[1]

Meanwhile, based on available data, opinions differed widely – and still do. For example, many in the private sector are (thankfully) moving to integrated clean technologies and away from 'end of pipe' solutions. Generally, new technologies are associated with fewer jobs. So those such as Noel Morrin, former Director of Business in the Environment, tend to be pessimistic about the employment opportunities concomitant with environmental progress. On the other hand, Friends of the Earth in their report *Working Future?* (November 1994) predicted that 700,000 new jobs could be created in the UK through policy changes in areas such as transport, energy, etc.

The following account discusses various aspects of the inter-relationship between environmental action and jobs. In private industry there is a mixed outlook, while in the public and community sectors, the job opportunities appear more obvious. Attention is also drawn to the possible redefinition of 'work' – suggesting that solutions to the unemployment crisis are likely to lie outside a narrow search for 'jobs'.

## PRIVATE INDUSTRY

Worldwatch has stated that the polluting industries usually associated with manufacturing industry represent a minimal and declining source of jobs (Renner 1991). Their decline is not due to environmental pressures, but is primarily the result of structural adjustments. It is estimated that only 1 per cent of industry closures are due to environmental considerations: environmental compliance costs are, for example, generally less than 2 per cent of turnover. Frequently, those companies which do not survive exhibit fundamental flaws, and while it is possible that environmental pressures may tip them over the edge, the environment is rarely a significant factor in corporate demise.

For industry as a whole, it is those companies which take positive environmental action that are likely to thrive in the long term, creating a better climate for protecting or increasing jobs. Studies by SustainAbility (Elkington with Dimmock 1991) and others have demonstrated that it is companies which exhibit excellence in all aspects of their operations which tend to take the environment seriously. In the UK a 1991 study (ECOTEC 1991) showed that the companies winning business were those treating the environment as a core business issue, along with quality, price, distribution and other traditional considerations.

Of course, given other trends, such as the move to 'flatter' organisations, corporate success does not automatically translate into job growth, but attending to environmental performance is certainly a necessary condition for success.[2]

## THE ENVIRONMENT INDUSTRY

The 'environment industry' itself is defined in numerous different ways – the term frequently referring to what could more accurately be described as 'environmental protection'. A note of caution should be sounded here. Many environmental job predictions are based on taking 'environmental protection' expenditure and applying a factor for the number of jobs generated per pound/dollar spent. As 'environmental protection' tends to refer to 'end of pipe' remedial measures, any job increases are likely to be temporary. As industry moves to integrated pollution control systems, the tendency will be towards

*Table 4.1* Environmental protection market

| | |
|---|---|
| World | $200bn (1990) to $300bn (2000) |
| Germany, US, Japan | 50% |
| EU | 25% and losing ground |
| UK | Imports now = exports |
| | 10 years ago, exports = 8 × imports |
| | Lack of awareness, information and training |
| Jobs | 1.3% total EU employment/1.2m jobs |
| | 200,000 in UK by 2000 |
| | Many high wage, skilled |
| SMEs | 200,000 environmental SMEs in EU |
| Taiwan | $200m to $1.5bn (2000), £35.6bn 1991–96 |
| Singapore | 'Leading-edge' clean technology |
| South Korea | $11.5bn 1991–96 + a no-cars scenario |
| China | 250 coal-fired power stations needing flue gas de-sulphurisation and seeking EC 'technology transfer' |

static job numbers or even decreases. We may well be deluding ourselves if we think that there are likely to be many jobs in 'environmental protection'.

The Organisation for Economic Co-operation and Development (OECD) has predicted a potential global turnover of £300 billion for the environment industry by the turn of the century (OECD 1992). Less attention has generally been paid to the greater local possibilities, such as in the Far East (Table 4.1). Clearly, such forecasts represent enormous business potential. However, whether and where this translates into *additional* jobs depends on a complex mix of factors. Key among these is where the most appropriate technologies are being produced: we know that the most advanced technology tends to be developed in those countries with the strictest environmental regulation.

## ENVIRONMENTAL MANAGEMENT

'Environmental management' is a similar story to that for actual jobs. As with environmental protection, the trend is towards integration. Many of those interviewed for the Directorate General V (DGV) study consider environmental responsibility needs to be integrated into every activity. The environment will become part of everyone's job – much as Health and Safety is currently. While a few environmental specialists will be required, most employers require the same engineers, chemists, etc., as they always have done, but now they need them knowledgeable and sensitised to the environment. The demand for environmental specialists seems more likely to decline, rather than grow, as environmental tasks are taken on by regular internal functions. Even the once burgeoning environmental consultancy market has been experiencing consolidation and stabilisation.

The need for the integration of environmental awareness into all roles is particularly acute in small and medium-sized enterprises (SMEs). It is these businesses which collectively pose a greater threat to the environment than their larger counterparts, yet it is this sector that often finds it hardest to respond. For this reason SMEs need help and support. As one response, Business in the Environment produced a do-it-yourself guide to conducting an environmental audit (BiE 1991). The implication of this for jobs is that no additional support will be needed for the foreseeable future as the task can be carried out internally or through consultants.

It is therefore not surprising that 80 per cent of environmental graduates are not getting jobs. Perhaps some educational institutions may even be guilty of jumping on a popular bandwagon – responding to apparent demand (from potential students), rather than actual demand (from prospective employers). While obviously not all courses are vocational, a greater degree of clarity on likely job prospects would be welcomed by many students. Those institutions which are moving to integrate the environment into their courses through appropriate cross-curricula arrangements will be likely to provide the most vocationally relevant education and training.

Nevertheless, there are huge employment opportunities in pursuing best practice in the environment. The Friends of the Earth study *Working Future?* illustrated some major opportunities that could accrue from specific policy adjustments (Table 4.2). Two of these areas include recycling and energy, which will be examined below, and other areas briefly touched on will be tourism, the public sector and local initiatives.

## RECYCLING

Following a study in the US in 1991 (reported by Renner for Worldwatch), we have known that recycling produces a far greater number of jobs than other forms of waste disposal such as incineration or landfill (Table 4.3).

*Table 4.2* Protecting the environment and conserving resources in the UK

|  | New jobs |
| --- | --- |
| Next 10–15 years | 700,000 |
| Saving to taxpayer in unemployment benefits £3b | |
| Environmental goods/services – if polluters pay | 200,000 |
| Recycling 40% domestic waste | 2,450–11,500 |
| Returnable beer/soft drink packaging | 3,200–4,000 |
| Improving water quality | 690,000 |
| Transport – £900m to rail vs roads (in 1995) | 16,000 |
| Energy efficiency – £1.25b/year on homes | 45,000–138,000 |

*Source*: FOE, *Working Future? Jobs and the Environment*, 1994

*Table 4.3* Recycling materials/resource use, waste = food

---

*Waste minimisation* = the name of the game (i.e. *reduce*, re-use, recycle)
Waste management companies underperformed the market by 14% (1993)
Product design = materials savings of 10–30% (Dutch study)
   + design for durability, repair, re-use, disassembly and resource recovery
Repair and reconditioning = labour intensive
Car reconditioning = 56% more labour than new car production
   (and = 42% energy saving)
Recycling of waste is cheapest and provides more jobs
One million tons of waste
   recycled      =   2,000 jobs
   incinerated   =   150–1,100 jobs
   to landfill     =   50–360 jobs

---

*Source*: Data for Vermont, USA, cited by Renner 1991

One of the factors which has tended to hold back recycling investment is the development of appropriate products from the recyclate materials. An example of an innovative approach and of what can be achieved is that of Deja Shoe, whose products are sold in the UK by Vegetarian Shoes. These highly fashionable items are made entirely from recycled materials: poly-styrene cups, tyre rubber, plastic milk jugs, ground shoe soles, recycled clothes and recycled magazines are just some of the things that go to make up this popular product.

In Edmonton, Canada, a similar entrepreneurial spirit has produced a commercial recycling business that contributes $4.5 million per year economic impact to the city as a whole. Seventy per cent of the employees of the Edmonton Recycling Society have a disability.

The famous blue box kerbside scheme in Canada in one town alone created 5,000 direct jobs and thousands of others indirectly in the sorting of the waste stream and the production of this waste into other materials.[3]

New York is the home of the 'We Can' scheme, based on the five-cent deposit paid on all cans and bottles that are sold in the city. Despite the deposit, many people leave their cans in the streets and parks. Unemployed and homeless people began collecting them and returning them to the stores. As the stores were unhappy about these customers, a charity was established to receive the cans and claim the deposits back from the drinks companies. In a short time the charity had collected back $12 million in five-cent pieces and paid out $4 million in wages to the people now employed in sorting and handling the cans. It is thought that if the Bottle Bill were to become a national scheme in the US, it would result in the collection of $1.4 billion in five-cent coins. This money could then be spent on finding work for the unemployed and on environmental activity.

In reply to a question as to whether environmental jobs are 'good' jobs, a person who works at We Can said 'you can make a living out of anything if you do it right' (quoted from an interview for the BBC Radio 4 programme 'Costing the Earth').

Recycling needs to be considered in the context of waste as a whole. Waste minimisation is the generic term, for the hierarchy which runs from *reduce*, to *re-use* and then to *recycle* materials. The critical point comes at the moment of product design – designing for durability, repair, re-use, disassembly and resource recovery. This strategy has potentially a great influence on job numbers, in addition to the labour intensity of recycling activity (repair and reconditioning is far more labour intensive than the work involved in the original production – for example, 56 per cent more so in car production). To maximise the opportunities for repair, reconditioning and recycling, these aspects need to be considered in the original design specification of a product.

Graphically illustrating the principle of 'waste = food' on a geographical (rather than single industry) basis, an integrated approach has been taken in cities such as Kalundborg in Denmark where, through co-operation between various enterprises and the city authorities, the waste from one process becomes a valuable input for the next.

# ENERGY

Energy efficiency is one area in which it has been relatively straightforward to evaluate the potential employment effects of increased activity. Table 4.4 illustrates some examples of studies predicting the effects on employment of energy conservation in Europe.[4] One key advantage of expenditure on conservation rather than energy generation is that it tends to have beneficial social effects – for example, the installation of insulation directly benefiting lower-income households.

As in the case of recycling, the environmentally preferable option also produces the greatest number of jobs in the energy field: wind power provides

*Table 4.4* Energy

| |
|---|
| Social and political effects |
|    nuclear concerns |
|    regional effects – e.g. 'dash for gas' |
|    Mansfield (Notts) – 5,000 colliery jobs lost in 1992 + 5,000 other jobs |
|    3,000 enquiries for 70 vacancies at a new fabric plant |
| Job creation – pollution control, energy conservation, renewable energy |

| | | |
|---|---|---|
| Conservation and renewables programme for the EU | = | 530,000 jobs by 2000 |
| Labour Party – insulation work in 500,000 homes | = | 50,000 UK jobs |
| FOE – £1.25b/year on UK fuel – poor homes | = | 54,000–138,000 jobs |
| CHP programme of 3,000 MW in nine UK cities | = | 8,000–12,000 jobs |
|    + valuable multiplier and responding effects | | |
|    + help to low-income households | | |

*Table 4.5* Renewable energy

EU goal – 20% of electricity from renewables by 2025
UK wind energy – manufacturing and installation jobs by 2005 = up to 18–30,000
UK solar energy – additional jobs by 2005 = 1,000
Renewables = more jobs than conventional energy, e.g. + 396% for wind
   capital requirements lower and labour needs higher
   employment is in local/rural economies
   clean and safe jobs
   many skills transferable from conventional to renewables
Generating 1,000 gigawatt hours of electricity per year:

| | | |
|---|---|---|
| nuclear | = | 100 jobs |
| coal-fired plant | = | 116 jobs |
| solar thermal facility | = | 248 jobs |
| wind farm* | = | 542 jobs |

Biomass energy = jobs in agriculture, fabricated metal products, retail trade

*Source*: After Renner 1991
Note: *Major UK opportunity = off-shore wind power – jobs + exports (ahead of US and Japan) but DTI 'watching brief' only

five times as many jobs as the nuclear industry for the same amount of energy generated (Table 4.5).

## TOURISM

Tourism is the biggest industry in the world. It depends on the environment for its continued existence and success, and has a responsibility to economies, cultures and the environment globally.

Considerable activity is being carried out by organisations such as Tourism Concern and Earthwatch in the UK to safeguard the planet and, as a consequence, the millions of jobs that are dependent on tourism being conducted in a sustainable fashion.

## THE PUBLIC SECTOR

The 1993 study for DGV showed that 50 per cent of EU structural funding on the environment passes through the public sector. It also reported on the massive backlog of environmental work that needs to be done: infrastructural improvement, clean-up, reclamation, etc. The job implications of an investment to clear the backlog are clear. Some commentators have even suggested that such an investment would be preferable to the billions of Ecu being poured into unemployment benefit around the EU at present.

## LOCAL INITIATIVES

There is evidence to show that local and regional expenditure on the environment results in healthy local and regional economies. A study in the US found that Louisiana was both the dirtiest and the poorest state. In contrast, the Ruhr in Germany, the most industrialised area of the country, is now renowned for the proactive stance taken to resolving the dilemmas of a declining economy based on old 'dirty' industries: 100,000 jobs have been created in 1,000 new companies all based on environmental technologies. In the UK, the town of Corby chose a green strategy for the town's development on the grounds that it was also the best way to attract industrialists and their families.

These are some examples of how local initiatives have been introduced to tackle a combination of social, economic and environmental problems. Four others of note are in Berlin (Germany), Denmark, Ontario (Canada), and Unst in the far north of Scotland.

In Berlin, the Environmental Improvement Programme was created to help SMEs improve their environmental performance and to have the best chance of succeeding as thriving (and job-rich) ventures. In addition to the availability of subsidies for investment in necessary equipment, environmental 'service companies' are set up to provide collective services (such as Combined Heat & Power) which the SMEs could not afford individually. The Programme is funded by the city, with EU support. To date, 3,000 jobs have been created, most of which have gone to the unemployed.

The Green Jobs project in Denmark, where the Danish General Workers Union has been working with the ministries of environment, housing and energy, has produced a range of schemes on renewable energy, energy efficiency and recycling. Using another Danish study of wide-ranging environmental action, it has been estimated that if similar programmes were implemented in the UK, these would create a million jobs. If the energy activities were spread across Europe, they alone would create 2 million jobs.

In Ontario, Canada, the Green Communities Initiative has produced massive improvements in household environmental performance (energy, waste, water, etc.), business for hundreds of local suppliers, and the motivation to create dozens of community-led initiatives to improve the local environment. A $40 million inter-ministerial grant enabled the initiative to be established. The initiative is expected to create 11,000 jobs over its first three years (1993–96). This high-quality employment offers opportunities to a wide variety of job-seekers, including engineers, environmental studies graduates and architects, some of whom help assess the work needed while others carry it out.

Finally, at the northernmost tip of the British Isles the island of Unst in the Shetlands won the 1994 Most Innovative Business in Britain award, for the Unst Isle's Telecroft. The island is economically dependent on fishing and oil. The *Braer* oil tanker disaster emphasised to the people the fragility of their economy. Even after the sea was cleared of pollution, the island's fishing industry suffered from a market perception of continuing pollution problems. The islanders therefore had to find an alternative sustainable way of working, to diversify the economy and provide a buffer against any future threats to the fish or oil revenues. The Telecroft was the answer.

In general, these local initiatives provide the most hope in combining environmental needs with employment generation. Their local nature also has important advantages for the social and economic value of such activities.

## WAYS OF WORKING

Much of the success of any of the initiatives mentioned above depends on finding different ways of organising elements of the economy; of creating new kinds of partnerships between what have hitherto been separate sectors of private business, public authorities and the community; finding new ways of considering the funding streams that pass through each sector is also an important element of success.

There is a need to rethink how we approach 'work' (rather than purely in 'jobs' terms). It is predicted that by the year 2000 only half of the industrialised world will be working in full-time jobs. Only a third of the UK workforce currently works in a nine-to-five job. It is now a question of seeing how individuals can create 'work' roles for themselves that are satisfying, make a contribution to society and the economy as a whole, and for which they receive various forms of compensation. In future, in a world characterised by increasingly 'portfolio' lifestyles,[5] some work may be paid employment, some voluntary, while other elements may be supported by some form of state payment or benefit.

## IN CONCLUSION

Whatever the specific employment effects of environmental action, it is implicit that we need to be pursuing the combined agendas of economy, society and environment, i.e. of sustainable development. The old agenda of 'jobs vs the environment' has little relevance in a world that must make environmental progress *and* must provide employment. The most effective energy will be that directed towards maximising the employment opportunities that *can* be found in environmental action.

> The real choice is not jobs or environment. It's both or neither. What kind of jobs will be possible in a world of depleted resources, poisoned water and foul air, a world where ozone depletion and greenhouse warming make it difficult to survive.
>
> (US steelworker/trade unionist)

## NOTES

1   Since the study (and the 'Careers in the Environment' conference, at which the ideas in this chapter were originally presented), some excellent work has been produced by the Forward Studies Unit at the European Commission: *Local Development and Employment Initiatives – An Investigation in the European Union*. This reports on local initiatives which are generating employment, classified into seventeen fields including 'environmental services' (including waste, water, natural areas and pollution). This provides some practical examples of where employment has been generated by environmental action: the type of research that the 1993 Wikima report for DGV recommended as most fruitful.

2   There are signs that the past decade's fashion for 'downsizing' may have outstayed its welcome. The adverse social and personal consequences are now being taken into consideration.

3   A version of this scheme is now being tested in a number of UK cities.

4   A relevant report comparing a number of studies is Linda Taylor, *Employment Aspects of Energy Efficiency*, Association for the Conservation of Energy, 1992.

5   A term coined by the management writer Charles Handy.

## REFERENCES

BiE (Business in the Environment) (1991) *Your Business and the Environment: A DIY Review for Companies*, BiE, London.

ECOTEC (1991) *The Implications of Environmental Pressures: A Report to Warwickshire County Council*, Coventry City Council and the BOC Foundation.

Elkington, John with Anne Dimmock (1991) *The Corporate Environmentalists*, Sustain-Ability, October 1991.

OECD (1992) *The OECD Environment Industry: Situation, Prospects and Government Policies*.

Renner, M. (1991) *Jobs in a Sustainable Economy*, Worldwatch Institute, NY.

Wikima Consulting (1993) *The Employment Implications of Environmental Action*, September 1993.

# 5

# GLOBAL CONVENTIONS AND AGREEMENTS AND EC ENVIRONMENTAL DIRECTIVES

*Kay Hunt*

## INTRODUCTION

This chapter describes how the UK Department of the Environment (DoE) has implemented the sustainable development policies it agreed at the 1992 Rio Earth Summit; it covers the Department's work both in the UK and globally. The chapter is intended to give a flavour of how international agreements are implemented in practice. Hilary Hillier (in chapter 1) has referred to the skills and aptitudes that are needed for specialists working in the European Environment Agency. It is more difficult to define the skills needed by general policy makers at the DoE, but the chapter aims to illustrate them by outlining the type of work in which policy makers are engaged.

The process of implementing an internationally agreed convention in national action plans can be quite complex. This chapter seeks to show how it can be done by taking as a case study how the UK prepared and is implementing its sustainable development strategy to fulfil its Rio commitments. It also briefly reviews the mechanisms that are being put in place for ensuring continuing progress.

## POLICY ORIGINS

The first thing to understand is that the sustainable development strategy was largely built on existing UK environmental policy. It did not require a U-turn or a major shift in direction. Much of what is in the UK strategy and of what was agreed at Rio accords with, and takes forward, the general environmental policies that the UK and many other countries already had in place. Before the Rio conference the UK's environmental policy had been developed and set out in *This Common Inheritance* published in 1990. This focused on four main areas:

1    It set out the UK's main aims, such as the precautionary principle, which requires protective action to be taken if the risk to the environment is very great, even if the science is uncertain. A key example is the policy on climate change, where the potential costs to the planet of failing to act are so vast that even though in the early stages the science was uncertain, it was better to take immediate action rather than wait for the science to be fully proven and then perhaps find that the necessary remedial costs were enormous or that corrective action was impossible.

2    It set targets, for example that of returning $CO_2$ emissions to their 1990 levels by the year 2000.

3    It set out some 350 commitments, such as to cut the government's own energy bill. To achieve this a number of measures to reduce energy consumption within the government estate are being implemented.

4    It considered new policy processes. To improve policy formulation, the government set up a network of 'Green' Ministers, who are each responsible for environmental issues within their Department. It also created a number of consultative groups to influence and inform government policy.

Two distinguishing features of this first comprehensive White Paper on the environment (*This Common Inheritance*) in 1990 were the commitments first to report annually on the progress in implementing remedial measures and then to review what further work needed to be done. Since 1990 the government has published a series of annual White Papers. Year by year these monitor the progress against each of the earlier commitments – including where necessary reporting on areas where less progress had been made than had been hoped. The White Papers also set out each year the government's new commitments as policy develops and where new initiatives need to be taken. They assess how integrated environmental policy is being put into effect in the work of all Departments across government, not just in the DoE.

The UK has a well-established system of collective Cabinet responsibility; this means that major decisions cannot be taken by any Department until they have been cleared or approved across Whitehall. The situation is very different in some other Member States, where individual ministries may wish to use the European Union as a lever to take forward a policy in their own country, for example if their environmental protection ministry is small and not very powerful within the government. This does not happen in the UK, since the Treasury and other Departments need to approve policy initiatives before they can be agreed in the international arena. This sometimes makes the UK rather slow in signing up to international agreements, particularly where the financial implications have not been well researched. But it does mean that once the UK *has* signed up, the government and the country are committed and the resources are available to ensure the appropriate actions will be taken. The UK therefore has a good record in implementation of such international agreements and directives.

To achieve collective Cabinet agreement a number of sub-groups have been formed to consider particular ranges of issues. One such committee examines environmental issues across government. The 1990 White Paper also introduced a new rule – that any policy proposals going before Cabinet should be accompanied by a statement of any *significant* environmental impact. A number of consultative committees have also been established with industry, local government and with the voluntary sector.

## DEVELOPING THE STRATEGY

The then Prime Minister, John Major, promised at Rio that the UK would produce its sustainable development strategy by the end of 1993. The document was in fact published in January 1994. Some people in government expected it to be a rather short, simple report describing what was already in place and what was already being done. But Ministers recognised that the strategy needed to reflect the significant shift in global policy agreed at Rio and to undertake a fundamental review of UK policy from the perspective of sustainable development. The review was to encompass not just environmental protection, but to take a much wider perspective and look at how to encourage economic development while minimising damage to the environment: to look twenty years ahead and to consider the global impact of various environmental and economic activities within the UK; and to consider too how local communities could be involved to ensure effective action at the local as well as the national level.

One of the ways the government considered it needed to go about this was to undertake more consultations with the public. The UK has always been quite good at consulting with various groups. As recommended in Agenda 21, Ministers were keen that the public in all its forms should be involved as much as possible, since achieving sustainable development will require an enormous change in people's lifestyles – in their patterns of travel, their energy consumption and their consumption patterns generally. Such a change is not something that any democratic government can seek unilaterally to impose. It requires a wide national debate and a huge shift in public perception and behaviour.

The UK set about its task first by organising a three-day seminar at a college in Oxford; about a hundred people with a close interest in environmental issues were invited to discuss the range of subjects that had been raised at Rio and how these should be implemented in the UK. A consultation paper was published, seeking a wide range of views. More than 500 responses were received. Some 40 consultative meetings were also held. The meeting on transport, for example, was held with civil servants from both the Departments of Transport and the Environment and with specialist business people, motoring associations, environmental and transport campaign groups, and academics, to promote a wide-ranging discussion. Another group discussed how the government could develop green accounts and indicators of sustainable development. And so on.

A national newspaper, the *Daily Telegraph*, published a series of articles about the issues raised by sustainable development and printed a questionnaire which generated some 8,000 responses. These were from a broad cross-section of the public, who said what they thought needed to be done to promote sustainable development. The EU also ran a workshop on development and the environment for those in national governments who were drawing up their strategies. This allowed the British government to hear how other countries were tackling sustainable development issues. The Spanish government held a workshop on environmental planning which also discussed strategies for sustainability, and how they were being prepared. This built on an earlier initiative by the Dutch government. The Organisation for Economic Co-operation and Development ran a workshop in Ottawa for developed and developing countries. The DoE was involved in all these discussions.

Because such a large number of people were invited to participate in the public consultation in the UK, expectations were naturally raised. It is sometimes difficult for people to understand that their own particular concerns are not necessarily going to be totally acceptable to government (or indeed to other interest groups). Proposals and suggestions may be too expensive, or 'off the wall', but some groups believe that simply because they have been invited to discussions with governments, their issue is going to be taken up in its entirety. Clearly, this cannot be the case.

Governments are exposed to pressure from many different directions. Such pressure is helpful in terms of considering how the debate should be taken forward nationally, but it does sometimes make it difficult to arrive at a consensus. After the consultation exercise some campaigning groups felt disappointed with the outcome. They had expected the strategy to take the UK farther than it actually did. The deadline the government had set itself of completing the strategy by the end of 1993 to some extent curtailed the debate, but the discussions on sustainable development are still actively taking place across the country. And the government welcomes that as a healthy sign that the issues remain live and relevant and of continuing concern to large groups of people.

## ORGANISING THE STRATEGY

Having decided what the strategy should cover, how was it organised? First, it began by examining the principles of sustainable development, to inform the debate and so allow people outside government to challenge the decisions and statements that were made in the strategy. The document then reviewed the state of the environment medium by medium – air, water and land –

looking twenty years ahead or more and extrapolating from present trends. It then reviewed different economic sectors – agriculture, transport, industry and so on – and suggested possible policy responses, assessing the roles of central and local government and of industry. It proposed different ways of approaching change, including the traditional route of regulation, as well as more novel paths such as encouraging voluntary action (e.g. the producer responsibility initiative) and using the market and economic instruments (e.g. through the landfill tax). This tax demonstrates one way in which the government is trying to reduce the amount of waste going to landfill and to move it further up the waste hierarchy.

This approach sends out the message that it will in future make fiscal sense to reduce waste. It is an important means of showing the government's determination to start to tax the processes and actions that it wishes to discourage, such as environmental degradation; and to impose less taxation on activities it wants to promote, such as employment. The strategy also reviewed the role of voluntary action by business and the voluntary sector and went on to look at the role of education, in schools and more generally.

At the beginning of each chapter in the strategy there was a standard checklist. This structure was valuable in helping to identify issues and forcing the authors to be honest about areas of difficulty where as yet sustainable development was not being achieved.

The chapters on economic sectors began by looking at the general framework of sustainability, and proposing trends for the next twenty years or so. They assessed problems and opportunities and reviewed the way in which responses were being formulated to check if they were right, and then to conclude how to proceed. For example, the transport chapter detailed what was necessary for a sustainable framework for transport. It projected that, on the basis of present trends, road traffic would double by the year 2025, and concluded that this would have unacceptable consequences for the environment and for the economy in certain parts of the country. Action had to be taken.

The most important element that was new about the sustainable development strategy was that it made much more explicit the relationship between environmental protection and economic activity. The DoE was no longer just concerned with protecting the environment but had explicitly to consider the complementary need to promote economic development. At the same time, the policy enshrined in the strategy ensured that those Departments which were primarily concerned with economic development – such as the Treasury, Trade and Industry and Transport – needed also to consider how to promote economic development in ways that protect and enhance the environment.

The strategy looked outwards at the UK's impact on the world, and inwards to Local Agenda 21 nationally. Agenda 21 referred to international, national and local situations.

The strategy generally looks much further ahead than is normal for government policy; it projected ahead twenty years, to the year 2012. In terms of transport it concluded that policies were needed that would influence the rate of traffic growth. The Royal Commission on Environmental Pollution – a body independent of government consisting primarily of respected experienced academics – has taken evidence from various sources and recently produced a considered report on transport and the environment. It suggested a number of ways in which the country might reduce its dependence on road transport. It is not easy, however, to engage people in considering the environmental impact they are personally having through their own travelling.

The Secretary of State for Transport has launched a public debate to try to get people to look at the issues and give their opinion on what should be done. The British government is not seeking, as some other governments are considering, to dictate draconian means of reducing traffic demand – for example by determining which people should be banned from driving on certain days of the week or when air pollution levels become too high. Whatever measures are decided to limit the need to travel, they will have to be acceptable to the public at large and to industry. The problem with transport is that people are inclined to think that what needs to be done is going to be done by somebody else. Also, that if the roads are made less congested then it will become easier for them personally to drive to work or for leisure!

## ASSESSING THE STRATEGY

So, what *did* the strategy achieve? It set out the principles of sustainable development in clear terms. It was fairly strong in its analysis of the problem and by helping to inform the debate allowed people to challenge the conclusions that the government had reached. It said that the best way to harmonise environmental protection and economic development was by bringing environmental costs and benefits right into the heart of economic decision-making, both in government and in the private sector. It confirmed the British government's belief that this is best done in a vigorous market economy, taking the optimum mix between regulation, economic instruments and voluntary action.

Ministers have concluded that privatisation of the water industry, for example, identified the true costs of water supply which in turn led to higher investment and more realistic charges. The strategy identified problems and opportunities, and these are being monitored through annual reports. These show in which areas action is being taken and what specific action is being implemented. The reports review and thereby improve the policy process. The government aimed at a dynamic strategy, and issued the first major document in an ongoing debate. It also established processes which are helping decision-making. Regular monitoring is continuing so that the effects of the new policies can be ascertained in detail.

What sort of judgements were made? The government decided that it wanted rapidly to review what was required and to proceed with the policy of developing economic instruments and green taxes (for example, those on energy). This is a difficult area, but progress is being made. As previously mentioned, the landfill tax has recently been introduced and the government is looking at a number of other measures such as sulphur trading, water abstraction and licensing charging. However the practicalities of implementing these are extremely difficult.

The government judged that the mechanisms for co-ordinating policy across government were generally effective. The system of consultative groups is being continued. New work on green accounting and indicators for sustainability is underway and the DoE published the first set of indicators of sustainable development in 1996 (DoE 1996). A strategy for environmental education is also being produced – not just to cover the national curriculum in schools but much more broadly for continuing education.

As for targets, many commentators considered that the government did not move policy forward far enough or set enough new targets for reducing pollution and achieving environmental improvements. Other countries have drawn up different types of plans for achieving sustainable development and in those plans the emphasis is often more on setting new policies and targets. The Netherlands, for example, is well known for its national environmental policy plans; quantitative targets have been set for each sector. But the UK's targets are ones that are known to be achievable and that the government is committed to attaining; they are more than just statements of aspiration and intent. They are essentially measures that can be achieved. Some of them may be regarded as modest, but they are progressive steps to achieving tangible improvements. And they are being achieved.

Other countries adopt different approaches to setting targets. Sometimes they are set purely to identify aspirations; for example, some Member States of the EU set targets which are more of a reflection of what they would like to do rather than what they think is possible. Often they may not know how they will achieve them or even if they are capable of being achieved. The UK takes a more pragmatic approach. First it discusses the issues across government, so that overall objectives are agreed and the extent to which progress can be made is assessed. Then it is able to set realistically achievable targets which it can effectively deliver.

Targets in the UK often derive from international negotiations such as those on climate change. But the government's annual report for 1995 set out in a consolidated table the main environmental targets that it had set and was working up, partly to counter the criticism of a lack of targets, but also to stimulate a review across government of their sufficiency. These also cover a number of areas, such as in waste strategy, where targets are being set for purely domestic reasons. The intention is that in succeeding annual reports more targets will be set, in order to promote policy and push it forward.

In parallel, local authorities are developing their own sustainability indicators. While the debate continues as to whether it is best to develop these initiatives from the top-down or from the bottom-up, local authorities are looking at indicators of sustainability which will be useful for their local communities. Some interesting indicators are emerging, although their local variability sometimes makes it difficult to make comparisons between areas. The development of indicators which are relevant in a micro-sense may not be applicable in a larger macro situation. It is not necessarily easy to combine them to reflect a national picture.

## SUPPORTING THE STRATEGY

The UK has also drawn up action programmes for the other topics agreed at Rio – climate change, biodiversity and forests. The UK was the first nation to produce, in January 1994, programmes and strategies for all four topics covered at Rio (including the overarching Agenda 21 programme). Its climate change programme confirmed the UK's commitment to reducing emissions of greenhouse gases to their 1990 levels by the year 2000. The UK is on target to exceed that figure and is pressing its international partners to agree to tougher reductions beyond the year 2000. It is necessary to take international action as climate change is a global problem.

The Biodiversity Action Plan consists of a thorough analysis of the problems and priorities in the UK. The plan itself does not set targets but it established a steering group consisting of government and a number of outside specialists to produce specific costed targets for biodiversity by the end of 1995. The process has included consulting with those outside the steering group to assess whether the right targets have been fixed.

The Forestry Programme is aimed at protecting the very few surviving ancient and semi-natural woodlands, the sustainable management of all existing woodlands and forests and a steady expansion of tree cover in harmony with the environment.

Since 1994 it has worked on a number of other strategic documents. Early in 1995 it published *Air Quality: Meeting the Challenge*, setting out the philosophy and proposed framework for a strategic approach to air quality issues in the UK. Complemented by a system of local air quality management where this is needed, the strategy will include air quality standards, objectives on ambient concentrations of the most significant air pollutants and measures to be taken to achieve these objectives.

A draft waste strategy is currently out for consultation. This has also set quantifiable targets – for example, the reduction of waste to landfill by 10 per cent over the next ten years, and a further 10 per cent over the following ten years. There are a number of other detailed targets and the DoE is seeking views nationally as to whether these targets are the most appropriate ones.

The Secretary of State for the Environment launched an initiative on town and country planning in 1995 which has led to widespread debate. It is hoped that this will set a number of targets to improve the design and the quality of building in the country and towns.

Other ways of pushing the government's strategy forward are being reviewed. For example, in the land use planning system the Secretary of State's guidance notes to local authorities are being revised to ensure that they fully incorporate sustainable development principles. Local authorities are the competent authorities responsible for licensing planning activity, so the government is concerned that they incorporate the latest thinking on sustainable development in their decision-making. For example, large out-of town supermarkets are now being discouraged in favour of the regeneration of inner cities and town centres.

There is still a need for new mechanisms to ensure that sufficient opportunities are being given to people outside government to offer their views on sustainable development. The government announced in the strategy its intention to set up three new bodies to facilitate this. They are all now in being.

First, it created the Government Panel on Sustainable Development, which is composed of five eminent people chaired by Sir Crispin Tickell and appointed by the Prime Minister to advise government and monitor the government's performance. The Panel has direct access to Ministers and to senior civil servants and discusses various sustainable development issues with specialists in particular areas to ascertain the effectiveness of the government's action on specific areas. It can give advice in private (which it has done on occasions) but it also publishes open reports. The first report was published in January 1995; this set out a number of policy proposals including one suggesting that the UK should have an Inter-governmental Panel on the oceans and to further international co-ordination to achieve a sustainable fishery policy.

Second, the government set up the UK Round Table on Sustainable Development. This consists of 35 people drawn from all sectors and it is chaired jointly by the Secretary of State for the Environment and by a senior academic, Sir Richard Southwood. The objective of this forum is to review some of the difficult issues and try to seek more general consensus across society about the way ahead. The Round Table was established in January 1995. The initial work of the Round Table was to interview 'Green Ministers' across Whitehall to evaluate what policies were being pursued in each Department. They looked initially at transport, economic instruments, environmental appraisal and energy. Further issues will be added at a later date.

Third, Ministers have set up a public campaigning group called 'Going for Green'. Its focus is to make people aware of the sorts of lifestyle changes that are necessary to achieve sustainable development. The group is run by a committee of prominent people working with a range of existing groups, giving publicity to the issues and bringing new initiatives to life. It is an attempt to get the message of sustainable development across in the widest possible way.

## CONCLUSION

This chapter has tried to show how in preparing the strategy and taking it forward policy makers at the DoE have attempted to involve all sectors of the community to establish a national plan for sustainable development. This will determine what needs to be done and ensure that the appropriate machinery is in place to implement and refine the plans in different areas. It has summarised the many areas for which the government is responsible in promoting the quality of the environment and pursuing sustainable development. It has also shown how complex the issues are, and why an increasing number of specialists are required both to develop and implement policy.

## REFERENCE

Department of the Environment, Transport and the Regions (1996) *Indicators of Sustainable Development for the UK*, London: HMSO.

# 6

# THE MEDITERRANEAN REGION

## The problem of integration of environmental issues in the policies of Mediterranean countries

*Antoni Alarcón*

## INTRODUCTION

To understand the importance of increasing the role of environmental managers and other environment professions in the Mediterranean region it is necessary to understand the cultural and historical background of the region and some of the environmental problems currently occurring.

The Mediterranean region is the cradle of ancient civilisations stretching back over 5,000 years. These cultures have left an indelible imprint along the entire Mediterranean coastline. The geographical and environmental conditions of the region have had a decisive influence on the development of coastal populations. This long history of habitation, together with the present high levels of demographic pressure, is significantly affecting the environment and its natural resources. In some cases environmental deterioration has reached critical levels in recent years. If swift action is not taken some of these problems could become irreversible.

The most seriously affected area is the coastal zone. This zone varies in its extent in each of the countries bordering the Mediterranean. It may stretch tens or hundreds of kilometres inland and from 12 to 200 marine miles out to sea.

The Mediterranean region is experiencing a significant increase in population. Of the 350 million people who inhabit this area, 130 million live within the coastal strip, which is also visited annually by 110 million tourists. Added to this seasonal increase there is a growing tendency for the population from the interior to migrate to coastal areas in search of better economic conditions and a higher standard of living.

The Mediterranean region displays a considerable degree of heterogeneity and common characteristics that define its regional identity. For example, the coastal zone includes a great diversity of ecosystems: wetlands, reefs, rocky coasts, sandy beaches, dunes, islands, etc., which coexist with built-up areas and large conurbations. The region's heritage is increasingly threatened by problems which respect neither borders nor government policies. Socio-political problems of an ethnic or religious nature have turned certain Mediterranean regions into battlefields, where the loss of human life is accompanied by the loss of cultural heritage and by environmental destruction.

To reverse current trends there is a need to study the causes of the present situation and integrate environmental policies in the economic development strategies of the countries in the region. There is a need to redirect mistaken economic policies and ineffective administrative and legal systems, as well as increasing awareness among the population as a whole and among all politicians. Only in this way will the whole of the Mediterranean region be able to work together towards sustainable regional development.

The 1975 Action Plan for the Mediterranean organised by the UNEP in Barcelona drew up agreements that have served as a basis for the improved integration of environmental issues in each country's policies.

## ENVIRONMENTAL PROBLEMS IN THE MEDITERRANEAN REGION

Many of the environmental problems in the Mediterranean region are, to a greater or lesser extent, common to all the coastal countries. As mentioned above, many of these problems are trans-national in nature and require international co-operation that may extend beyond the Mediterranean region.

Marine pollution, the disappearance of habitats and therefore threats to biodiversity, and fisheries problems are all clearly trans-regional. Other problems are confined to sub-regions and affect specific areas of the Mediterranean, the pollution of the Adriatic being an example. A final category is more specific in nature and affects only limited areas but has solutions that are more generally applicable. What follows is a brief description of some of these problems.

### Pollution and loss of water resources

This is one of the main ecological and socio-economic problems in the region. In a number of areas within the Mediterranean basin there is a shortage of drinking water.

This problem has increased as a result of population growth and an improvement in standards of living. According to published figures (from the Blue Plan), per capita consumption, which stood at 90 m$^3$/year in 1980, will rise to 110–130 m$^3$/year in 2025. In the southern countries it will increase from 45 m$^3$/year at the end of the 1980s to 65–82 m$^3$/year in 2025. The drought being suffered in certain areas of the Mediterranean intensifies this problem of resource availability.

Bad planning, together with various forms of pollution, contributes increasingly to the reduction in water resources. The northern Mediterranean has adequate water treatment processes but in the south more than a third of the population has no access to safe drinking water, with all the health problems which that implies. The distribution of water resources varies throughout the region. There is an overall surplus in the north but a shortage in the islands and in the south.

The over-exploitation of aquifers has led to many problems, both of pollution and contamination by salt water, which have reduced their usefulness. Urban and industrial pollution, and the overuse of chemical fertilisers and pesticides have damaged surface water resources: 20 of the 29 large hydrographic basins in the Mediterranean are highly polluted in their lower reaches.

Agriculture makes by far the greatest demands on water resources. In some cases these demands are increased by the European policy of subsidising specific crops.

Countries such as Algeria, Egypt, Libya, Israel, Morocco, Syria, Malta and Cyprus, and areas of Spain and Italy all have problems with water resources. It is apparent that in Cyprus and Malta, as well as in Israel and the Occupied Territories, this situation is damaging the regional development of these countries.

In most countries the price of water does not include the real cost of treatment and supply as this would lead to a continuous increase. This is due both to the difficulty of finding new resources and to the use of new and expensive treatment techniques to counteract increased water pollution. This situation will inevitably affect the economic policies of the whole Mediterranean region.

## Pollution

Inadequately treated sewage, hydrocarbons and industrial waste, discharges from shipping, agricultural run-off and the dumping of waste are some of the causes of pollution in coastal and marine areas. Eighty-five per cent of the pollution in the Mediterranean comes from terrestrial sources.

More than 70 per cent of urban waste water is untreated and is discharged into the sea either directly or through underwater outfalls. It is estimated that by the year 2060 the volume of waste water will have increased to 1,500 million $m^3$ from its present level of 400 million $m^3$.

The effects of this pollution are greater in coastal areas where combined sewage and rainwater systems have a negative effect on the quality of the coastal waters. Pollution from household sources is by far the largest in volume. However, given its organic and faecal content, and the absence of toxic elements, this type of waste is highly treatable through biological processes.

Unfortunately, and above all in the northern Mediterranean, a considerable and increasing volume of industrial waste water is discharged into urban sewage systems. This makes treatment difficult in conventional plants. (In the case of the Barcelona metropolitan area almost 35 per cent of the waste water in the urban sewage system is of industrial origin.)

Industrial waste contains more complex and dangerous elements such as heavy metals and organo-chlorates. This industrial pollution is more environmentally damaging because of its heterogeneity and longevity in ecosystems.

At various places in the Mediterranean industrial discharges have led to high levels of pollution. This is the case in Split and Rijeka in the Adriatic, Portman Bay in Spain, and Izmir and Istanbul in Turkey. In other cases rivers which run though large industrial zones discharge their pollutants into the Mediterranean (Ebro, Rhone, Po, Nile, etc.). Many of these bays contain much higher levels of heavy metals and organo-chlorates than recommended by the World Health Organisation (WHO).

Some of these problems have already been detected in various parts of the food chain. For example, it is known that the tuna caught in the western Mediterranean contains almost twice the level of mercury as that caught in the eastern Mediterranean or the Atlantic.

Another problem is the increasing eutrophication of the water in the Mediterranean. This is due to the discharge of nutrients (nitrates and phosphates) from chemical fertilisers used in agriculture, from industrial pollution and from household detergents. The Mediterranean is a sea poor in nutrients (oligotrophic) and this increase might represent a new food source for marine ecosystems. In fact, because of limited mixing between the coastal zone and the open sea, the nutrients concentrate excessively in areas of slowly circulating water (the vertical mixing of the water in the Mediterranean takes 250 years). An example of this problem, the concentration of algae in the upper Adriatic, fed by the pollution from the River Po, leads to grave environmental problems because of the decrease in oxygen in the water. This has a significant impact on water quality in the coastal zone with important consequences for the tourist industry.

Shipping is also an important source of pollution in the Mediterranean. More than 200,000 vessels of over 100 GRT use it every year and there are more than 2,000 vessels using it at any one time, 250 of which are oil tankers. Although there has not been a serious incident involving an oil tanker so far, the sea is polluted with hydrocarbons from the tankers' ballast water and from industrial waste. Of the 650,000 tonnes of hydrocarbon pollutants, 75 per cent have their origin in tanker traffic. Almost 30 per cent of this is discharged off the African coast in the eastern Mediterranean where it affects the coastal ecosystems.

Another source of pollution is the dumping of sludge from sewage treatment plants or industrial processes (prohibited in the EU since 1988). Plastics and other non-biodegradable waste from shipping also represent a problem along the Mediterranean coast, although this is diminishing due to stricter regulation.

## Loss of habitat and biodiversity

The loss of habitat is of particular significance to the environmental health of the region. Since the beginning of the century, rich, dynamic ecosystems such as wetlands, estuaries, dunes and lagoons have all been lost or ruined and this has also meant a substantial loss of biodiversity. Over the last fifty years a million hectares of these habitats have disappeared throughout the Mediterranean.

The destruction of wetlands is linked to the degradation of estuaries and the erosion of deltas. These areas are of central importance to the dynamic of the land–sea interface. Marshes are reservoirs of sediment and nutrients which create ideal conditions for the development of an important floral biomass. This in turn serves as a cover and food for a great diversity of invertebrates, fish, amphibians and other animals, and especially birds.

Dunes have an important role in coastal protection and they are also an important reserve of biodiversity. In the Mediterranean countries of the EU more than 75 per cent of the dune area has been lost. The threat to these areas comes from the increasing demand for sand as a building material, and for industry and tourism. As previously mentioned, the loss of biodiversity is linked to the loss of natural ecosystems and this refers to both the disappearance of species and the loss of genetic variation within species. Within the Mediterranean region there are a number of animal species threatened with extinction. In addition, over half the plant species threatened with extinction in Europe are to be found in coastal areas.

Overfishing both of species such as swordfish and tuna and smaller ones like sardines or anchovies presents another environmental problem. Although the Mediterranean is not as rich in resources as other seas, fishing is of great importance economically for the coastal populations. According to the Food and Agriculture Organisation (FAO), in the Mediterranean region 14 kilograms of fish are consumed annually per capita of which only 3.5 kilos are imported from other parts of the world.

## Soil erosion and deforestation

Erosion and soil loss are taking place at a high rate. The Blue Plan estimates a loss of productive agricultural land of the order of 300 million tonnes/year. Erosion is the result of a number of different processes. Intensive grazing is the most significant but water and aeolian erosion of unprotected and steeply sloping ground is also a cause of soil loss.

Only 5 per cent of the Mediterranean region is still forested and this area is concentrated in the northern part of the region. The characteristics of Mediterranean woodland expose it to a high risk of fire, accidental or deliberate.

Every year more than 200,000 ha of woodland are burnt. The loss of woodland promotes surface erosion, particularly on slopes, due to the strong seasonal rains that are characteristic of the Mediterranean climate. It is estimated that by the year 2050, 25 per cent of the present woodland will have disappeared.

The salinisation of agricultural land is another process of soil degradation. This results from the lack of proper drainage and the effects of evaporation leading to an accumulation of salts in the soil. Thirty-two per cent of the Nile delta is affected by this problem which has repercussions for its agricultural production.

The overuse of chemical fertilisers, pesticides and herbicides is another problem linked to both the deterioration of soil and the contamination of surface and underground water. According to the Blue Plan, 550 tonnes of pesticides are discharged into the sea every day.

## Solid waste

According to estimates, the production of solid waste is approaching 500,000 m³ of waste per day. The treatment and elimination of this waste takes place under very variable conditions throughout the Mediterranean basin. Waste disposals are often tips and poorly designed, leaching contaminates into water resources and the soil. The sharp increase in population has led to a significant increase in waste generation. This problem is most severe in the coastal area where it is difficult to find tipping sites.

Waste treatment and recycling plants are still not widespread in the region. Some have extremely old technology based on mining systems. Many existing incinerators do not comply with emission standards. Another problem is the elimination of industrial waste due to a lack of suitable treatment plants.

## Atmospheric pollution

Atmospheric pollution is increasing in the region. Most atmospheric pollutants are produced by industry, power stations, domestic heating and motor vehicles. Although the sources of this pollution are primarily concentrated in large urban areas, the pollutants reach the sea through air and water dispersal. Ninety per cent of the lead in the western Mediterranean comes from atmospheric pollution.

The use of motor vehicles has doubled since 1980 and is expected to double again before the year 2000. The effects of smog, not only on public health but also on historic buildings, are well known.

## Coastal erosion

Coastal erosion is increasing. Human-induced changes to the coastline – the construction of breakwaters and marinas, the reinforcing of beaches, building along the coastline, etc. – together with a reduction in the natural sediment deposited in all hydrographic basins, have led to increased erosion in coastal areas, affecting over 30 per cent of the coastline.

The primary consequence of this process is a significant loss of sand from beaches to the point where, in many places, the area immediately behind the beach has had to be protected from the waves so that roads and built-up areas are not threatened.

The regeneration of beaches is a very costly process that often damages the marine environment. Dredging sand from the sea bed can affect not only benthic populations but also their breeding grounds. Moreover there is no guarantee that this process will be enough to stop beach erosion.

Another serious problem is the erosion of the deltas in the region. In the delta of the Llobregat, for example, the lighthouse for the port of Barcelona which was situated 300 metres inland a century ago is now on the shoreline protected by a breakwater.

## THE CAUSES OF ENVIRONMENTAL PROBLEMS

Environmental deterioration in the Mediterranean region is primarily due to the high level of population growth and the lack of adequate environmental policies. Economic policies must therefore include new elements aimed at achieving sustainable development. These policies must incorporate new ideas about all environmental resources. An example is pricing policy.

As mentioned earlier, water charges do not reflect the real price of water. This contributes to a deterioration in water resources. If the price of water remains low, demand will continue to increase. The price will also not cover the real environmental costs. These environmental costs must therefore be included in all industrial processes and all those processes related to the exploitation of natural resources.

Ineffective regulations have also led to environmental degradation. The countries in the region have negotiated various binding environmental agreements. The EU has also produced legislation and environmental regulations in a number of areas: water, waste water, solid waste, the transport of dangerous material, atmospheric pollution, etc. Most of these regulations have been incorporated into national legislation. However, the level of compliance in many countries is low, either because of the lack of enforcement or, in many cases, because application of the regulations would have a negative effect on the economic policies of the countries concerned.

It is important to consider the difficulty of implementing environmental regulations because in many cases the problem is cross-border in nature and sometimes there is a long delay before the decrees which complement the laws are brought into effect. It is also important to admit that environmental problems require a new way of working, which may run up against a legal system unused to operating in such an interdisciplinary area as environmental protection.

However, the most serious problem is the lack of management and organisation. The management of many natural resources in the Mediterranean region is split among a multitude of different bodies in each country. This complicates the implementation of new environmental policies, especially when solutions have to be found at regional level. Water is a clear example because of the multiplicity of organisations that are involved throughout the water cycle.

Another cause is a lack of awareness of environmental problems by the public. The adoption of environmental policies and the reduction of administrative obstacles will only be possible with a high degree of public support. The case of recycling is one example. However much legislation and however many policies are introduced to minimise, recycle and retrieve waste, if there is no awareness among members of the public of the importance of recycling and consuming recycled products, the policies will fail.

Tourism is undoubtedly a prime cause of environmental damage which is linked to demographic growth. The Mediterranean is a region oriented towards tourism. The paradox is that the more success it has as a tourist destination, the more visitors come and the more damage there is to the environment, its principal attraction. In the long term its future as a tourist destination therefore depends on the quality of its environment. This indicates objectives that are clearly opposed to the present policies of large-scale, low-cost tourism.

Clearly the solution has to lie in the sustainable development of tourist centres where the various tourist zones and activities are managed and controlled.

## ELEMENTS FOR IMPROVING THE ENVIRONMENT

Analysis of the various environmental problems outlined above suggests the need to incorporate necessary elements to develop a policy of sustainable development within the framework set down by economic policies.

All elements such as regional planning, pollution, resources, etc. must be brought together, as action cannot be taken in one area without taking into account its inter-relation with all the others.

Environmental policies must be developed within a general framework that takes into account all the factors involved. Control and management of water resources is of no use without the same level of control over waste, for example. Moreover, given the regional character of the Mediterranean basin, it is necessary to work in a much wider context than the nation-state: i.e. at an overall regional level. Coastal planning needs a level of consensus that goes far beyond any one country's own coastal area.

International agreements on the environment are an extremely important tool. There are already innumerable treaties and pieces of legislation in existence, of both a general and a specific nature, concerned with various aspects of environmental protection; some more general ones include the Rio treaties (1992). The EU has also issued numerous decrees on environmental protection: environmental impact evaluation (85/337/EEC), the protection of habitats (92/43/EEC), the quality of waste water (92/271/EEC), the protection of birds (79/409/EEC), the quality of bathing water (76/160/EEC), etc.

In 1992 a meeting of EU Environment Ministers asked the Commission to prepare an integrated strategy on coastal planning.

The application of these international agreements will only be possible if individual countries are willing to implement their own national and regional programmes. It is also extremely important to involve local administrations in improving environmental planning. One example is the Association of Municipalities of the Barcelona Metropolitan Area (MMAMB) and its policy to reclaim its coastal environment, even though this is a complex area (500 km$^2$ with a population of over 3,200,000) which includes natural areas, industrial areas, a large infrastructure, etc. For the past year an attempt has been made to incorporate environmental processes into the planning system.

This link between the environment and development is especially relevant to MMAMB projects for reclaiming the Llobregat and Besos rivers and the Llobregat delta. The recuperation of the whole environment of the Llobregat is part of a larger project known as the 'Delta Plan' which includes the development of the whole area, with construction of roads and environmental amenities, and the extension of the airport and the port of Barcelona, as well as the restoration of natural areas. At the end of 1995 the Official College of Biologists and the various administrations held an experts' seminar in Barcelona on the re-use of waste water in Mediterranean countries. This forum provided an opportunity to exchange knowledge and ascertain the state of new technology for water re-use and regeneration.

The establishment of collaborative networks linking various levels (national, regional and local) has an important role in facilitating communication between communities and the possibility of resolving similar problems. Various networks already exist: Eurocities, Eurisles, Coast, Restore and Hydro. There are also numerous European programmes concerning coastal planning and environmental protection: ENVIREG, LIFE, EPM, etc.

It is important to work together and combine economic policies with environmental policies that enable us to achieve sustainable economic development to protect and promote the coastal area of the Mediterranean. However, this cannot be achieved without appropriately trained and skilled personnel. General awareness raising of the importance of the environment to all professional specialisms, such as planning, economics, law, etc., is vital to ensure the successful integration of environmental considerations into all policies and planning. In addition, education and awareness raising of the environment to the consumer and voting public are also essential to this process. The countries of the Mediterranean region still have a considerable way to go before environmental employment is widespread in all sectors of the economy but it has been recognised, albeit by a small minority thus far, as being crucial to the environmental well-being, indeed survival, of the region.

# 7

# THE ENVIRONMENT AND INDUSTRY

## Legislation and voluntary standards schemes

*Rita Raum Degrève*

The different approaches to introducing environmental standards that have evolved include:

1   Voluntary measures, e.g. responsible care schemes;
2   Legislative measures, e.g. emissions controls;
3   Economic and fiscal measures, e.g. carbon tax.

Some of the difficulties associated with these include, for example, the problems local authorities experience in knowing which approach to take, the political connotations of any form of taxation and the political/economic effects of legislation (i.e. on exporting/importing and trade), and the need to overcome the resistance of business and industry to legislation. There has been a noticeable shift towards the voluntary approach (e.g. such as eco-labelling and EMAS).

However, the voluntary approach is often more innovative and effective as its origins within industry foster greater co-operation between businesses. Agreements for standards originating from industry itself tend to provide longer-term measures to reduce environmental effects as they need to be shaped into and around business strategies. Self-regulation by industry is highly effective as it is a natural result of peer scrutiny, public scrutiny and consumer pressure.

The very existence of industrial standards can itself stimulate further action by individual businesses. Standards may be heavily dependent on extensive consumer awareness and could potentially stifle competition to become even more environmentally sound (i.e. beyond the levels set by standards). Larger (multinational) companies are now leading the field in producing cleaner, more environmentally sound technologies. However, different approaches will be appropriate according to the specific nature of the structure and dynamics of different industrial sectors.

## OUTCOMES

Environmental scientists (chemists, ecologists, etc.) are increasingly required to research environmental unknowns, and to progress and develop more environmentally benign industrial technologies. As legislation develops and regulation intensifies, more accurate monitoring and regulation of industrial outputs to the environment and more technical personnel will be required. In this sense, 'technical' will include eco-auditors, environmental management specialists, environmental lawyers and environmental economists. There is an increasing need for training and education of these developing specialisms.

The process of environmental technology innovation must be encouraged and supported at all levels from small-scale SMEs to multinationals. In particular, the education of the SME sector to foster greater environmental awareness is crucial, and such education must be readily usable, understandable and cheap. It was recognised that greater emphasis must now be placed on fostering and developing links between SMEs and academia and other education and research establishments. This is necessary to overcome cultural barriers in communication between these groups, and increase the sensitivity of each group to the other's needs and objectives.

All sectors of society, and industry in particular, now require environmental skills to be integrated into traditionally specialist areas. Although environmental specialists will still be required, environmental awareness and underpinning knowledge must be an integral part of all vocational areas. This necessitates a reorientation of all job training to incorporate environmental considerations.

However, this integration needs to be more extensive in some areas than in others. For example, it is important for the management and planning of multinational corporations to acquire and demonstrate a greater awareness of global conventions, co-operation agreements (to facilitate technology transfer), and trans-boundary pollution – more so than for the average SME. The development of interdisciplinary skills within local authorities and central government in particular is crucial, to facilitate information flow with industry, and to develop infrastructures conducive to improving industrial environmental performance – e.g. transport infrastructures.

The further development of interdisciplinary skills in those vocations concerned with both environmental and employment matters is also necessary.

There will be increasing employment opportunities within the environmental services sector, for example for waste management specialists, and it is vital that this sector should continue to receive appropriate development support.

Finally, the development of more multi-sectoral communications and networks to establish cross-sectoral concerns and priorities is necessary. These can then be fed back into the individual sectors, incorporating their own specific considerations. (An example of such an approach is carried out by the German Environment Agency.)

# 8

# THE IMPACT OF EC ENVIRONMENTAL PROGRAMMES AND LEGISLATION ON EMPLOYMENT[1]

## *James Medhurst*

## INTRODUCTION

The introduction of policies to improve the environmental performance of industry is a continuing, albeit uneven process. Its progress is largely dependent upon business cycles and the perception and identification of environmental problems. The increase in environmental legislation and programmes inevitably affects the economy overall and influences the number and type of employment opportunities offered by industry.

Traditional views hold that environmental programmes reduce employment, causing investment to be directed away from those opportunities offering the best return. More recently, the emphasis on 'sustainability' implies that unless the environmental impacts of industrial activity are reduced to manageable and acceptable limits such activity cannot be sustained and the survival of individual companies will be jeopardised.

This chapter does not comment on these two positions, but reports on some of the direct linkages between environmental policy and employment opportunity and, in particular, examines the role of European Commission (EC) legislation and programmes. The EC is generally regarded as having been a major catalyst for change and continues to exert a strong influence on the formation of environmental policy and of the frameworks within which subsequent environmental impacts are evaluated.

## ENVIRONMENTAL EMPLOYMENT

This chapter examines the following areas:

1   Definition of environmental employment: use of a simple economic frame-
    work (demand-side/supply-side).
2   Key aspects of EC activities with particular significance to the EC
    programme which directs environmental investment, and their impact
    on the number of employment opportunities.
3   Implications for the type of employment opportunities.

## Definition and framework

In the context of this chapter environmental employment refers to those jobs
provided in:

- the pollution control and waste management industry (abbreviated to the
  environmental protection industry);
- the water supply industry;
- the environmental management activity in industry and public authorities;
- 'soft' environmental activities including conservation and amenity
  provision.

This list in not exhaustive and the possibility of extending this is considered
later. Employment issues arising from the above will be discussed below using
a simple supply–demand framework to avoid double counting.

Direct employment impacts are defined as those which are generated as a
known consequence of environmental policy, and which can be overtly identified. A typology (Table 8.1) of impacts can be identified and divided into
'supply-side' and 'demand-side'. The supply-side employment impacts relate
to the expansion of the pollution control and waste management industry
consequent upon increased environmental expenditure (and are not solely a
function of investment levels). This also includes the employment associated
with new environmental infrastructure programmes.

The demand-side employment impacts arise from the direct response of
the economy to environmental policy. This includes the employment impact
in environmentally sensitive industries, usually considered as those with high
pollution control expenditure, such as energy and chemicals. However, sensitivity is not just a function of the level of pollution control requirements.
Sensitivity is determined by the use, directly or indirectly, of environmental
resources at all stages of the production/product life cycle.

The demand-side impact must be considered not only in terms of the
increased expenditure on pollution control and the presumed opportunity cost
associated with the redirection in investment from production to pollution
control (the conventional view) but also in terms of the strategic adaptation
of industry to environmental pressures in the longer term (e.g. the diversification from conventional power generation technologies to renewable energy

*Table 8.1* A typology of direct employment impacts of environmental policy

*Supply-side impacts*

1 Employment generated in the supply of pollution control goods and services and waste management and other environmental services

2[a] Employment generated in the construction, supply and operation of new environmental infrastructure/clean-up/improvement programmes

3 Employment generated in the water supply industry

*Demand-side impacts*

4 Employment impact in sensitive industries

  a[b] Short-term (adjustment impact) (includes issues of SMEs, investment cycles, etc.)

  b Long-term (adaptive impact) (includes changes in competitiveness and industrial structure)

5 Employment impact consequent upon changes in environmental conditions

  a Sectoral impacts

  b[c] Spatial impacts (e.g. impacts on urbanisation)

*Notes:*

[a] The possibility of opportunity costs, in the short term, associated with the diversion of investment for environmental purposes should be taken into account

[b] Sensitive industries are those most exposed to environmental pressures as a consequence of their use of environmental resources, at any and all stages of the product life cycle

[c] Also consequent upon changes in sectoral competitive advantage

technologies). The demand-side impact also includes the sectoral consequences of improved environmental conditions (a sustainability argument). For example, the improved economic performance of tourism consequent upon reduced coastal water pollution may create employment opportunities.

Finally, it is worth noting that both the supply-side and demand-side impacts are influenced by the type of environmental policy adopted. For example, BATNEEC dictates the range of suitable production technologies, while economic instruments permit flexibility in the response of industry. Furthermore, the hypothecation of environmental taxes will generate direct employment impacts.

### Mechanisms for generating and retaining employment

Environmental pressures create a demand for environmental goods and services which in turn generates employment. These pressures also require improved environmental management practices in industry which generates a requirement for new (improved) management and technical knowledge competence.

The articulation of these environmental pressures, resulting from consumer preferences and social aspirations for a better environment, represents a mechanism through which environmental employment is generated and retained. These mechanisms are based on:

- Administrative activities, specifying environmental regulation, its enforcement and compliance;
- Markets, as preferences for a better environment are reflected in market prices;
- Social dialogue through which social and community aspirations are defined.

These mechanisms vary in the strength of their influence through time and between regions and sectors. Increasingly social dialogue and market-based instruments are becoming the primary mechanisms. In particular, social dialogue and voluntary agreements affecting the balance between environmental and commercial performance will have a related effect on employment. Social dialogue has a particular role to play in response to short-term pressures on industry to reduce employment to finance capital investment in environmental management activity. Specific and targeted responses to minimise the risk to and to retain employment are therefore required.

## Extensions of the definition of environmental employment

The definition of environmental employment previously noted is based upon a set of clearly definable activities which are directed to improving the environmental performance of industry. These activities form the basis of most empirical estimates of environmental expenditure and environmental employment opportunities. However, the pursuit of sustainable development requires an ever expanding definition of environmental employment to encompass employment in all those activities which result in environmental improvements. For example, employment in renewable energy activity, as this may displace conventional fossil fuel-based activity, can be deemed to be 'environmental'. Similarly employment in waste recycling or the production of clean technologies can be defined as environmental, even though such activities might be driven by non-environmental interests.

Ultimately, however, the term 'environmental employment' loses its meaning as all economic activity and associated jobs become 'sustainable'. Thus the original definition, where the *intent* of improved environmental performance underpins the classification, is retained and excludes employment in activities which have beneficial environmental *effects* but where this is incidental to the main purpose of the activity. It also follows that, as the economy progressively becomes environmentally sustainable, the term refers to a transitory (albeit potentially long-lasting) component of the economy.

# EC PROGRAMMES AND LEGISLATION

## Background

The European Commission is directly responsible for a number of expenditure programmes investing in environmental activities and therefore generates environmental employment opportunities. In addition, the EC continues to be responsible for driving forward the environmental policy debate and for proposing new legislation and initiatives. The impact of EC legislation is difficult to quantify, since it is an integral element of environmental pressures acting on industry. The specific attribution of employment impacts to the EC is therefore confined to the expenditure programmes.

## The role of community programmes (environmental improvement)

The role that Community programmes can play in supporting job generation is of particular significance given the objective of reducing unemployment in Member States (MS), partly by public programmes. The use of public programmes to create employment through environmental improvement programmes has been a traditional anti-recessionary tool; and a number of countries have undertaken such programmes. These programmes are often labour intensive with a low cost per directly created job; they are targeted at unemployed and disadvantaged groups and integrated with programmes to aid SMEs at a local level. However, such programmes are unlikely to create many permanent jobs and the scale and relevance of training does not contribute generally to the long-term integration of unemployed persons.

## The role of community programmes (environmental infrastructure)

In addition to employment creation from programmes of environmental improvements, there are also Community programmes which fund environmental investment in infrastructure and technological development. Table 8.2 summarises Community programmes for environmental actions.

EC programmes accounted for some 3,000 Mecu of environmental expenditure in 1995. As the EC co-funded up to 50 per cent of total investment (except for JRC expenditure), these programmes support a total environmental expenditure of approximately 5,500 Mecu. Structural Fund expenditure is the largest source of environmental project funding, estimated at 1.7 billion Ecu in 1995, of which 1.1 billion Ecu was spent in Objective 1 regions. This represents a significant proportion of total environmental expenditure in those regions. Environmental expenditure under the Structural Fund is set to grow during the 1990s to reach an estimated 2.2 billion Ecu in 1999. These

Table 8.2 Budgetary resources for environmental actions[a]

| Programme | Programme value (Mecu) | Duration (Years) | Estimated expenditure 1995 (Mecu) |
|---|---|---|---|
| Research | | | |
| • 4th Framework Programme (1995–98) | 852 | 4 | 213 |
| • Other programmes (industrial technologies, energy) | 135–270[b] | 4 | 50 |
| Demonstration | | | |
| • LIFE (1991–95) | 400 | 4 | 100 |
| Structural Funds | | | |
| • (1994–99) | 11.300[c] | 6 | 1,700 |
| Structural Funds | | | |
| • (1993–2000) | 7,500[d] | 8 | 937 |
| Total expenditure | 20,187–20,322 | | 3,000[e] |

Source: European Commission (various data sources)
Notes:
[a]  Environmental actions include environmental research, environmental protection, environmental infrastructure, waste management, water treatment, assistance for clean technologies and related environmental training
[b]  Assumes 5–10% of funds spent on environment
[c]  Assumes 8% of funds spent on environment
[d]  Assumes 50% of funds spent on environment
[e]  With the exception of research expenditure, all programmes are 50% cost shared. Total expenditure is therefore approximately twice the budgetary allocation; a total expenditure of 5,500 Mecu in 1995

expenditures include investment on environmental infrastructure such as water and waste water treatment plant, sewerage, solid waste disposal and industrial pollution control facilities.

Substantial finance for environmental investment is also provided by the Cohesion Fund, which aims to reduce economic and social disparities within the EC by contributing to infrastructure projects and environmental investment programmes in the four poorest Member States, Greece, Portugal, Spain and Ireland. Funding is equally split between environmental and transport projects. The type of environmental investment projects supported is similar to that financed by the Structural Funds.

Together, the Structural Funds and the Cohesion Fund provided funding of over 2.6 billion Ecu for environmental projects in 1995, of which over 2.0 billion Ecu was in Objective 1 regions. Allowing for co-funding, the Structural and Cohesion Funds generated approximately 5.2 billion Ecu of environmental infrastructure projects per annum, of which 4.0 billion Ecu was in Objective 1 regions.

*Table 8.3* Environmental expenditure: employment ratios for environmental infrastructure projects in Objective 1 regions

| Infrastructure project | Environmental expenditure employment ratio[a] | |
| --- | --- | --- |
| | Capital related: direct and first round indirect (Ecu/jobs year) | Operational related: on-site only (Ecu/full-time job) |
| Public water supply | 35,000 | 2,000,000 |
| Waste water management | 40,000 | 1,230,000 |
| Municipal solid waste management | 75,000 | 55,000 |

*Note*:
[a] Capital related and operational related employment ratios refer to the capital investment in Ecu required to generate either one full-time job or one job-year equivalent. This assumes that the expenditure necessary to operate the project would be forthcoming
*Source*: *Exchange of Experience within the Context of ENVIREG: The Impact on Employment of Environmental Expenditure in Objective 1 Regions: A Report to DGXVI*, ECOTEC Research and Consulting, November 1994

## ATTRIBUTABLE EMPLOYMENT IMPACTS

Analysis by ECOTEC has revealed capital investment ratios for both investment and operational employment in water supply, waste water management and municipal solid waste management projects (Table 8.3). Using average capital employment to investment ratios of Ecu 50,000/job-year for investment jobs and 1.1 million Ecu per full-time operational job, environmental investment supported each year by the Structural Funds and Cohesion Fund can be estimated to generate 100,000 job-years, or 10,000 full-time jobs per year, assuming that 1 job is equivalent to 10 job-years (i.e. a person is employed for a year), and 5,000 full-time operational jobs. The latter are permanent and cumulative, with investment in the 8 years between 1993 and 2000 creating an estimated total of 40,000 new jobs; 77 per cent of new employment will be created in Objective 1 regions. In addition, it is estimated that the Structural Fund and Cohesion Fund generated induced employment of around 5,000 full time equivalent jobs in 1995. Thus the total employment impact from direct, indirect and induced effects is equivalent to 20,000 full-time jobs per year.

## WIDER EMPLOYMENT IMPACTS

The employment impact of these programmes, especially in Objective 1 regions, lies not only in the direct and indirect employment supported by the investment but also in the employment potential associated with economic development which would otherwise be prohibited due to the absence of environmental infrastructure. Thus expenditure in water supply, waste water treatment and waste management infrastructure enable tourism, industrial and commercial developments which might otherwise not have been possible. However, the induced employment cannot be defined as 'environmental'.

## ENVIRONMENTAL EXPENDITURE AND EMPLOYMENT NEEDS: A CASE STUDY OF CONTAMINATED LAND

The job creation potential of environmental policy is significant if the employment opportunities arise in areas where there is a particular shortage of job opportunities. The opportunities for generating employment in Objective 1 regions has been discussed above. The potential for creating employment in Objective 2 regions has been considered by reference to the remediation of contaminated land.

Objective 2 regions are generally characterised as areas of severe industrial decline. In these areas land previously used for industrial purposes is often contaminated, thus restricting redevelopment and urban regeneration. Measures and expenditure on clean-up and site remediation will, it is thought, create employment opportunities in areas of greatest job need, both directly and indirectly, by removing development constraints.

There is a need to establish whether the land remediation market provides new employment opportunities in Objective 2 regions. Estimates of the stock and distribution of contaminated land in the EU (Table 8.4) confirm the highest concentration in northern Member States, especially the UK and Germany. Data for the UK (Derelict Land Survey) suggests that over half of contaminated

*Table 8.4* Number of contaminated sites in EU countries

| Country | Estimated number of sites | Estimated number of sites requiring clean-up |
| --- | --- | --- |
| Belgium/Luxembourg | 20,000 | 5,000 |
| Denmark | 7,000 | 2,000 |
| France | 100,000 | 20,000 |
| Germany | 200,000 | 50,000 |
| Greece | 5,000 | 1,000 |
| Ireland | 1,000 | 200 |
| Italy | 30,000 | 10,000 |
| Netherlands | 110,000 | 30,000 |
| Portugal | 4,000 | 800 |
| Spain | 25,000 | 5,000 |
| UK | 100,000 | 30,000 |
| *Total EU* | 602,000 | 154,000 |

*Source*: ECOTEC/Frost and Sullivan 1992

land is located in Objective 2 regions. With both the availability of public funding and the increased environmental awareness of industry, the market for remediation is estimated at 1.4 billion Ecu (1992) and is expected to grow to 4.0 billion Ecu in 2000: an average annual growth rate of 14 per cent.

Contaminated land remediation is a relatively labour intensive activity compared to other sub-sectors of the environmental protection market. A significant proportion (15–20 per cent) of expenditure relates to consultancy, including site investigation, analysis of samples, development and supervision of remedial work, and post-remedial monitoring. Clean-up activities account for 80–85 per cent of the market, and involve a large amount of earth moving and soil handling as well as specialist engineering and treatment.

ECOTEC data on turnover and employment in the environmental protection industry, obtained from POLMARK, indicate an average turnover/ employment ratio of 0.1 million Ecu. This implies total employment in this sector of 13,500 in the European Union in 1992.[2] Employment is forecast to total 33,600 by the end of the century. Based upon a crude pro-rata figure this suggests that up to the year 2000 some 10,000 gross direct jobs might be created in Objective 2 regions to reclaim contaminated sites. Additional employment would also be generated as a result of economic development which would otherwise not have occurred.

## OCCUPATIONS IN THE ENVIRONMENTAL SECTOR

### Current evidence

The occupational characteristics of employment related to the environmental sector have been identified in a number of studies. US research has identified in overall and detailed terms the occupations associated with environmental protection (Table 8.5). In the European Union CEDEFOP has undertaken a series of 'mini' exercises to identify occupations which have some responsibility for environmental management in selected industries and services. This analysis is based on detailed profiles of selected positions in industry. This analysis does not cover the environmental protection industry. As many of the activities of the environmental protection industry relate to engineering and technical services there are arguably few distinctive occupational characteristics of employees in this industry.

Land remediation is a good illustration of one of the types of new environmental employment opportunities which have developed. Remediation of contaminated land involves a combination of both highly specialist as well as general skills. Expertise in a range of disciplines including chemistry, engineering, geology, hydrogeology, environmental science, ecology and project management are central to this area. In addition, less qualified technicians

*Table 8.5* Environmental protection-related jobs created in the US economy, 1992, by major occupational group

| Major occupational category | Jobs (thousands) |
| --- | --- |
| Managerial and Professional Speciality Occupations | |
| • Executive, administrative and managerial occupations | 464 |
| • Professional speciality occupations | 330 |
| Technical, Sales and Administrative Support Occupations | |
| • Technicians and related support occupations | 109 |
| • Sales Occupations | 576 |
| • Administrative support occupations, including clerical | 601 |
| Service Occupations | |
| • Protective service occupations | 27 |
| • Service occupations, except protective | 370 |
| Farming, Forestry and Fishing Occupations | |
| • Farm operators and managers | 27 |
| • Other agricultural and related occupations | 41 |
| • Forestry and logging occupations | (*) |
| • Fishers, hunters and trappers | * |
| Precision Production, Craft and Repair Occupations | |
| • Mechanics and repairers | 204 |
| • Construction trades | 288 |
| • Extractive occupations | (11) |
| • Precision production occupations | 200 |
| Operators, Fabricators and Labourers | |
| • Machine operators, assemblers and inspectors | 359 |
| • Transportation and material moving occupations | 174 |
| • Handlers, equipment cleaners, helpers and labourers | 200 |
| Total | 3,981 |

*Source*: Management Information Services, News Release, Washington DC, 8 March 1993
*Note*: * is less than 500 jobs

are employed to take and analyse samples and undertake routine monitoring work. The skills required for clean-up operations vary according to the remediation technique adopted. However, all projects will to some extent involve specialist engineering expertise, as well as tasks such as general earth moving, requiring machine operators.

A list of the types of organisations and occupations usually involved in land remediation projects is given in Table 8.6. While any project is likely to involve a combination of skills, the division of services between consultants, contractors and the client varies between projects. For example, project management may be undertaken in-house or contracted out. Some projects involve the appointment of independent consultants who will design the clean-up operation, appoint contractors and manage the clean-up operations. In other cases, a contractor may provide a complete package, managing the investigation and clean-up of the site as a whole.

*Table 8.6*   Agencies and occupations involved in land remediation

| Agencies | Occupations |
|---|---|
| Advisors | Environmental Consultants |
| | Geological/Geotechnical Consultants |
| | Civil Engineering Consultants |
| | Ecological Consultants |
| | Chemical Engineering Consultants |
| | Laboratory Analysis Consultants |
| | Quantity Surveyors |
| | Landscape Architects |
| | Project Managers |
| | Financial Consultants |
| Contractors and Sub-Contractors | Civil Engineering Contractors |
| | Chemical Engineering Contractors |
| | Site Investigation Contractors |
| | Waste Management Contractors |
| | Laboratory Service Suppliers |
| | Specialist Land Remediation Contractors |
| | Sewerage Undertakers |
| | Landscape Contractors |
| | Land Surveyors |
| | Grouting Contractors and Suppliers |
| | Plant and Machinery Hire Companies |
| | Manufacturers of Geotextiles and Geomembranes |
| | Construction Materials Suppliers |
| Skill Needs | Chemists |
| | Engineers: Civil, Geotechnical, and Environmental |
| | Geologists |
| | Hydrogeologists |
| | Environmental Scientists |
| | Ecologists |
| | Project Managers |
| | Technicians |
| | Machine Operators |

# CONCLUSION

## Research and policy context

The above account has described the current levels of employment and occupational characteristics associated with the environmental sector, related to EC programmes. The analysis is based upon recent estimates of environmental expenditure and some empirical research into employment activities. The results should only be used to provide a broad indication of the scale and character of activity rather than as exact measures.

As noted in the Introduction, activity in the environmental sector is fundamentally a derivative and side effect of pursuing environmental policy objectives and responding to environmental pressures. The employment impacts in other areas of the economy, especially in the longer term, are likely to be more profound than the levels and types of employment associated with the environmental sector, and to a large extent this will depend upon the willingness to define and pursue sustainable development in all economic sectors.

To understand these wider and potentially far-reaching changes a variety of research approaches and perspectives is required. The policy initiatives which flow from fully integrating environmental interests within other policy domains need to be defined in order to understand probable future employment changes in the context of sustainable development. The approach used in the research described above represents only a small part of a much wider investigation which is in its infancy.

## Mechanisms for sustaining employment

Employment in the environmental sector is, as noted, primarily generated as a consequence of the pursuit of environmental objectives. For example, the requirement to comply with defined standards of environmental performance generates a demand for environmental goods and services.

As described above, the availability of public funding and the increased environmental awareness of industry will increase the market for remediation. In 1992 this was estimated at 1.4 billion Ecu and is expected to grow to 4.0 billion Ecu by the year 2000, representing an average annual growth rate of 14 per cent. As previously mentioned, contaminated land remediation is a relatively labour intensive activity compared to other sub-sectors of the environmental protection market.

Government and Community programmes therefore have a dual role in both defining and driving the pursuit of environmental pressures and in part financing environmental improvement activities.

## Occupational characteristics

The increasing requirement for environmental management competencies is likely to be reflected in additional responsibilities for existing employment positions rather than an increase in new types of job.

Available research has documented employment characteristics in companies which have environmental management pressures rather than those associated with the environmental protection industry, although there have been developments to define and improve skills in the waste management industry. The documentation indicates that the growth in environmental management skills relates to all managerial, technical and operative levels within companies, but with an emphasis on scientific, engineering and technical competencies.

The occupational changes described above relate primarily to traditional employment positions, mainly in manufacturing industry and reflected in male-dominated, highly structural and graded full-time positions.

### Employment policy initiatives

It is apparent that the generation of employment in the environmental sector is a 'side-effect' of environmental policy. It therefore follows that the retention and generation of employment in relation to environmental policies and environmentally driven changes in consumer behaviour requires specific employment initiatives. The development of initiatives at local and regional levels aimed at improving environmental performance while minimising the frictional costs of adjustment is especially noteworthy in this context.

In the longer term the pursuit of sustainable development requires the integration of environmental and labour market policy, as well as with other policy domains, to ensure that the pursuit of environmental objectives is complementary to the pursuit of economic, employment and social objectives. The range and character of these policies, the relevant mechanisms and the necessary research still remain to be fully defined.

## NOTE

1   The basis of this chapter is a report to the EC (DGV): *Job Creation and New Occupations in Various Sectors of the European Union's Economy*, a Report by ECOTEC Research and Consulting, 1994.
2   A new report published by Eurostat provides an updated analysis of those employed in EU eco-industries: *Data Collection on EU Eco-Industries*, Eurostat, 1997.

## REFERENCE

ECOTEC Research and Consulting Limited (1994) *Exchange of Experience within the Context of ENVIREG: The Impact on Employment of Environmental Expenditure in Objective 1 Regions: A Report to DGXVI.*

# 9

# EXPANSION AND PROFESSIONALISATION OF THE EUROPEAN ENVIRONMENTAL EMPLOYMENT SECTOR[1]

*Monica Hale*

## INTRODUCTION – THE ENVIRONMENTAL 'MARKET'

Over the past five to ten years increasing interest in the environment has led to more people seeking careers in the environment sector. Coupled with this interest has been a revolutionary change in the perception of 'environmental jobs' and the nature and status of such jobs. This change is in part explained by the realisation by governments that 'a healthy economy is dependent on a healthy environment' (M. Thatcher, former UK Prime Minister, in a speech to the Royal Society, September 1988).

Consequently the demand for expert advice and assistance to both business and industry and local and central government in environmental policy formulation, environmental management and conservation has rapidly grown. In addition, industry-specific environmental skills and knowledge are increasingly required in existing professional, industry and business skill areas. The further application of statutory regulations as well as voluntary codes of practice to both the public and private sectors, in areas such as pollution control and sustainable resource management, has meant that personnel with the appropriate environmental skills are needed to find practical work-based solutions to such measures.

In addition to the new legislative requirements, the commercial logic of 'going green' has also been more widely recognised. This can result in lower costs from increased energy efficiency, recycling initiatives and careful purchasing policies. Investment in state-of-the-art environmental technology and sound management practices also results in tangible efficiency and cost benefits, as well as providing image-improving positive publicity.

Career opportunities have expanded as a result of the increased importance and relevance of environmental issues to all sectors of economic activity. In the late 1980s and early 1990s the demand for environmental consultants was more or less outstripping supply. It has been said that the growth in the environmental consultancy sector has proved to be a reliable barometer of environmental activities in the community as a whole (ENDS 1995). Even during the recent economic recession the environmental jobs market (particularly with reference to environmental consultancy) was relatively recession-proof (ENDS 1992).

It is notoriously difficult to gain accurate data on the numbers employed in the environment sector, so consequently analysis is likely to yield an underestimate of employment in environment management as it refers only to those who have a major responsibility for pollution control and whose cost can be separately identified.

In the UK in 1988 there were around 200 people engaged in environmental consultancy of varying types and specialisations. These were mainly small operators chasing a market worth around £100 million per year. Currently the business is worth about £400 million per year and has around 400 to 500 operators, of whom more than 70 have sales of over £1 million. There are a number of environmental consultancies who have exceeded £10 million and a few are now prominent internationally (Figure 9.1) (ENDS 1995).

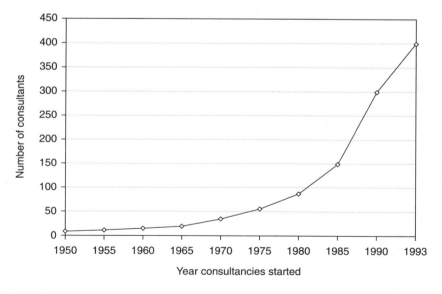

*Figure 9.1*  Cumulative increase in the number of environmental consultancies in the UK, 1950–93

Before the early 1970s, environmental consultancy was mainly carried out as part of civil engineering contracts or within laboratory, analytical or planning services. Environmental consultancy only began to be a service in its own right twenty years ago, and many of the now largest consultancy companies were established around this time. From the early 1980s the number of environmental consultancies expanded rapidly, reaching a peak growth rate in 1990 when around 45 new businesses entered the market. In 1992, 1993 and 1994 the number of new entries levelled off to about 30 per year. New entrants are currently mainly unemployed environmental specialists from industry (and non-specialists – which creates specific problems for the environment industry), and other consultancies starting up on their own.

ENDS report that the number of environmental consultancies in the UK has risen from 149 in 1985 to 339 in 1992 (including 20 major players), while turnover reached £400 million (524 Mecu) in 1992, up from £130 million (170 Mecu) in 1986. The number of UK professionals working full time on environmental contracts rose from 3,846 in 1990 to 6,477 in 1992, with a total of 19,000 environmental consultancy contracts being awarded in a single year – 1992. The *Environment Business Journal* reports that consulting job numbers in the US have grown by 57 per cent from 1988 to reach 158,000 in 1992.

In 1992, it was estimated that there were approaching 500,000 people employed in the environment industry in the United Kingdom and that there was evidence that this number was increasing (ENDS 1992). Also the potentially wider careers market for environmental specialists across Europe and North America was also expanding. However, in the most recent market assessment it was found that while the demand for environmental consultants is likely to rise, this will not be at the rate forecast two years ago. At that stage, based on the steady rate of growth up to then, it was expected that the sector would be earning £1 billion by the year 2000, but now the projection has been revised to about £700–850 million (ENDS 1995). It is thought there are two main reasons for this downward revision:

- Many clients adversely affected by the recession are more insistent on getting value for money, and a fiercely competitive pool of consultancies is helping them achieve this.
- The new and rapidly growing phenomenon of environmental managers in business is now defining a different role for the consultants they employ.

While there are job opportunities in the short term, the Commission of the European Communities (CEC 1993) emphasises that it is important to recognise the way in which various parts of the environment industry have tended to develop. In the early days many small companies came into the market, often staffed by people previously employed in traditional large companies. There is then a process of consolidation as environmental specialist businesses combine or are taken over by larger companies. The period of consolidation often suggests a halt to the growth in job numbers.

It is also important to bear in mind that environmental policy initiatives require staff for research, planning, training, monitoring and enforcement in the public and private sectors and in voluntary organisations. In some cases such tasks will be absorbed within existing responsibilities.

There is a general shortfall in the number of staff available to conduct environmental management work in the public sector: this has also been identified within the European Commission's own work and in national and local governments (CEC 1993). The UK National Audit Office (NAO) suggested that the Pollution Inspectorate (Her Majesty's Inspectorate of Pollution – HMIP) would need twice its current staff by 1994 to fulfil its role in monitoring compliance with the Environmental Protection Act (1990) (Oates 1993). This situation changed after April 1996 when the new UK Environment Agency became operational. This combined the functions of HMIP and the National Rivers Authority. The remit of the Agency is to protect and enhance the environment and to prevent pollution through a more integrated approach to environmental management and regulation.

At the end of 1991 the ILO suggested there was a need to increase current employment levels for public administrative staff by 100 per cent to 150 per cent to meet the requirements for fully enacting existing legislation (ILO/Lewis 1991).

When assessing European environmental career opportunities, additional considerations which have to be taken into account include the recognition and transferability of skills and qualifications across Europe and other international boundaries as well as European language capability.

In response to this 'information gap' the London Guildhall University 'Careers in the Environment' initiative organised a series of events and publications to inform careers guidance officers, employers and others of the nature of environmental careers and the qualifications necessary to enter the environmental careers market (Buxton et al. 1993; Hale 1995a and b).

## ENVIRONMENTAL EMPLOYMENT AND SUSTAINABLE DEVELOPMENT

Sustainable development gained prominence at the Earth Summit in Rio de Janeiro in 1992 and is based on the premise that unless the environmental impacts of industrial and business activity are reduced, such activity, and the survival of companies, cannot be guaranteed. There are thus direct links between environmental policy and employment opportunity.

Policies directed at improving the environmental performance of industry continue to increase and stricter environmental legislation affecting the operations and outputs of companies is also coming into force. This is reflected in environmental employment opportunities. Thus, there are several factors which must come together if sustainable development is to be successfully worked towards. These include:

1   A cadre of environmental 'professionals' needs to be available to advise, organise and implement programmes of environmental action in all sectors of activity (governmental, industrial, community, etc.).
2   There needs to be an environmentally literate and aware public willing to take action for the environment and who will take heed of the advice offered by the environmental 'professionals'.
3   Full employment must be a goal of all countries – many of the 'new jobs' will result from environmental action plans.

This chapter will concentrate on the area of the environmental professionals. However, it should be remembered that unless the economic, political and social climate is right there will be no demand for environmental professionals. This point was emphasised in an International Labour Office report which recalled the Bruntland Report stipulating the requirements for achieving sustainable development (ILO 1992):

• An economic system that is able to generate surpluses and technical knowledge on a self-reliant and sustained basis;
• A social system that provides for solutions for the tensions arising from disharmonious development;
• A political system that secures effective citizen participation in decision-making.

## WHAT IS ENVIRONMENTAL EMPLOYMENT?

It can be said that all jobs are 'environmental' as virtually all economic activities have an impact on the environment. Some of these activities have a more obvious effect on the environment than others, however. An all-encompassing definition of environmental employment is difficult to construct and even more difficult to achieve general agreement about.

One of the problems of definition is the differentiation between 'environment industry', 'environmental management', environmental protection, etc. A number of researchers in this field have taken 'environmental management' and 'environmental protection' to be sub-sectors of the overall environment industry (CEC 1993). Table 9.1 is based on dividing the 'environment industry' into two broad categories: those who produce and supply specialist environmental goods and services (labelled 'environmental protection'), and those in the public and private sectors who require, purchase and use those

*Table 9.1* EC environmental expenditure and direct employment 1992/2000

| Environmental sector | Expend. within $EC^a$ | Numbers employed (000) | | | | % EC Jobs$^b$ |
|---|---|---|---|---|---|---|
| | (1992 prices billion Ecu) | 1992 | 2000 | Increase | % Increase | |
| Environmental protection | 48$^c$ | 370 | 636 | 266 | 72 | 34 |
| + exports$^d$ | | 92 | 192 | 100 | 50 | |
| Industry environmental management$^e$ | 15 | 168 | 288 | 120 | 72 | 15 |
| Public authority environmental management | | 333 | 573 | 240 | 72 | 30 |
| Water supply | | 226 | 389 | 163 | 72 | 21 |
| Total environment industry employment | | 1,189 | 2,078 | 889 | | 100 |

*Source*: Adapted from estimates by ECOTEC (1993)
*Notes*:

a   'Environmental protection' and 'environmental management' are taken as being 75 per cent and 25 per cent, respectively, of 'total environmental expenditure'.
b   This refers to relative employment numbers when exports are excluded from the environmental protection figures. The inclusion of exports would increase the relative importance of the environmental protection market to 39 per cent of total employment in the environment industry.
c   Adjusting for imports of 9 per cent (OECD estimate – OECD 1992) the estimate for EC *production* for the environmental protection industry is reduced to 43 billion Ecu.
d   Employment associated with exports to non-EC countries is estimated at 92,000 jobs in 1992 and 192,000 in 2000 (calculated using an OECD estimate of a 20 per cent additional output for non-EC markets and an ECOTEC estimate of a 'doubling' of jobs by 2000 due to export potential). While employment associated with exports may not be as directly influenced by EC policy production for the internal market, it is impacted by the range of EC environmental, industrial and employment policies, and is therefore considered appropriate for inclusion in the overall employment figures in this table.
e   This refers to *internal* management activities; for example, in 'sensitive industries'.

services and have also to manage the environmental effects of product, process and resources, etc. (labelled 'environmental management'). As can be seen from the table, it is estimated that in 1992 500,000 people were employed directly in 'environmental management' in the EU. Of these, 67 per cent were in public authorities (333,000) and the remainder in industry (168,000) (ECOTEC 1993).

The OECD has identified three broad types of 'environmental service' jobs:

● *Technical Engineering*: site assessment, process design, control specifications, project management – included in 'environmental protection' figures;

- *Environmental Consulting*: impact assessments, environmental audits, monitoring and risk management;
- *Management Services*: financial analyses, database management and expert systems, of which there are now over 100 directly applied to environmental tasks.

Medhurst (see chapter 8) defined environmental employment as jobs in the:

- Pollution control and waste management industry (abbreviated to the environmental protection industry);
- Water supply industry;
- Environmental management activity in industry and public authorities; and
- 'Soft' environmental activities including conservation and amenity provision.

By contrast, a more descriptive attempt at defining the profession has been made by the Institute of Ecology and Environmental Management (IEEM 1995) which is based more on the definition of the knowledge and skills an environmental manager requires with reference to 'ecological management' (this is of course only one part of the employment management area – Medhurst's definition is more all-embracing). However, the IEEM does illustrate the level of detail required to differentiate the various areas in which environmental management has evolved. Ecologists and environmental managers are:

> Professionals who have a sound knowledge of ecology and environmental management through academic studies or professional training, and who have a minimum of three years experience in relevant professional practice. In particular, professional ecologists and ecological managers should be competent to apply their ecological knowledge (in a direct or advisory capacity) to study, classify, protect and manage ecosystems, their constituent species, and the processes which affect ecosystems.
>
> This must be understood as applying ecological principles to strategic considerations as well as those relating to the implementation of policies and projects. The practice of ecology and ecological management is not solely a scientific and technical one. At senior level in particular, it involves competence in management and mediation among many interests. It draws on innovative and creative capabilities in development and managing solutions to problems as well as evaluating them. It requires a sensitive awareness of political and ethical issues as the profession is typically practised in complex institutional contexts.
>
> (IEEM 1995)

These contrasting attempts to define the 'environmental profession' illustrate one of the major problems of defining this profession: the Medhurst definition is based to some extent on the sector of activity where environmental managers may be found whereas the IEEM defines what environmental managers actually do and what underpinning knowledge and skills are necessary to carry out such work. However, the latter definition is confined to only one of the many task-based areas of environmental management.

Medhurst bases his definition upon a set of clearly definable activities which are primarily directed at improving the environmental performance of industry. While from the environmental employment point of view this may not be the most informative way of describing the environmental sector, it is these activities that currently form the basis of most empirical estimates of environmental expenditure and environmental employment opportunities.

With the increasing tendency to relate economic and environmental factors to sustainable development there is now an expanding definition of environmental employment which may deliver environmental improvements. Thus, as Medhurst illustrates, employment in waste recycling or the production of clean technologies can be defined as 'environmental', even though such activities may be driven by non-environmental interests. For the purposes of this chapter, an 'environmental job' will be taken as one where the majority of the job specification is related to environmental considerations or improvement.

The environment is a multi-disciplinary area of work and study. It encompasses a great variety of specialisms and areas of expert knowledge. Consequently, the definition of this employment area will vary according to which of the many different fields of expertise is being reviewed. Each of these areas requires a different knowledge base. It is a characteristic of this area of employment that no single person can be expected to cover every facet of it.

The concept and importance of professional institutes in defining the environmental employment sector and how this relates to the emerging recognition of and increase in the environmental jobs market will be discussed later in the chapter.

## HOW MANY JOBS ARE THERE IN THE ENVIRONMENT?

Whatever definition is used to establish the boundaries of environmental employment, the demand for environmentally-trained specialists *and* environmentally-aware personnel who may not necessarily be considered environmental specialists arises from the direct response of the economy to environmental policy and practice. This includes the employment impact in environmentally 'sensitive' industries, particularly those with high pollution control expenditure (e.g. energy and the chemical industry) at every stage of the production/ product life cycle.

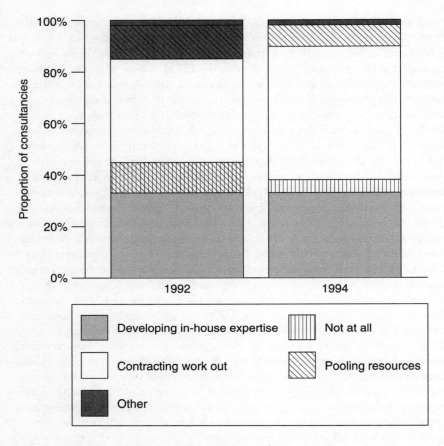

*Figure 9.2* In-house staff vs consultancy, 1992–94

The type and nature of employment in the environment sector is not necessarily the same as that for other employment sectors. As mentioned in the
Introduction, environmental consultancy has been one of the main sources
for employment in this sector. During the past few years, according to an
ENDS survey of clients' reactions to environmental concerns (ENDS 1995),
the impact of the economic recession, particularly staffing cut-backs, has had
an effect on the number of clients developing in-house expertise rather than
contracting work out to consultants. A typical reaction quoted was from
Kodak's environmental manager, who commented that 'Our own resources
are diminishing, now we are buying in the expertise.'

The changes during the past few years are shown in Figure 9.2 based on the
ENDS survey which shows, with reference to environmental consultancies, that
more industry contacts than before are responding to environmental concerns,
and fewer are pooling resources with other companies. But rather than develop

the necessary skills in-house, clients are relying increasingly on external input from environmental consultancies (ENDS 1995).

Whether to use in-house staff or a consultancy depends on a number of particular circumstances. Employing a consultancy is often the quickest and simplest method of solving particular environmental dilemmas. Consultants largely trade on knowledge, so they have to keep up to date with developments and develop particular expertise to remain competitive. Many companies, however, combine the use of in-house staff and external consultants to varying degrees.

In the EU it has been estimated that direct employment supported by environmental expenditure was approximately 1.2 million jobs in 1992, including the water supply industry. This represents 1.3 per cent of total EC employment and is projected to increase by a further one million by the year 2000. To this can be added at least 200,000 jobs in 1992, in 'soft' environmental activities (such as nature conservation, heritage preservation, coastal protection and amenity provision such as parks and open spaces). The Commission of the European Communities has estimated that 'environment related' employment could double these figures (CEC 1993).

In the UK in 1990 environmental employment was estimated to be 109,000 or 0.4 per cent to 0.6 per cent of all jobs (ECOTEC 1990). German environmental employment was put at 430,000 – about 1.7 per cent of the total labour force. The UK was estimated to have over 100,000 environmental jobs (13 per cent in regulatory agencies, 23 per cent in the 'polluting' industries and 64 per cent supplying pollution control equipment). In France, the ILO 1989 figures showed 360,000 workers (1.6 per cent of the labour force) engaged in environment related employment. The Danish Metalworkers (1987) suggest an environmental industry employing 10,000 people and representing half of Denmark's export production.

Around two thirds of employment in the EU 'environmental protection' industry is located in the northern countries. This is estimated as representing 370,000 jobs, plus 92,000 in production for exports (ECOTEC 1993) and is distributed as follows:

- 30 per cent in Germany;
- 15 per cent in France;
- 10 per cent in the UK;
- 9 per cent in Italy.

The CEC (1993) also reports that 'environmental management' provides a further 500,000 jobs, while environmental management skills are also being integrated into a range of existing roles, such as chemists and engineers. It was emphasised that the public sector is vital to the growth of environmentally focused jobs, accounting for more than half of the total spending on environmental equipment and services in Europe.

One of the fastest growing job areas in the environmental employment market is environmental auditing, often associated with monitoring compliance and pre-acquisition auditing. Jobs are being created in:

- Financial auditing firms (who provide the security of being a known firm);
- The insurance industry which underwrites enormous potential environmental liabilities and is therefore needing to carry out auditing for its own purposes: their auditing departments are now offering services to others;
- Independent consultancies.

## THE DEVELOPMENT OF THE ENVIRONMENTAL 'PROFESSIONAL' IN EUROPE

One of the main problems the environmental market faces, which is particularly manifest in the environmental consultancy field, is the proliferation of underqualified and often unqualified people setting themselves up as 'environmental consultants'. As this area has been one of perceived growth and expansion, and in many instances fairly lucrative, and not regulated by an official or institutional body (i.e. such as environmental health officers), a number of people have been attracted to this sector. Consequently, the quality of work and consultancy has often been poor to say the least and has in some instances brought the profession into disrepute. The situation in the UK has reached the point where one of the environment and business magazines ran an article on 'Environmental Cowboys'.

Invariably these 'consultants' are undercutting well-qualified, experienced personnel on the basis of price, and consequently securing significant contracts. Clients, who are themselves unaware what to look for in terms of the 'environmental credentials' of tenderers, will generally go for the lowest price without fully realising the quality of the job which will result. This situation also emphasises the need for the environmental management profession to reach a point where it is highly institutionalised, if not regulated (this latter essentially implying an environmental manager needing a 'licence to practise').

The environmental profession is fully aware that standards of work are very varied. Its reaction has been to establish trade associations and several systems of accreditation for both organisations and individuals to stamp quality into environmental work.

## PROFESSIONAL INSTITUTES IN THE ENVIRONMENTAL SECTOR

Over the past five years there has been the recognition that if the environmental area is to gain the acceptance and to be held in the same regard as other 'professions' (i.e. lawyers, engineers, the medical profession, etc.) then it must implement the structures which regulate any other profession.

Thus the emerging professional environmental institutes have developed their own code of practice (to which members as a condition of their membership must adhere), professional services (such as professional indemnity insurance), a continuing professional development (CPD) or other educational requirement, and have issued guidelines for professional practice (for example, guidelines on tendering, model service agreements, etc.). Importantly, institutes need to communicate their existence to potential employers and hirers of environmental services. The institutes must also educate and communicate with the buyers of environmental services and employers of environmental personnel as to what to look for by way of professional 'credentials' (i.e. appropriate institutional membership) as well as academic achievements when engaging personnel or contracting a consultancy.

While this scenario has been the case for most of the 'established' professions for decades, this is a new development in the environmental area. In the UK alone there are several 'environmental institutes', some of which include:

- IEEM – Institute of Ecology and Environmental Management
- IEM – Institute of Environmental Management
- IEA – Institute of Environmental Assessment
- EARA – Environmental Auditors Registration Association
- IWEM – Institute of Water and Environmental Management

This list is by no means comprehensive but serves to illustrate the increasingly fine dividing line that separates the various specialist functions of those employed in the environment sector. It has been said that this burgeoning of environmental institutes may serve to weaken the profession by the distribution of small membership institutes across a range of small professional bodies. This may well point to the need for either an amalgamation of some of these institutes or the development of an 'umbrella' body representing all the environment institutes, much as the Engineering Council which has approximately 70 engineering member institutes and can thus present a unified approach to issues affecting the profession.

There are a number of professional associations and institutes established in most countries in Europe, for example:

- Association Française des Ingénieurs Ecologues (AFIE)
- Réseau EcoConseil

- Association Française des Eco-conseillers
- Verein der Geoökologen (VdG)
- Bund der Ökologen Bayerns (BOB)
- Vereinigung der Umweltwissenschaftlichen Berufe Deutschland (VUBD)
- Institute of Ecology and Environmental Management (IEEM)
- Associazione Svizzera degli Ecologi Professionisti
- Schweizerischer Verband der Oekologinnen und Oekologen
- Association Suisse des Ecologues Professionels (ASEP)
- Institue of Environmental Health Officers (IEHO)
- Institute of Environmental Sciences (IES)
- Landscape Institute (LI)
- Association of Local Government Ecologists (ALGE)

In addition, for many years a number of the biology/geography orientated institutes have had environment committees, for example, the Institute of Biology in the UK – which primarily, however, deals with the interests of 'biologists' and cannot operate the specialised services needed by the increasingly complex requirements of environmental managers.

More professional bodies outside the strictly 'environmental' field are also taking seriously environmental issues and the environmental impact their members may have while carrying out their duties. For example, the Engineering Council has recently issued guidance to their members on environmental issues and stipulated that members undertake environmental CPD.

The co-ordinating body across Europe for environmental institutes is the European Federation of Environment Professionals (EFEP).

## SKILL CHALLENGES IN THE ENVIRONMENT SECTOR

Environmental considerations are now included in the employment debate in the UK and in the rest of Europe. For example, in *Labour Market and Skill Trends 1991/92* (Department of Employment 1992), it was stated that the four main skill challenges for Britain in the 1990s were highlighted as:

> international competitiveness; the introduction of new technologies; action on the environment; and population changes. Inevitably there are complex links between the challenges and local or sectoral initiatives which will need to recognise these.
>
> (Department of Employment 1992)

This report acknowledges that 'environmental concerns have led to increasingly stringent control over pollution and other environmental hazards' and that 'business faces new legal requirements covering the technologies they use in the disposal of waste'. There is also recognition of the impact of consumer pressure in changing product ranges, packaging and production processes. Countryside conservation and energy efficiency are cited as creating new demands on businesses and their workforce.

The main uncertainty of the UK Department of Employment was the pace at which consumers and taxpayers would make resources available for environmental improvements, rather than *if* environmental concerns would feature prominently in the jobs market. The key labour force skill requirements the report identified were:

- The technical skills to create solutions to raw material, production and waste disposal problems;
- A general level of environmental awareness in the workforce to form the basis of effective company policies.

Skills shortages do not always manifest themselves in reported recruitment difficulties. Employers may respond to them by reducing the level of service they offer or accepting reduced efficiency rather than by putting more effort into recruitment. Consequently some skills gaps are not easy to quantify. Environmental skills and knowledge shortages generally fall into this category. This is important to consider when reviewing the results of labour market assessments and training needs analyses produced by statutory and non-statutory bodies as they may not detect the underlying demand for additional environmental skills.

Because the environment skills marketplace is still comparatively young, matching available skills with those needed is often difficult. The nature of this mismatch is not necessarily one of qualifications (although this is true in some cases) but more a lack of experienced personnel: particularly those with the experience to work with industry, understand its problems and identify realistic solutions (ENDS 1992).

Concern about the lack of environmentally qualified staff, and hence about the quality of environmental work (particularly in business and industry), has led to initiatives for the accreditation of environmental impact assessors, environmental auditors and environmental managers.

A severe skills shortage hampered the environmental consultancy profession in the late 1980s and early 1990s when demand for well-qualified environmental consultants far outstripped supply. At the time of the third edition of the ENDS *Directory of Environmental Consultants* (ENDS 1992), 58 per cent of the consultancies believed there were insufficient numbers of suitably qualified staff on the market. The position has now improved with the corresponding figure for the fourth edition of the *Directory* (ENDS 1995) being 43 per cent. This figure is still high and should warn potential buyers of such services to beware of consultancy teams built from staff without the right qualifications and skills.

The problem also has as much to do with lack of experience as formal qualifications. Experience, particularly at senior consultant level, is widely quoted as in short supply, as is the ability to write reports! However, it is business management skills that are currently in most demand by consultancies, i.e. someone to liaise with clients, develop the business and manage the specialists.

On the scientific side, the ENDS survey (ENDS 1995) found that hydrological skills were still in most demand. Other types of staff in short supply included ecologists, noise and vibration specialists, chemists and chemical engineers, process engineers and environmental auditors.

## SKILLS REQUIREMENTS AND PRIORITIES

Recent research has shown that there is no numerical shortage of postgraduate environmental scientists (Court *et al.* 1995), with the possible exception of hydrogeology and soil science. Employers are, however, increasingly demanding scientists with MSc qualifications. This is largely due to the increase in activities which require a combination of expertise in a main discipline and specific types of technical expertise. These areas may include Geographic Information Systems, remote sensing and waste management techniques. Employers consider that it is not the level of qualification that is important but the specialist nature of the expertise required, which meant that few first degree graduates would possess the required skills.

Court *et al.* found a mismatch between the postgraduate environmental science training most commonly supported by research councils and that demanded by business and industry. The larger proportion of environmental science higher degrees supported were in agriculture and fishing sectors and mineral extraction. There were no higher environmental science qualifications supported in energy production and the distribution and waste sectors. When this is compared to the pattern of demand, agriculture, forestry and fishing and mineral extraction industries account for a relatively small proportion of environmental science employment. From research evidence Court *et al.* suggest that the energy production and waste industries have a demand for environmental scientists. In the case of the waste industry this is likely to grow.

The key issues with which employers are primarily concerned are the growing realisation that environmental issues need to be tackled from a variety of perspectives and an increasing awareness that scientific expertise on its own is not sufficient. A further issue concerns the level of numeracy of environmental scientists.

Employers are concerned about the availability of environmental scientists with a particular combination of qualifications, skills and experience. The desired combination of skills was generally a good in-depth knowledge and understanding of a core discipline, the ability to communicate with and understand scientists from other disciplines, and a range of personal skills. These concerns have important implications for the training of environmental scientists.

Environmental issues require input from a range of disciplines. Environmental scientists in the workplace will need to contribute to an understanding of processes related to the environment. They will need to work with scientists from a range of disciplines and to be able to understand arguments presented in more than one specialism. This requires individuals who have an in-depth and broadly based understanding of their own specialism to be able to communicate it to non-specialists. There is also a perceptible awareness in some sectors of the need for expertise in crossing the natural science–social science divide.

Scientists who lack personal transferable skills will not find employment in the business sector. Essential generic skills include communication skills (particularly an ability to communicate with non-specialists), team-working skills, project management skills, and an awareness of the business world and the wider social and political context within which environmental issues are addressed.

The need for numerate, computer literate scientists to work on environmental issues is also of prime importance. In a number of areas this may include the need for highly numerate environmental scientists capable of understanding statistical analysis and mathematical/computer modelling techniques. The demand for such skills is not confined to the 'hard science' subject areas: changes within other disciplines, and the need for predictive capability in the environmental area generally, mean that scientists with modelling skills are increasingly required in a wide range of activities.

## ADDRESSING EMPLOYMENT TRAINING NEEDS

While companies and organisations can respond to changing skills needs by employing (either on a permanent or contractual basis) individuals with the required skills and expertise, the development of in-house capabilities and understanding is also necessary. There are many instances whereby existing personnel have been required to take on the environmental remit, alongside their other duties. If the greater proportion of their time is spent addressing environmental aspects within that organisation then this may constitute an 'environmental job', but the person performing these duties may not have received the appropriate training or have the relevant experience necessary for such work. These skills will have to be engendered by additional training and experience gained over time.

In such instances a crucial process which will have to be undertaken is a training needs analysis (TNA). This should be carried out on a regular basis and should be an integral part of decision-making on annual training budgets. The process can be summarised in four stages (Laffan and Bromhead 1996):

1   Identification of necessary skills (company wide);
2   Identification of individuals requiring specific training;
3   Identification of the level of skill currently possessed;
4   Identification of the skills gaps.

'Skills' include a combination of awareness, specific skills, information, knowledge and the necessary tools required by an individual to meet an organisation's needs. To equip employees with specific skills and knowledge the training undertaken will have to be job specific: for example, training for a site waste management team may include the necessity for detailed knowledge of waste legislation, the waste management hierarchy, administrative procedures, etc. (Laffan and Bromhead 1996).

## CONCLUSION

While over the past five years there has been a continuing upward trend in environmental employment, there is evidence that the pace of this increase has slowed down (ENDS 1995). This could be due to a number of factors. It may be that companies are now better able to cope with the demands of environmental pressures (i.e. from legislative requirements, consumer demand, supply chain requirements, etc.) from within their own staff resources. This may result in less need to call in consultants, and with the increasing knowledge of relevant environmental effects and options for remedial action, employers are now better able to resource these needs from within. Therefore the employment of environmental 'specialists' may not be detected in the research carried out on environmental employment in companies as the environment becomes increasingly integrated into other aspects of jobs.

There is a possibility that with the move towards integrating environmental considerations and environmental applications into educational courses at higher and specialist levels (Department for Education 1993; Hale 1993), the position of environmental manager or environmental consultant may dwindle or vanish altogether. It may even repeat a similar pattern of fewer demands for programmers in the computer industry, as software 'packages' for PCs are now extensively used.

Ultimately, the term 'environmental employment' may lose its meaning as all employment and all economic activities and associated 'jobs' become 'sustainable'. Thus the original definition which Medhurst uses of an environmental job where the *intent* of improved environmental performance underpins the classification is retained, and excludes employment in activities which have beneficial environmental *effects* but where this is incidental to the main purpose of the activity. As the economy progressively becomes environmentally sustainable, the term 'environmental employment' may increasingly refer to a transitory, although potentially long-lasting, component of the economy.

A recent example of this scenario may be cited from the Chemical Industries Association. In their *UK Indicators of Environmental Performance 1994* one of the parameters used to judge investment in the environment of this sector is the proportion of capital spent annually on remedial environmental measures (Chemical Industries Association 1995). For the past four to five years this has been increasing. But now for the first time since these figures have been collated there has been a fall in this proportion. The CIA interprets this situation as demonstrating two tendencies:

1  As *new* plant is being installed it is already specified and fitted with pollution reduction mechanisms, thus reducing the need to invest large sums in end of pipe solutions.
2  Retro-fitting pollution reduction equipment is generally a one-off expenditure and will not show up in the year-on-year environmental measures expenditure being collected by the CIA.

While these are logical explanations, a full site-based assessment of the underlying reasons for this reduction in environmental expenditure has not yet been undertaken to verify these assumptions.

The combination of increasing UK and European legislation, a shift in taxation policies to pollution-related charges, the establishment of environmental standards such as ISO 14001 and voluntary environmental initiatives, will result in an increasing requirement for environmental knowledge and skills. This will not only be in the form of additional environmental specialists, as already established professions and careers will increasingly have an environmental component.

The CEC (1993) have predicted that while the increase in external environmental experts is likely to continue in the medium term, auditing, monitoring and computer-based management of environmental performance can increasingly be expected to be brought in-house. In addition, in line with research on corporate demand for environmental training, it is likely that those in existing posts within industry will be trained to undertake the new environmental tasks, with a relatively small increase taking place in the number of in-house environmental specialists.

While implementing corporate environmental policy within operating sites has often tended to be via operating technical committees in a 'command and control' process, many companies are now seeing the value of 'establishing environmental protection as a discrete component of every employee's job description' (much as Health and Safety has become). This is seen to be a more cost-effective way to reduce environmental risks (CEST 1993).

In 1991, the British Trades Union Congress (TUC) Environmental Action Group suggested increased demand for environmentally trained professional, managerial, scientific and technical staff in the key sectors of chemicals, water supply, electricity, food processing, metal manufacture and motor vehicles. Thus, managing the environment is likely to require the 'sensitising' of many existing occupations to environmental requirements, rather than enormous increases in posts for environmental specialists. While the total number of people working in environment related jobs will increase, it will not be at the rate previously projected.

## THE LONDON ENVIRONMENT CENTRE 'CAREERS IN THE ENVIRONMENT' INITIATIVE

The 'Careers in the Environment' initiative was started in 1993 by the Faculty of Human Sciences, London Guildhall University, in response to the lack of accurate and accessible environmental careers information for school leavers, graduates, postgraduates and mid-career changers. Enormous changes in job types and resultant career opportunities have taken place in this sector over the past decade (Hale, 1993, 1995a and b). Rapid expansion of the environmental jobs market has taken place, from the traditional nature conservation-related areas to positions in business and industry, the service sector, and local and central government.

To assist in the dissemination of information about environmental employment and training issues and to investigate the nature and extent of these developments, the 'Careers in the Environment' initiative has:

- Organised a National Conference (October 1993) and National Workshop (November 1993) on 'Careers in the Environment';
- Published *Careers in the Environment* (the proceedings of the above events) (1995);
- Published the *Careers in Ecology and Environmental Management* booklet with the Institute of Ecology and Environmental Management (1993), second edition (1994);
- Organised the 'Careers in the Environment across Europe' conference (May 1995);
- Prepared papers, workshop reports and outcomes for the 'Careers in the Environment across Europe' conference for publication as *Environmental Employment and Sustainable Development* (1998);
- Contributed to the preparation of the publication on environmental employment and training in conjunction with the European Federation of Environment Professionals to be published in *Network 21* (1995/96);
- Prepared a project for a 'Careers in the Environment' video for Careers Officers; and

- Is currently formulating a research project on environmental employment and training.

In addition, staff involved in the initiative have contributed to a number of other conferences and publications, both within the UK and overseas.


## NOTES

1  Based on an article which appeared in *Business Strategy and the Environment* (1996), Vol. 5, 242–51.


## REFERENCES AND FURTHER READING

Buxton, R., Gentil, E. and Hale, M. (1993) *Careers in Ecology and Environmental Management*, London Guildhall University.

Cahn, M. (1995) Environmental Careers in Europe. In Hale, M. (ed.) *Careers in the Environment, Proceedings of the National Conference and Workshops*, London Guildhall University.

CEC (Commission of the European Communities) (1993) *The Employment Implications of Environmental Action*, CEC, DGV, Employment, Industrial Relations and Social Affairs, Brussels.

CEST (Centre for the Exploitation of Science and Technology) (1993) *Environmental Profiles of European Business*, from the Royal Institute of International Affairs Energy and Environment Programme, UK.

Chemical Industries Association (1995) *The UK Indicators of Environmental Performance 1994*, CIA, London.

Court, Gill, Jagger, Nick and Moralee, Janet (1995) *Skills Requirements and Priorities in the Environmental Sciences*, Institute for Employment Studies, University of Sussex.

Department for Education (1993) *Environmental Responsibility: An Agenda for Further and Higher Education*, HMSO, London.

Department of Employment (1992) *Labour Market and Skill Trends 1991/92: Planning for Growth*, Department of Employment, London.

Department of Trade and Industry (1991) *The Single Market: Open for Professions, UK Implementation*, HMSO, London.

ECOTEC (1990) *Training in the Environmental Field within the Community*, report to the European Commission, 1990.

ECOTEC (1993) *Sustainability, Employment and Growth: The Employment Impact of Environmental Policies*, Discussion Paper Two, May 1993.

Ellis, J. B. (1995) The Range of Vocational Areas and Career Structures in the Environment: An Overview. In Hale, M. (ed.) *Careers in the Environment, Proceedings of the National Conference and Workshops*, London Guildhall University.

ENDS (Environmental Data Services Ltd) (1992) *Environmental Consultancy in Britain: A Market Analysis*, ENDS, UK.

ENDS Environmental Data Services Ltd) (1993) *Environmental Managers in Business*, ENDS, UK.

ENDS (Environmental Data Services Ltd) (1995) *Directory of Environmental Consultants*, fourth edition, ENDS, UK.

Friends of the Earth (1994) *Working Future? Jobs and the Environment*, Friends of the Earth, London.

Hale, M. (1993) Careers in a Changing Environment, *Newscheck*, Careers and Occupational Information Centre/Department of Employment, 5–8.

Hale, M. (1995a) Promoting Environmental Education across Professions: The 'Careers in the Environment Initiative', In Leal Filho, W., MacDermott, F. and Murphy, Z. (1995) *Practices in Environmental Education in Europe*, University of Bradford, 119–35.

Hale, M. (ed.) (1995b) *Careers in the Environment, Proceedings of the National Conference and Workshops*, London Guildhall University.

Hale, M. (1996) Sustainable Growth and Environmental Employment in Europe, *Business Strategy and the Environment*, Vol. 5, 242–51.

IEEM (Institute of Ecology and Environmental Management) (1995) *The Profession of Ecology and Ecological Management: What You Need to Know*, First Report, May 1995, IEEM, UK.

Institution of Environmental Sciences (1993) *Environmental Careers Handbook*, IES, London.

ILO (International Labour Organisation)/Lewis (1991) *Employment and Training Implications of the Waste Management Industry*, Research Note by Keith Lewis, Geneva, November 1991.

ILO (International Labour Organisation) (1992) *Environment and the World of Work*, Report to the Director-General of the International Labour Office to the International Labour Conference, 1990, second impression, International Labour Organisation, Geneva.

Laffan, Jane and Bromhead, Alistair (1996) Establishing Training Needs, *Environmental Assessment*, Vol. 4, Issue 2, June.

Oates, Andrea (1993) *Industrial Relations and the Environment – United Kingdom*, for the European Foundation for the Improvement of Living and Working Conditions, Working Paper No. WP/93/09/EN.

Shovelton, R. (in press) Employment Implications of Environmental Action: A Report to the EU Directorate General V, this volume, chapter 4.

TUC (1991) *Industry, Jobs and the Environmental Challenge*, TUC Environmental Action Group, TUC, UK.

# 10

# SUSTAINABLE DEVELOPMENT AND THE EUROPEAN JOBS MARKET

*Jørn Pedersen*

## INTRODUCTION: THE EUROPEAN FOUNDATION FOR THE IMPROVEMENT OF LIVING AND WORKING CONDITIONS

The European Foundation for the Improvement of Living and Working Conditions, an autonomous EU body, was established by a Council Regulation in 1975 to assist the formulation of future policies. Through the Foundation's research and information activities it provides the EU institutions, particularly the Commission and the European Parliament, as well as the Member States, with a scientific basis against which to develop medium- and long-term policies for the improvement of social, socio-economic, environmental and working conditions. The Foundation also serves as a forum for discussion on these issues, bringing together EU and government policy-makers, including politicians, representatives of the social partners, international organisations and NGOs, and not least researchers and other experts.

One of the main areas of the Foundation's work is the socio-economic aspects of the environment and sustainable development policies. In 1993 the Foundation, with the Commission's Directorate-General for the Environment, initiated a project on the employment potential of sustainable development policies. The main purpose at that time was to contribute to the discussion in the EU of how the move towards sustainability could be used as an instrument for furthering growth and job creation. The project's first output was a working paper for discussion, entitled, 'The Potential for Employment Opportunities from Pursuing Sustainable Development' prepared by ECOTEC (see Medhurst, chapter 8). The Foundation's work on employment and sustainability is expected to continue for another couple of years. At present the research is focusing on the micro level while market-based instruments are being discussed in a research group which may develop into a research network. Close co-operation between the Foundation, the Commission's Directorate-General for

Research and Development and its Directorate-General for the Environment has been established, including the provision of financial support.

This chapter will highlight some of the most significant sectoral and cross-sectoral trends in our society and their implications. It will attempt to identify the changes required to achieve sustainability, the measures and approaches involved and the likely impact and potential of this process in terms of economic activity and employment.

## EUROPEAN POLICY FRAMEWORKS

We are today at a crossroads where we know that the path we have been following for the last few decades is no longer viable and that urgent radical changes in our society, based on innovative thinking, are needed. This is largely accepted in developed countries. At the global level, we are faced with key issues which must be addressed effectively as soon as possible. Developed countries have a consumption pattern based on excessive use of resources, many of them non-renewable, and through various policies developing countries are being encouraged to deplete their resources to satisfy our own short-term needs, thus jeopardising their medium- and long-term development prospects. Over the last few decades, a population explosion has occurred in the developing and so-called industrialising countries, contributing to even more poverty and constituting a major threat to life on earth. These two elements, resource consumption and population growth, have had a detrimental impact on the environment and living conditions in many parts of the world. Ecosystems have been destroyed, varieties of flora and fauna have disappeared and global climate change is a serious problem.

It is within this context that the concept of sustainable development emerged and was defined in the report of the World Commission on Environment and Development (1987) (the so-called Brundtland Report) as 'development which meets the needs of the present without compromising the ability of future generations to meet their own needs'. Although the problems in Europe were not of the same magnitude as those in many other parts of the world, it was clear that we would be affected by the situation elsewhere. Also developed countries were partly to blame for this situation and it was clear that our own environment had deteriorated considerably and would suffer irreparable damage if we did not change our policies and lifestyles. Hence, the concept of sustainable development has been adopted by the European Union and integrated into its policies.

The adoption of this principle is reflected most distinctly in the EU's Fifth Environmental Policy and Action Programme which defines sustainable development policies as 'policies and strategies for continued economic and social development without detriment to the environment and the natural resources on the quality of which continued human activity and further development

84

depend'. This definition points to three key dimensions of sustainable development:

- Economic;
- Social;
- Environmental and resource consuming.

These three elements interact to the extent that it is unlikely that we would be successful in achieving sustainable development without considering them together as part of the same effort, using the potential of each of them to strengthen the total effect. Importantly, this thinking is also reflected in the Treaty on European Union which not only states that 'environmental protection requirements must be integrated into the definition and implementation of other Community policies' but also sets out as its principal objectives the need to promote:

- A harmonious and balanced development of economic activities;
- Sustainable and non-inflationary growth respecting the environment;
- A high degree of convergence of economic performance;
- A high level of employment and social protection;
- The raising of standards of living and quality of life;
- Economic and social cohesion and solidarity among Member States.

It is within this broad framework that we have to consider sustainability and its potential for growth and employment creation.

The services of the Commission were well aware of this from the outset as the Fifth Environmental Policy and Action Programme stated in its sub-chapter on industry that the intention was to use environmental policies and measures reflecting stringent requirements, improved resource management and a broad mix of instruments to stimulate investment, innovation and competitiveness, thus 'turning an environmental concern into competitive advantage'. It was therefore not surprising that the Commission, in the light of the recession and the high rate of unemployment, decided to assess the possibility of using environmental improvements and the move towards sustainability as an instrument for economic growth. Several initiatives were launched, not least at the behest of Jacques Delors, including European seminars in 1993 on 'Environment and Development' and in 1994 on 'Towards a European Model for Sustainable Development'.

A communication by the Commission was followed up, in 1993, by a White Paper on 'Growth, Competitiveness, Employment – The Challenges and Ways Forward into the 21st Century'. This document, as indicated by its title, goes far beyond policies and strategies for future developments and environmental and resource management performance, but such policies are a crucial element in the ideas and proposals set out in the paper. It suggests that the economic development model followed over the last few decades has been inefficient insofar as it has led to 'under-use' of the workforce, both in terms of quantity and quality, and to excessive use of natural and environmental resources. A new sustainable growth model is therefore required to strengthen growth, competitiveness and employment as well as the environment and the quality of life.

A key aspect of this process is the widespread implementation of clean technology. This should be supported and supplemented by a complete review of existing macro and sectoral policies and their aims in the light of the requirements of sustainability, and the development of a consistent set of market incentives which would be integrated into the new policies so as to ensure that market prices exclude all external effects.

While the changes and adaptations following from the new policies will have to be dealt with at all levels (European, national, local) the White Paper sets out five priority areas specifically for EU action:

- Making the most of the single market;
- Supporting the development and adaptation of small and medium-size enterprises;
- Pursuing the social dialogue;
- Creating the European infrastructure networks (transport and energy);
- Preparing and laying the foundations for the information society.

The last two areas were considered the key to enhanced competitiveness and the choice of them was seen as an opportunity to study aspects of employment and living conditions in the light of technical progress.

This document has been debated extensively in the EU and in national contexts. Several proposals are regarded as furthering the move towards sustainability. However, it should be considered for what it is, i.e. a document for discussion launching the debate on our future society and how we can achieve our economic, environmental, social and other objectives in an interactive and integrated approach to policies in these areas, ensuring that we move towards sustainable development.

Thus, this leads to an examination of existing trends and the policies required in a few key sectors if sustainability is to be achieved. In addition, the implications in terms of economic activity and employment need to be assessed.


## ENERGY

Energy is one of the key sectors in any effort to achieve sustainability, as it is, directly or indirectly, not only responsible for more environmental problems than most other sectors but is also the basis of virtually all economic activity.

Therefore a major dilemma exists of having to reduce the environmental impact of energy quite dramatically, which also means reducing energy consumption while, at the same time, ensuring that economic activity remains largely unaffected.

The policies and measures adopted to date at national and European levels do not appear to be very successful in this respect. This is not surprising considering there are no easy solutions and that Member States' energy policies differ considerably. These are based on a variety of considerations with different priorities in the national context (e.g. economic, development or environmental, easy access to a specific energy source, existing investments in plants, etc.). In addition, many countries seem to be looking for an international agreement enabling them to introduce adequate measures which would solve the dilemma without affecting their competitiveness, but such agreements may be a long way off.

Meanwhile, we are experiencing a rise in energy consumption of 1–2 per cent per annum as energy efficiency measures introduced in the late 1970s are increasingly inadequate and can no longer offset the steady increase in the transport sector. During the period 1980–89 the transport sector's share of total energy consumption rose from 24.6 to 31.2 per cent while that of industry and private households, including the tertiary sector, declined from 35.5 and 37.7 to 31.2 and 35.2 per cent respectively (Figure 10.1).

The energy consumption per capita in Europe is at 3.5 toe[1] comparable to that of Japan and less than half of that of the US at 8 toe.

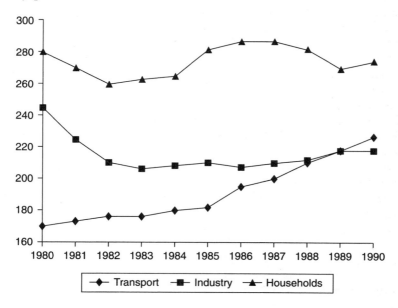

*Figure 10.1* Energy consumption by sector in Europe

A 'business as usual' scenario prepared by the Commission in 1992 and covering the period until 2005 indicates that total energy demand may rise by 1.3–1.6 per cent per year over the next ten years, reflecting annual increases of 2 per cent in the transport sector, 1.4 per cent in private households and the service sector and 0.4 per cent in industry. The annual demand for coal is expected to fall by 1.3 per cent while for gas and electricity it may rise by 2 per cent. Only a slight increase in oil consumption, approximately 1 per cent, is foreseen and a relative fall in the consumption of industry, private households and the service sector is expected. Renewable energy sources may be further developed but their market share is unlikely to increase significantly due to the lack of incentives. Public opposition in addition to competition from gas may mean the use of nuclear energy for electricity generation will remain at the same level as currently. Such development would, together with various measures introduced over the years, result in a reduction, albeit insufficient, of $SO_2$ and $NO_x$ emissions. It would also result in a considerable increase in $CO_2$ emissions which will not, as planned, be stabilised at the 1990 level by the year 2000. Recent developments already show this to be the case.

Sustainability in the energy sector will have to be based on radical changes breaking the present trends. It will require substantial improvements in energy efficiency through various national and European programmes and measures, a major R & D effort to ensure diversification of energy sources away from present carbon-intensive energy consumption and a strengthening of the role of renewable energy and new energy technologies. Accompanying major changes in attitudes and behaviour throughout society would have to take place, supported by the education and training of users, agreements with industry and, probably most effectively, by economic and fiscal instruments. Finally, as it is unlikely that we will be able to move towards sustainability at this stage without relying, to some extent, on nuclear energy, it is necessary to find solutions to the safety and waste problems in this area.

Despite these efforts, we may not be able to achieve sustainability in the energy sector within the EU for a considerable period of time due to development in Central and Eastern Europe and the expected major economic expansion and increase in energy consumption in the so-called industrialising countries such as China. It is worth noting that, before enlargement, the EU was only responsible for 13 per cent of global $CO_2$ emissions.

Considering the significant changes required to achieve sustainability coupled with what is happening on a global scale, it is unlikely that a successful reduction in emissions will take place until 2030 or later. A variety of programmes and measures aimed at more sustainable development need to be implemented both nationally and at European level, some of which are already occurring. It is within this context of a gradual move towards sustainability, which is politically acceptable, that future employment perspectives must be examined and the potential of the various measures to contribute towards growth and job creation assessed.

Present trends as well as sustainability oriented policies will lead to further redundancies in the European coal industry, as a result of economic rather than environmental considerations, as it is heavily subsidised in some Member States. By contrast the gas industry can probably look forward to a prosperous future as gas is becoming increasingly popular. This will have a positive impact on employment prospects both in the gas industry itself and in associated equipment manufacturing industries. Renewable energy, notably solar energy and biomass, may be a major growth area offering good employment opportunities for engineers, skilled and semi-skilled workers, particularly in manufacturing industry, but this will largely depend on whether governments will make this a priority area for national energy supply and, hence, provide sufficient incentives. The development of new energy technologies, energy saving equipment and the pressure to reduce $SO_2$ and $NO_x$ emissions will have beneficial effects for employment at all levels in the relevant branches of manufacturing industry. Likewise, energy efficiency programmes will also generate employment, particularly for energy consultants (engineers), and the same will probably benefit from an introduction of an energy or $CO_2$ tax in industry.

## TRANSPORT

Transport is not only a vital part of economic activity in modern society but also enables us to exercise our right to mobility. Virtually no mode of transport is neutral in terms of its effects on the environment as the latter is affected both by transport itself and by the infrastructures and ancillary structures required for the movement of people and goods. Road transport is usually perceived as the main culprit in this respect and, hence, a major threat to achieving sustainability due to the range of serious problems associated with it in relation to the environment, including energy consumption, health, safety, noise, etc.

The important role of transport in our society, particularly its contribution to GDP and employment, and the individual's right to mobility have, until recently, made it difficult to impose restrictions on activities in this sector. This situation is now slowly changing, both at national and European levels, although a number of inconsistencies still prevail, e.g. in relation to the development infrastructures which are not compatible with policies aimed at encouraging a change to other modes of transport. It is also worth noting that in the transport sector we are not faced with the same dilemma as in the energy sector as alternative solutions are usually available if the political will is there and is supported by the public.

This is partly reflected in the trend or 'business as usual' scenario whereby various measures in countries such as Denmark, The Netherlands, Germany and the UK (despite some growth in the overall mobility demand), are likely

*Table 10.1* Energy demand and emission indicators in road transport under different driving circumstances

| Type of vehicle | | Fuel Consumption 1/100km | Emission of pollutants (in g/vehicle km) | | | | | |
|---|---|---|---|---|---|---|---|---|
| | | | CO | No$_x$ | HC | CO$_2$ | SO$_2$ | Part. |
| Private Car | | | | | | | | |
| Petrol | urban | 11.6 | 45.0 | 1.2 | 6.4 | 315 | – | – |
| | non-urban | 5.3 | 12.5 | 1.6 | 1.3 | 160 | – | – |
| Diesel | urban | 9.4 | 1.7 | 0.8 | 0.5 | 331 | 0.08 | 0.40 |
| | non-urban | 5.8 | 0.7 | 1.7 | 1.0 | 201 | 0.06 | 0.23 |
| Bus | | | | | | | | |
| | urban | 33.0 | 18.0 | 15.5 | 12.0 | 1158 | 1.70 | n/a |
| | non-urban | 32.0 | 3.8 | 15.0 | 2.7 | 1123 | 1.50 | n/a |
| Delivery Van | | | | | | | | |
| | urban | 16.0 | 55.4 | 3.0 | 6.0 | 498 | 0.18 | n/a |
| | non-urban | n/a | n/a | n/a | n/a | n/a | n/a | n/a |
| Heavy Goods | | | | | | | | |
| | urban | n/a | n/a | n/a | n/a | n/a | n/a | n/a |
| | non-urban | 33.0 | 8.0 | 17.5 | 2.8 | 1158 | 1.59 | n/a |
| Motorcycle | | | | | | | | |
| | urban | 6.0 | 15.6 | 0.1 | 14.0 | 163 | – | – |
| | non-urban | 3.5 | 8.5 | 0.2 | 4.7 | 106 | – | – |

*Source*: COM (92) 46f.
*Note*: n/a = no data available

*Table 10.2* Final energy consumption by sub-sector (per cent) (year 1989)

| | Road | Rail | Air |
|---|---|---|---|
| EUR 12 | 26.0 | 1.0 | 3.5 |
| Belgium | 21.5 | 0.6 | 2.4 |
| Denmark | 21.2 | 0.9 | 5.8 |
| France | 28.0 | 0.9 | 3.0 |
| Germany | 24.0 | 0.8 | 2.8 |
| Greece | 28.3 | 0.5 | 7.7 |
| Ireland | 21.1 | 0.6 | 5.2 |
| Italy | 28.1 | 0.6 | 1.7 |
| Luxembourg | 23.0 | 0.1 | 3.5 |
| Netherlands | 18.6 | 3.9 | 3.6 |
| Portugal | 31.6 | 1.0 | 6.1 |
| Spain | 33.4 | 1.0 | 4.7 |
| United Kingdom | 25.9 | 0.7 | 5.0 |

*Source*: *The State of the Environment in the European Community*, Vol. III

to lead to a reduction in car emissions to the 1990 level by between 2010 and 2030. Conversely, in countries like Spain, Greece, Portugal and Ireland, major investments in road building programmes, largely funded by the EU, will encourage greater use of both new and old vehicles. In these countries a move towards sustainability can only be ensured by more stringent EU regulations and directives (as well as local action), particularly as no long-term policies to rationalise and change the structure of the transport sector are envisaged. Some cities in most Member States may be forced to introduce a no-car policy in their central areas; and relief roads around cities may contribute to generating even more traffic.

The same scenario also indicates that high-speed trains may divert some traffic away from air routes, but the nuisance caused by aircraft (noise, land-take and stratospheric $CO_2$ emissions) can be expected to increase up to 2010 and beyond.

A *sustainable development scenario* will have to be based on a substantial reduction of road transport and a stabilisation of air traffic at levels marginally higher than at present. This will require various national and European-wide measures, some of which are already under discussion and partly agreed at EU level:

- Development of a Trans-European Network of high-speed trains for passengers and goods linked to the existing national networks, plus further development of the latter so they are compatible with each other and are linked to adequate port facilities and inland terminals to enable a transfer of goods from ships to rail and rail to road, or vice versa.
- Discouragement of long-distance haulage transport, e.g. by a European licensing system involving high registration and annual disc renewal taxes as well as very stringent requirements for exhaust emissions and road worthiness.
- Encouragement of shipping for transport of goods, e.g. by exemption of taxes and levies on bunker oil, accompanied by development of port facilities and incentives to shipyards, insofar as the existing shipping capacity is insufficient.
- Increase in fuel prices of 5–7 per cent per year in real terms over a twenty-year period.
- Improved and integrated land-use and traffic management aimed at reducing the distance between home, workplace and shops; providing a wider choice of adequate and comfortable modes of transport, including efforts to retain the urban population and workplaces within the boundaries of, preferably existing, urban areas; encouraging higher densities of key nodes of public transport networks; planning for a balanced urban system and a better mix of activities in cities, and contributing to the regeneration of existing towns and cities rather than creating new structures in peripheral locations.

- In central areas of cities – effective parking policies; priority measures for pedestrians and cyclists; priority measures to encourage the use of public transport; traffic calming measures; and environmental and social awareness programmes aimed at the public.

The move towards sustainability in the transport sector is going to be a gradual process over approximately forty years and will be the result of a combination of major changes in transport structures; the need for new infrastructures; and the role of vested interests. Integrated planning systems will also be required, some of which are not yet fully developed. Technological developments over this period may offer alternative solutions, so it is advisable to focus on short- and medium-term changes when assessing possible employment opportunities.

The introduction of a progressive increase in fuel prices by 5 per cent per year in real terms in Member States (as in Britain) will lead to fewer private cars on the road and, in time, to a reduction in the number of cars overall. This would be a more effective measure if combined with further development of public transport. Such measures will adversely affect the car industry but will be beneficial to the manufacturers of public means of transport, some of which are also car manufacturers. The restriction on cars in cities, high parking fees and the growing emphasis on car-free cities may lead to the same result.

The combination of shipping and haulage which is favoured by the Commission and the existence of excellent port facilities close to major economic centres in Europe may in the medium or long term bring about major changes in employment structure and reinvigorate the European ship-building industry. Such a structural change will, however, require better planning in both industry and the service sector.

Opposition to the development of hypermarkets and shopping centres on the periphery of cities, which is emerging in some Member States, could, combined with better land-use and traffic management, lead to the revival of some city centres. The additional employment created as a result would more than compensate for job losses in the peripheral areas.

## HUMAN SETTLEMENTS

Human settlements may not be a sector of economic activity, but they do provide a spatial dimension to all activities in society. The interaction taking place in such settlements reflects existing and past developments and the problems caused by them. Importantly, past experiences may also indicate a number of likely future developments and trends, thus enabling preventive action instead of remedial solutions to be found. This is, for instance, the case when looking at the present demographic trends in the European Union, illustrated in Tables 10.3 and 10.4.

*Table 10.3* The population in Europe

| Country | Area ('000 km²) | Population ('000) 1.1.1990 | 1.1.1991 | Density (by km²) 1.1.1991 | Est. pop. ('000) 2000 | 2020 |
|---|---|---|---|---|---|---|
| Total EC 12 | 2,368,0 | *343,299,9 | 344,924,7 | 145,7 | 350,152 | 340,731 |
| Belgium | 30,5 | 9,947,8 | 9,987,0 | 327,4 | 9,893 | 9,423 |
| Denmark | 43,1 | 5,135,4 | 5,146,5 | 119,4 | 5,233 | 5,019 |
| Germany* | 356,6 | 79,112,8 | 79,700,5 | 223,5 | | |
| Greece | 132,0 | 10,046,0 | **100,200,0 | **77,3 | 10,116 | 10,141 |
| Spain | 504,8 | 38,924,5 | 38,993,8 | 77,2 | 39,381 | 37,230 |
| France | 549,1 | 56,577,0 | 56,893,2 | 103,6 | 57,883 | 58,664 |
| Ireland | 70,3 | 3,506,5 | **3,518,3 | **50,0 | 3,486 | 3,464 |
| Italy | 301,3 | 57,576,4 | 57,746,2 | 191,7 | 57,611 | 53,484 |
| Luxembourg | 2,6 | 379,3 | 384,4 | 147,8 | 394 | 410 |
| Netherlands | 41,5 | 14,892,6 | 15,010,4 | 361,7 | 16,019 | 16,979 |
| Portugal | 92,1 | 9,878,2 | 9,858,6 | 107,0 | 10,577 | 10,460 |
| United Kingdom | 244,1 | 57,323,4 | 57,485,8 | 235,5 | 59,039 | 60,672 |

*Source*: Eurostat
*Notes*:
\* Situation after 3 October 1990
\*\* Provisional

*Table 10.4* The population by age group and sex in 1990 (per cent of the total population)

| Country | Less than 15 yrs Male | Female | 15–64 yrs Male | Female | 65 yrs and over Male | Female | Total Male | Female |
|---|---|---|---|---|---|---|---|---|
| Total EC 12 | 9.4 | 8.9 | 33.7 | 33.6 | 5.6 | 8.8 | 48.7 | 51.3 |
| Belgium | 9.3 | 8.8 | 33.7 | 33.3 | 5.9 | 9.0 | 48.9 | 51.1 |
| Denmark | 8.7 | 8.3 | 34.1 | 33.2 | 6.4 | 9.2 | 49.3 | 50.7 |
| Germany | 7.7 | 7.3 | 35.3 | 34.4 | 5.2 | 10.1 | 48.2 | 51.8 |
| Greece | 10.2 | 9.6 | 33.0 | 33.6 | 6.0 | 7.7 | 49.2 | 50.8 |
| Spain | 10.2 | 9.8 | 32.9 | 33.0 | 5.5 | 7.9 | 49.1 | 50.9 |
| France | 10.3 | 9.8 | 32.9 | 33.0 | 5.5 | 8.5 | 48.7 | 51.3 |
| Ireland | 14.3 | 13.5 | 30.8 | 30.2 | 4.9 | 6.4 | 49.9 | 50.1 |
| Italy | 8.5 | 8.0 | 34.2 | 34.6 | 5.9 | 8.8 | 48.6 | 51.4 |
| Luxembourg | 8.9 | 8.5 | 35.1 | 34.1 | 5.0 | 8.5 | 48.9 | 51.1 |
| Netherlands | 9.0 | 8.6 | 35.1 | 34.0 | 5.3 | 8.0 | 49.4 | 50.6 |
| Portugal | 10.7 | 10.2 | 32.2 | 33.8 | 5.4 | 7.8 | 48.3 | 51.7 |
| United Kingdom | 9.8 | 9.3 | 32.8 | 32.6 | 6.3 | 9.4 | 48.8 | 51.2 |

*Source*: Eurostat

These trends, resulting primarily from falling birth rates rather than increases in life expectancy, illustrate some of the problems which may be facing the younger generation of today and their children – for example, a considerable rise in pension contributions and health care costs as well as the likely introduction of a later retirement age.

There has also been a trend in Europe of increasing urbanisation which, in itself, could have been beneficial in environmental, economic and social terms; however, it was often based on poor planning. A high level of traffic in many cities is one of the consequences of this inadequacy. The problems in many cities (crime, poverty, etc.) are also becoming increasingly difficult to tackle by means of traditional instruments and institutions, so new approaches are needed which include a close co-operation between public and private sectors and the involvement of citizens in decision-making. Furthermore, a concentration of economic activity in a few densely populated centres in Europe may leave many regions with few development prospects.

As part of the move towards *sustainability*, measures will have to be found to solve some of the major problems of cities. Integrated land-use and traffic management schemes need to be part of a comprehensive approach in this respect. It will also be necessary to discuss, at the European level, issues such as Europe-wide planning and the spatial distribution of activities, and to agree policies which may more effectively meet the needs of regions outside the centres of economic activity without weakening the latter in the international context.

Employment prospects or more sustainable trends may emerge from the present, and good planning followed by urban regeneration will have a positive effect.


## INDUSTRY

During the 1980s industrial production increased at a slower pace than economic activity in general. The share of manufacturing industry as a percentage of GDP shows that this share diminished both in terms of the total value of production and, for some countries, also in terms of the total volume of manufactured products.

This development has been accompanied by major changes within the manufacturing sector. The decline in mining and heavy industries is beneficial to the environment, but growth industries such as electronics, informatics and pharmaceuticals have an environmental impact, particularly in relation to the final product. The increasing number of new products being launched by several branches of industry is likely to complicate the situation even more.

Environmental pressures depend, to a large extent, on the structure of industry, its geographical concentration and the wealth of a country. Thus, industries manufacturing intermediate products (e.g. steel, aluminium,

*Table 10.5* Manufacturing sector's share of GDP, 1970–90 (current prices)

| | Share (in % of GDP) | | | Annual variation (in %) | |
| | 1970 | 1980 | 1990 | 1970–80 | 1980–90 |
|---|---|---|---|---|---|
| Denmark | 18.5 | 17.2 | 16.5 | −0.7 | −0.4 |
| France | 29.9 | 24.2 | 21.0 | −2.1 | −1.4 |
| Germany | 38.4 | 32.8 | 31.2* | −1.6 | −0.5 |
| Italy | 27.1 | 27.8 | 22.4 | 0.3 | −2.2 |
| Netherlands | 25.8 | 17.9 | 20.1 | −3.6 | 1.3 |
| UK | 28.7 | 23.2 | 18.9** | −2.1 | −2.6 |

*Source*: OECD
*Note*: * 1989; ** 1988

cement, glass, chemicals, paper) typically constitute a much heavier environmental load than those specialising in, for instance, consumer goods.

Various measures and initiatives in Member States show that industry has increasingly become aware of the need for environmental protection and is prepared to take action either on its own or in co-operation with central and local government. Environmental expenditure in industry has also risen substantially over recent years and has led to a reduction in pollution levels in many regions. Efforts to reduce the polluting effects of industry are, however, primarily concentrated in certain regions of the EU where environmental awareness is already well developed, started much earlier than in other regions, and was followed up by adequate legislation which was implemented and enforced. There has also been a concentration of effort in specific branches of industry and primarily in larger companies which were able to access financial and manpower resources easily. Moreover, many industrialists are currently confronted with a multitude of environmental constraints at a time when financial pressures are greater than five or six years ago. There is therefore a temptation for many business leaders to postpone environmentally oriented investments as they have no short-term positive impact on the financial performance of the company.

Undoubtedly, industry has a major role to play and will have to provide a substantial contribution towards achieving sustainable development but it is, at this stage, unclear how the changes required are going to be implemented in detail.

The EU strategies outlined in the Fifth Environmental Policy and Action Programme are primarily guidelines or proposals which will have to be elaborated in the light of further studies and analyses on their possible consequences before they can form the basis of new macro-economic and sectoral policies. Once this has been completed, more specific legislation and action agreed upon by the Member States in consultation with the social partners and industry can be enacted. The subsequent implementation of new measures will largely be left to individual Member States, which are likely to adopt a variety of approaches and apply different levels of, for example, economic and fiscal incentives. The general level of environmental awareness in each Member State, and hence the political feasibility of certain decisions, will be an important factor in this respect.

International agreements may be needed in a number of areas, not least when it comes to the use of market-based instruments, such as eco-taxes, or other measures which are likely to increase the costs of production and provision of services as this will affect the competitiveness of the European business sector. Part of such additional costs may be offset by businesses becoming more effective in their use of resources and by a decline in labour costs resulting from the shift in taxation away from labour towards the use of resources. However this may be insufficient to ensure an acceptable degree of competitiveness in all sectors.

A cautious response to the changes needed is likely to enable industry to adapt to the new situation, but it may leave sufficient scope for some Member States to move more rapidly forward. A gradual introduction of market-based incentives and more stringent environmental requirements is needed. In addition a number of other measures must be implemented such as incentives to introduce clean technology, and to disseminate knowledge of this through major improvement in economic information systems on the environment. It is worth noting that investments in clean technology tend to be rather modest in some Member States, although there are considerable variations, increasing slowly in recent years.

Emphasis on the development of genuine and widespread environmental awareness, both in industry and among the public, will be a major challenge. Not only does it call for comprehensive education and training programmes, but also for a much better understanding of motivational processes.

An important issue is the growth in the number of small and medium-size enterprises with limited financial and human resources and insufficient expertise to tackle their environmental problems adequately. The development and creation of new networks providing these companies with advice and information on environmental issues will be needed and will have to be financed partly by public funds. Regulatory agencies at the local level may also have to take on the role of advisers to smaller businesses.

In this whole process of change it is essential that there is coherence between strategies at macro and micro levels. This means that the policies and measures adopted must be clear in their message to the business sector, allowing it sufficient scope for flexibility in its choice of approaches. This was emphasised in the Fifth Environmental Policy and Action Programme. Experience has shown that the application of a strict proscriptive system is unlikely to bring about the innovations which are required to ensure the long-term competitiveness of European industry.

Lastly, the social partners, industry and the business sector at large will have to be involved in the introduction of the various changes to ensure their co-operation in the implementation process.

We may at present be far away from sustainability in European industry, but the new EU strategies launched over the last few years have been well received by governments. The increase in environmental awareness in industry and the business sector and the introduction of new and environmentally friendly company strategies coupled with the achievements of some individual companies are promising signs. If we succeed in turning this development into real competitive advantages there could be considerable additional employment prospects in industry, as suggested by the Commission. If we do not succeed there will be a risk that part of European industry, particularly in the less developed regions, could become obsolete.

## CONCLUSION

In conclusion what will be required as part of the sustainable development process includes the following:

- There will be a need for a radical change in attitudes and ethics throughout society, not least among the public who will have to learn to behave more responsibly and to accept a number of restrictions and measures.
- Politicians and policy-makers, in general, will have to adopt a long-term approach and innovative thinking.
- A re-think of the adequacy of our existing systems and institutions, including the decision-making process, which may become more decentralised in certain areas will need to take place.
- Many measures will have to be introduced gradually at different speeds in various regions to avoid major shocks leading to a breakdown of activities which can be made sustainable.
- Assistance to developing countries must be better targeted and reflect the concept of sustainability, e.g. through energy programmes, programmes against desertification, reforestation, water supply, sustainable agriculture, etc.

## NOTE

1   toe stands for ton oil equivalent.

# 11

# ENVIRONMENTAL CAREERS AND ENVIRONMENTAL SCIENTISTS[1]

*Nick Jagger*

One of the problems with discussing 'environmental' careers is that the concept is relatively new, so that the boundaries of what is and what is not an environmental career are not clear. Sometimes it seems as if the term 'environmental' is like a little green label attached to a type of job to make it more attractive.

Increasingly there are environmental dimensions either to what people do, or how they do it, in many types of career (Jacobs 1994) as environmental concerns (Anon 1994) and regulations increase (ECOTEC 1993a). There is also what has been termed the 'environmental industry' (ECOTEC 1994). Another area of interest is the 'environmental manager' or 'environmental executive' (James and Stewart 1995). This chapter will not discuss the latter types of career.

The study focused on postgraduate 'environmental scientists'. The number of environmental scientists compared to 'other' environment professionals is relatively small and it is easier to define who they are. A simple way to define environmental scientists is to include those whose postgraduate training was sponsored by the Natural Environment Research Council (NERC). The Mission Statement of NERC lists the following subject areas within their remit:

> terrestrial, marine and freshwater biology and Earth, atmospheric, hydrological, oceanographic and polar sciences and Earth observation.
>
> (NERC 1994)

This group of scientists are pursuing what school leavers probably consider 'environmental careers'. For instance they study global warming and the ozone layer (indeed it was NERC scientists who first reported the hole in the ozone layer over the Antarctic). They also study water pollution, marine life, ecology and ocean circulation.

*Table 11.1* Numbers of postgraduate environmental scientists, other scientists and all postgraduates 1981 and 1991

|  | 1981 10% Sample | 1981 Estimate | 1991 10% Sample | 1991 Estimate | Growth 1981 to 1991 |
|---|---|---|---|---|---|
| Postgraduate environmental scientists | 353 | 3,530 | 827 | 8,402 | 138.0 |
| Postgraduate scientists | 6,234 | 62,340 | 10,964 | 111,394 | 78.7 |
| All postgraduates | 19,741 | 197,410 | 39,171 | 397,977 | 101.6 |

*Source*: OPCS (1984), (1994)

Even here there are difficulties in defining environmental jobs as the numbers of environmental scientists increase and new related academic disciplines emerge. Statisticians are usually slow to respond to these rapid changes and their classification systems fail to reflect the new realities. Equally, the NERC remit while being focused on the environment includes a wide range of academic disciplines.

Using a narrow definition of environmental scientists, that is geologists and other environmental scientists, from the Office of Population and Census Statistics (OPCS) subject classification, some basic information can be extracted from the 1981 and 1991 Qualified Manpower Reports based on the Censuses of Population (OPCS 1984 and 1994). This shows that the number of postgraduate 'environmental scientists' in Great Britain has increased from about 3,530 in 1981 to 8,402 in 1991. This represents an increase of 138.0 per cent compared with an increase of 78.7 per cent in the numbers of all postgraduate scientists (Table 11.1).

The table also shows that the numbers of postgraduate environmental scientists have increased at a faster rate than the overall number of postgraduates and, more importantly, faster than other postgraduate scientists. This may be in part a problem of definition in that in 1981 atmospheric physicists might have been more likely to report themselves as 'physicists' and be coded as physicists, while in 1991 they might have reported themselves as 'atmospheric pollution scientists' and been coded as environmental scientists. However, environmental science has become an increasingly popular subject, especially at the Masters level. This can be seen from the listings of available postgraduate courses, which although the categories are constantly changing do indicate a growth in the numbers of Masters courses and the numbers of universities offering to supervise PhDs in this area.

Figure 11.1 shows the age profiles of postgraduate environmental scientists, derived from the Census Qualified Manpower Reports. The growth in the area and the relative youth of some of the subjects included are reflected in the age profiles. This mainly reflects the ageing of the 1960s cohort when there was a rapid expansion of this area. In 1981, 66.9 per cent of the popu-

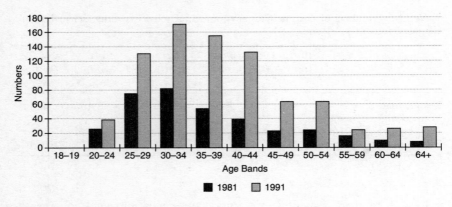

*Figure 11.1* Age profiles of environmental scientists in 1981 and 1991

lation of postgraduate environmental scientists were below 40 years of age compared with 59.7 per cent in 1991.

The 1991 Qualified Manpower Report also allows an examination of the sectors of employment of the narrow definition of environmental scientists. This shows that over half work in the other services sector, largely due to the importance of education which accounts for about 30 per cent of environmental scientists. The next largest sector of employment is business services. The interviews with experts in the area indicate that this represents the importance of environmental consultancies as employers of environmental scientists. The energy and water supply industries, primarily the oil and gas exploration companies and the water industries, are also important employers of environmental scientists with nearly 15 per cent. The other important sectors are research and development and the remainder of other services which includes local and national government (see Table 11.2).

Table 11.3, also derived from the 1991 Census of Population, shows the occupations of environmental scientists. As expected for a group with postgraduate qualifications, over 70 per cent are in professional occupations, while nearly 40 per cent are in the other professional occupations category, which includes teachers and lecturers. Almost exactly one third are practising scientists. Nearly 15 per cent are employed as managers and administrators and nearly 9 per cent as associate professionals.

Based on the Census data, university first destination data and interviews with experts, the majority of environmental scientists are employed in the following areas:

- Academia – as researchers and lecturers;
- Research institutes – as researchers;
- The regulatory bodies – both developing regulations and monitoring their implementation;

*Table 11.2* Sectors of employment of environmental scientists from the 1991 Census Qualified Manpower tables

| *Employees and self-employed* | *10% Sample numbers* | *% of those in employment* |
|---|---|---|
| **Total persons** | 847 | |
| **Employees and self-employed** | 728 | 100.0 |
| Agriculture, forestry and fishing | 7 | 1.0 |
| Energy and water supply industries | 107 | 14.7 |
| Extraction of minerals and ores other than fuels: manufacture of metals, mineral products and chemicals | 8 | 1.1 |
| Metal goods, engineering and vehicles industries | 15 | 2.1 |
| Other manufacturing industries | 11 | 1.5 |
| Construction | 11 | 1.5 |
| Distribution, hotels and catering; repairs | 17 | 2.3 |
| Transport and communication | 9 | 1.2 |
| Banking, finance, insurance, business services and leasing | 141 | 19.4 |
| Business services | 135 | 18.5 |
| Remainder of banking, etc. | 6 | 0.8 |
| Other services | 395 | 54.3 |
| Public administration, national defence and compulsory social security | 53 | 7.3 |
| Education | 220 | 30.2 |
| Research and development | 52 | 7.1 |
| Remainder of other services | 70 | 9.6 |
| Industry not stated or inadequately described | 2 | 0.3 |
| Workplace outside UK | 5 | 0.7 |
| On a government scheme | 6 | |
| Unemployed | 24 | |
| Economically inactive | 89 | |

*Source*: OPCS (1994)

- Oil and gas – primarily as geologists;
- The utilities, especially the water supply industries;
- Environmental consultancies – in a wide range of functions.

The main determinants of demand for environmental scientists by these sectors will be assessed in each of these main categories and the use of environmental consultancies in response to environmental regulation will be summarised below.

The numbers employed in academia and the research institutes are largely determined by the levels of funding for environmental research. As a proportion of UK government and European Union science funding environmental funding has been rising (OECD 1994 and European Commission 1994).

British scientists have been remarkably successful in obtaining international funding for their research as a consequence of that research being highly

*Table 11.3* Occupations of environmental scientists from the 1991 Census

|  | 10% sample numbers | As a % of employed |
|---|---|---|
| **Total persons** | 847 | – |
| **Employees and self-employed** | 728 | 100.0 |
| Managers and administrators | 106 | 14.6 |
| Professional occupations | 523 | 71.8 |
|   Natural scientists | 244 | 33.5 |
|     Chemists | 5 | 0.7 |
|     Biological scientists and biochemists | 31 | 4.3 |
|     Physicists, geologists and meteorologists | 171 | 23.5 |
|     Other natural scientists | 37 | 5.1 |
|   Other professional occupations | 279 | 38.3 |
| Associate professional and technical occupations | 63 | 8.7 |
|   Scientific technicians | 16 | 2.2 |
|     Laboratory technicians | 13 | 1.8 |
|   Other associated professionals etc. | 47 | 6.5 |
| Clerical and secretarial occupations | 16 | 2.2 |
| Craft and related occupations | 4 | 0.5 |
| Personal and protective service occupations | 4 | 0.5 |
| Sales occupations | 4 | 0.5 |
| Plant and machine operatives | 2 | 0.3 |
| Other occupations | 1 | 0.1 |
| Occupation not stated or inadequately described | 5 | 0.7 |

*Source*: OPCS (1994)

regarded. The numbers employed in the regulatory bodies are directly related to the nature, scope and levels of regulations. The numbers of geologists employed in the oil and gas industry appear to be relatively erratic and dependent on the amount of exploratory activity. This is in turn dependent on crude oil prices and the levels of known reserves.

The determinant of employment levels in environmental consultancies is more complicated. The growth in this sector has partly been determined by the more general trend for larger companies to use outside consultants rather than maintain in-house expertise. However, a more important factor has been the changing nature of environmental regulations. Increasingly regulations are changing from the use of BATNEEC (Best Available Techniques Not Entailing Excessive Cost) as a criterion to that of impact assessments. This means that the emphasis on compliance with the regulations has changed from an understanding of the process engineering involved and its costs to an understanding of the ultimate impact on the environment (Christie 1994). Industry needs to have an understanding of process engineering but often has little technical knowledge of the consequent environmental impacts. This gap has largely been filled by environmental consultancies.

The levels of funding for environmental research and the nature, scope and levels of environmental regulation are largely determined politically, while the political determination is mainly driven by levels of public environmental concerns. Therefore both the growth in numbers of environmental scientists graduating from the universities and those entering related employment can be associated with rising public environmental concerns.

## ACKNOWLEDGEMENT

I wish to acknowledge the contributions of Dr Gill Court and Janet Moralee, who have worked with me on this research project. However, any errors and omissions in this paper are my responsibility.

## NOTE

1 This paper is based on research currently being undertaken by the Institute for Employment Studies (IES) for the Natural Environment Research Council (NERC).

## REFERENCES

Anon (1994) Public concern for the environment rides the recession, ENDS Report 232, 18–20.

Christie, I. (1994) *Britain's Sustainable Development Strategy: Environmental Quality and Policy Change, Policy Studies*, Vol.15, No.3, 4–20.

Connor, H. and Jagger, N. (1993) The labour market for postgraduates, Report No 257, IES, Brighton.

Connor, H., Court, G., Seccombe, I. and Jagger, N. (1994) Science PhDs and the Labour Market, Report No 266, IES, Brighton.

DoE (1993) *Environmental Appraisal of Development Plans: A Good Practice Guide*, HMSO, London.

DoE (1994) *Environmental Appraisal in Government Departments*, HMSO, London.

ECOTEC (1993a) The potential for employment opportunities from pursuing sustainable development, A report to the European Foundation for the Improvement of Living and Working Conditions, ECOTEC, Birmingham.

ECOTEC (1993b) *A Review of UK Environmental Expenditure: A Final Report to the Department of the Environment*, HMSO, London.

ECOTEC (1994) *The UK Environment Industry: Succeeding in the Changing Global Market*, HMSO, London.

European Commission (1994) *The European Report on Science and Technology Indicators, 1994*, EUR15897, Luxembourg.

Jacobs, M. (1994) Green Jobs? The employment implications of environmental policy, WWF, Godalming.

James, P. and Stewart, S. (1995) The European Environmental Executive: from technical specialist to change agent and strategic co-ordinator?, AMRG 951, Ashridge Management Research Group.

Land Use Consultants (1994) *Evaluation of Environmental Information for Planning Projects: A Good Practice Guide*, HMSO, London.

OECD (1994) *Main Science and Technology Indicators*, OECD, Paris.

OPCS (1984) 1981 Census Qualified Manpower Great Britain, HMSO, London.

OPCS (1994) 1991 Census Qualified Manpower Great Britain, CEN 91 QM, HMSO, London.

OST (1993) Review of allocation, management and use of government expenditure on science and technology, HMSO, London.

Pike, G., Jagger, N. and Connor, H. (1993) Flows of Scientific Research Skills to and from Industry, an IMS report for the OST.

Wood, C. and Jones, C. (1991) *Monitoring Environmental Assessment and Planning, A Report by the EIA Centre for the Department of the Environment*, HMSO, London.

# 12

# THE ENVIRONMENT – NEW QUALIFICATIONS, NEW COMPETENCIES

## Challenges and perspectives for employment and training

*Odile Mear-Harvey*

## INTRODUCTION

As early as 1987 Recommendation 87/567 of the Commission related to women's professional training recommended the EU Member States to:

> develop awareness and information measures so as to offer women and those around them images of women engaged in non-traditional activities particularly those related to occupations of the future; encourage the participation of girls in higher education . . . making efforts to steer them towards key areas of new technology.

Subsequently, in accordance with the objectives of the Third Action Programme for Equal Opportunities (1991–95) it was considered essential that women, and young girls in particular, be kept better informed of the most recent economic, structural and technological changes affecting and possibly widening their career choices and job-seeking strategies. Promoting women's contribution to the vital issue of sustainable development as expressed in the Agenda 21 (post Earth Summit Action Plan, 1992), was also a priority.

In this context a Portuguese EC civil servant, Mrs Margarida Pinto, initiated a study to address an information deficit about new qualifications and new competencies in the field of the environment.

### Objectives

This exploratory and qualitative study involved over 600 students and teachers from 34 environmental courses throughout Belgium, France, Germany, Greece and the UK. These were postgraduate courses specialising in environmental law, waste management, and environmental studies/management. Informal exchanges also took place with representatives of prospective employers. The data collected were analysed from the point of view of both employment and training.

First, from the training angle, the study aimed at:

- Presenting a few representative examples of environmental training on offer in the above mentioned specialisations;
- Analysing major emerging trends by specific area of specialisation;
- Highlighting women's participation in these courses wherever significant.

Second, from the employment angle, the research aimed at:

- Analysing personal and professional variables most favourable to the student's entry to the environmental employment market;
- Analysing variables pertaining to the training institution favouring the student's successful entry to the environmental employment market;
- Identifying adequacies and inadequacies between training institutions and prospective employers emphasising cases of good practice;
- Shedding light on employers' views regarding the role and employment of women in the environmental field.

## Methodology

The choice of participating Member States, regions and teaching institutions was made on the basis of the following criteria:

- Balance between smaller and larger countries of the EC, and between north and south;
- Areas eligible for EC Objective 1 and Objective 2 funding;
- Established academic reputation of the training institution;
- Trans-national and/or international dimension of the course;
- Innovative character.

*Target groups*: students and heads of courses
*Level of training*: postgraduate, bac – 4/5 in France (continuing education was excluded)
*Research instruments*:
1 A student questionnaire – 20 questions (14 closed/6 open)
2 A teacher questionnaire – 40 questions (28 closed/12 open)

A total of 775 student questionnaires were distributed between September 1992 and the end of March 1993; 622 of them were returned and 612 could eventually be fully exploited. The rate of participation was 80 per cent. This unexpectedly high return of questionnaires was due to the author's personal visits to 28 out of 34 courses, and above all to the co-operation of heads of courses, faculty and administrative staff on the spot. At this point it is important to emphasise that this study remains a qualitative one. It does not assume to be a statistical one *stricto sensu*. However, given the high rate of return of questionnaires, it was possible to provide results in quantitative and graphic form on the basis of the 34 courses surveyed. These may also be indicative of overall trends.

The study is divided into two parts. Part I outlines the background to the survey: national and EU environmental structures, policies and recent trends in the growth of environmental employment. Part II describes the survey results and some recommendations. For the purposes of this chapter, attention will be given to the second part of the study and the results of the survey.

### Distribution between national and foreign students

Out of the 612 students who took part in the survey, 15 per cent were foreigners. The highest proportion were on Belgian courses at the Centre for Environmental Sanitation in Gent and at the Fondation Universitaire Luxembourgeoise in Arlon, as well as on UK courses, notably at Imperial College Centre for Environmental Technology and at Sunderland University.

### Full-time and part-time studies

Most of the sampled students follow environmental studies on a full-time basis and even those previously involved in professional activities usually prefer to dedicate themselves fully to such intensive further training or retraining. Recent updates suggest, however, that due to growing difficulties in finding employment, new applicants prefer to embark on a two-year, part-time course while continuing employment rather than risk losing their current job. Similarly, several teaching institutions are now offering this as a possibility as of 1994/95.

### Financing of studies

The individual ID card of each of the 34 participating institutions (Appendix 1 of the study) shows a wide variety of tuition fees depending on whether they are private or state-run institutions and on the field of specialisation. Fees range from free to moderately priced at around the equivalent of £200, but can even reach up to £7–8,000 p.a.

Fees applying to foreign students may be different in some countries, notably in the UK. Updates also suggest that some privately run training courses even had to lower their fees in 1994/95. In addition, half the students self-finance their courses, while 29 per cent have some form of grant, scholarship or other type of funding. Finally, 10 per cent continue to be paid by their employer while taking the course. It has been suggested that such sudden philanthropy was prompted by the desire to avoid even higher costs of continuing education in certain areas, in specialisations such as waste management for example. It is worth noting that 2 per cent were offered a pre-employment contract with full tuition costs borne by their future employer.

## SETS OF VARIABLES FAVOURABLE TO THE ENTRY OR RE-ENTRY TO THE ENVIRONMENTAL EMPLOYMENT MARKET

### Variables pertaining to the student

In addition to official qualifications, diplomas and technical competencies, prospective employers seek a set of human and professional qualities in job applicants. These include the student's motivation in environmental studies and a personal professional project, aptitude for linguistic and computing skills, job market approach strategy, mobility, perception of career prospects, and last but not least ecological commitment.

### Results of the Students'/Teachers' Survey

The following is a brief summary of participating institutions and students' basic characteristics:

| | |
|---|---|
| *Distribution per country* | Belgium 10.7%; Greece 13.5%; Germany and UK 25%; France 25.6% |
| *Distribution per specialisation* | Law 18%; Waste 24%; Management 26%; Studies 31% |

Under 'Studies' are grouped general environmental studies and environmental science courses including environmental engineering and professional training known as *eco-conseil*/eco-adviser/*umveltberater*.

| | |
|---|---|
| *Distribution per sex* | Men 58%; Women 42% |
| *Distribution per sex and per country* | In France, Germany and the UK the distribution reflects the national trends of women's rates of participation in higher education. It should also be noted that prospective employers such as Belgian municipalities prefer employing women in environmental positions, especially in eco- |

advisers' jobs, as they consider them to be closer to the day-to-day preoccupations of citizens.

*Distribution per age group*

49%    20–24
32%    25–30
19%    over 30

The 19 per cent over 30 belong to the eco-adviser training courses (Namur, Strasbourg, Reichenback) and most of them are registered job seekers.

This sub-group is also found in trans-national courses such as the European Masters, in Environmental Management at Imperial College's Centre for Environmental Technology (ICCET), the Institut d'Ingéniérie et de Gestion de l'Environnement de l'École des Mines de Fontainebleau, Mastere Juturna in Angers, and Herford in Germany. This confirms that mature students are returning to further training after some professional experience, often in the environmental field. In addition, at the Institute of Ecology of the University of Essen there were a number of students with teaching qualifications, mostly in biology, who were not able to find a teaching position and were trying to escape unemployment following a conversion course.

## Motivation

The majority of students were highly motivated. Their primary reason for choosing their current studies was that they were particularly interested in the subject matter (36 per cent) and second, because this might lead to the sort of job they wanted (32 per cent). Only 17 per cent of them thought it would give them a better chance of finding employment. Only 1 per cent made their decision on the basis of guidance and careers advisory services. At the first presentation of the study at the University of Louvain a number of career advisers commented that they had little documentation on new environmental courses let alone environmental career prospects. This situation is not helped by the fact that only 10 out of 34 courses keep records of their students' employment destinations.

To many employers, strong motivation of an employee is undoubtedly an asset. The Human Resources Manager of a Franco-Danish eco-industrial group commented: 'The young people we hire must be extremely motivated and even passionately interested in their field of specialisation. Strong motivation is a source of innovation and in these new types of competencies, one always needs to be imaginative, innovative and inventive.'

## Ecological convictions

In reply to the question, 'Is it necessary to be a convinced ecologist to become a good environmental professional?', the Head of a Brussels-based Agricultural

Federation is adamant. 'Should I recruit an environmental professional, I would not choose a militant ecologist. I am in favour of sustainable development but I could not accept to be systematically barred from setting up indispensable job creating infrastructures of development especially in backward agricultural regions.'

A French environmental consultant commented: 'The environment is a state of mind; one should be convinced without confusing militantism and voluntary work despite the necessarily high personal implication required from environmental executives.'

However, there is an excessively high rate (54 per cent) of 'no answers' to this question: is this discretion or a lack of interest? The 46 per cent of militants belong to various associations for nature protection and green political parties.

British students show the highest score for participation and commitment to the environmental cause (82 per cent), the average for the other four countries being around 30 per cent. In all countries the WWF, along with the British Trust for Conservation Volunteers (BTCV) or a similar type of organisation is the most often quoted, well ahead of Greenpeace or political parties such as Les Verts, Die Grune, Ecolo, etc.

From an employment point of view, employers tend to prefer applicants who have done voluntary work with such organisations as the British Trust for Conservation Volunteers or a local environmental protection organisation.

## Mobility

At the time of the introduction of the EU single market, the question of mobility was an important one for Directorate General V (DGV). Almost half of the survey respondents were willing to look for employment in another EC country, over one-third of them said they might envisage that possibility while almost one out of five firmly rejected it. About one out of three would also be willing to work outside the EU. This confirms trends highlighted in *Social Europe* of March 1990 in a study of young people from Germany, France, Italy, Eire and the United Kingdom. Students confirmed that they were ready to go abroad for two main reasons:

1   To avoid unemployment in their own country.
2   To embark on a career strategy with a first employment opportunity in a foreign country. In some countries – Greece, for example – 'some professional experience or at least a postgraduate training abroad has become a prerequisite to landing a job', an environmental engineering consultant in Athens observed.

## Linguistic skills

It has become commonplace to regard environmental concerns as trans-boundary. Regarding the internationalisation of environmental markets, all the employers contacted during the study reiterated how being able to work in several languages is important for future environmentalists. Given the arrival in Europe of competitors such as those in the waste management sector looking for highly qualified locals, and given the internationalisation of such groups as ABB, Deutsche Babcock AG, George Wimpey, etc., linguistic ability and multicultural interpersonal skills are positive advantages to gaining employment.

## Computing skills

Among environmental law students, computing skills do not seem well developed. Few environmental software packages are mentioned by name. There are a number of possible reasons for this. Yet employers using Aspen technology or Cap Gemini software, etc., commented that they would welcome job applicants familiar with these new tools for eco-auditing or pollution simulation modelling.

## Job hunting strategy

In response to the question, 'How will you go about seeking a job at the end of your present course of studies?' 27 per cent of the respondents considered they would contact employers directly; about 20 per cent would use job advertisements in the national and regional press; and a similar percentage would rely on the specialised press. Only 3 per cent would use alumni associations, whereas 8 per cent would use their personal and family acquaintances. Since the survey, students have started alumni associations to draw on their networking resources in order to enhance their chances in the environmental job market. In several cases, female students are the driving force behind these associations. Despite examples of prominent women, such as the Norwegian Prime Minister, Gro Harlem Brundtland, and Corinne Lepage, a well-known environmental lawyer appointed by President Chirac, the question should be asked, 'Is the environmental job market less accessible to women?'

## Variables pertaining to teaching institutions

In this section the academic reputation of three groups of training courses is examined: the pioneers of the 1970s, the adventurers of the 1980s, the 'nouvelle vague' of the 1990s. In the last category, 12 out of 34 training institutions under review were established after 1990, of which 7 were formed in 1992. Speaking at Louvain, Professor André Renoux commented that each of the 90 French universities boasts some type of environmental course, meaning that French universities produce about 2,500 environmental specialists each year. Obviously this far exceeds the absorption capacity of the French environmental jobs market. Since the survey, some training institutions, for instance INSA in Lyon, have ceased offering some environmental courses.

The role played by the guidance and career services is most important and the type of assistance the teaching institution can offer a student looking for work is also a significant factor. Both these aspects were reviewed in the survey. On the whole less than 10 per cent of the student population received any assistance from their teaching institution. Co-operation with industry through internships, sandwich courses and joint research projects was also described in the survey report. Sixteen out of the 34 environmental courses offered a period of 'stage' ranging from two weeks to three or six months. Special mention should be made of sandwich courses as they are highly regarded by employers.

One of the most important concerns is that of the adaptation of training to employers' needs. According to the teachers' questionnaires improvements that need to be made include:

- more effective interdisciplinary approach;
- better use of practical training (longer internship, more sandwich courses, on-site visits);
- more teamwork between students and teachers;
- strengthened co-operation with local authorities;
- better information on regulations and environmental legislation;
- better integration into the regional dimension;
- better integration into the international dimension.

The course elements which should be considered both by teachers and students as likely to be most useful in their future profession are as follows (in order of importance):

*Law*

CONTENTS

- Principles of environmental law
- EU environmental legislation
- National environmental legislation
- International environmental legislation
- Waste legislation

OTHERS

- Internship
- Contact with environmental specialists
- Multidisciplinary approach
- Teamwork
- Practising English

## Waste

CONTENTS

- Waste processing technologies
- Eco-toxicology
- Waste legislation

OTHERS

- Contacts with waste specialists
- On-site technical visits
- Communication techniques

## Management

CONTENTS

- Environmental legislation
- Waste and pollution processing treatment
- National and international environmental institutions and structures

OTHERS

- Interdisciplinary approach
- Internship
- Communication and negotiation techniques

## Eco-conseil

CONTENTS

- Environmental legislation
- EU and national environmental institutions and structures
- Regional and local authorities

- Waste management
- Water pollution

OTHERS

- Communication, negotiation and mediation techniques
- Internship
- Contact with professionals
- Multidisciplinary approach
- Teamwork
- Data processing skills

## Employment prospects

The Commission's White Paper on 'Growth, Competitiveness and Employment, Challenges and Ways Forward into the Twenty-first Century', emphasises the employment potential of the environment sector. 'On the basis of the latest estimates, this world market in environmental products and services is worth some 190 billion Ecu per year and could reach Ecu 270 billion by the year 2000.' For the European Union alone, 'This could average Ecu 2.5 billion per annum 1993–2000 which by the end of the century could have created 100,000 permanent jobs and 200,000 jobs related to supply of equipment, construction and contracting services in these areas.' Where stands the dream and the reality?

At the time of the survey (September 1992 to the end of March 1993), both students' and teachers' responses were optimistic ones. Obviously, many still felt exhilarated from the Earth Summit in Rio (1992). Employers contacted at the time were also generally bullish, some of them witnessing impressive growth rates with markets opening in both the east and south.

To the question 'How would you rate your employment prospects as related to your present studies?' about one student in two thought that his/her prospects were fairly satisfactory (52 per cent), one in four considered that they were not very good whereas one in ten viewed them as excellent. The most optimistic perspectives came from German and British students. The spectacular development of environmental consultancies in the UK, the prospect of cleaning up the 'Augean stables' in former East Germany, as well as the international reputation of some environmental centres in both countries, largely account for this overwhelming optimism. However, such confidence in the future is tempered by the location and notably the Objective 1 and Objective 2 areas of Newcastle, Le Mans and the Ruhrgebiet.

The same question asked of heads of courses revealed more cautious answers expressed through quite a few diplomatic 'don't knows', but the overall picture was an optimistic one. However, it must be asked what the situation is today.

Ten heads of courses out of 34 (two per country) were asked follow-up questions:

How many of the students who took your environmental course in 1992/93 (in other words those who took part in the original survey)

1 Have obtained employment?
2 Are still seeking employment?
3 Are engaged in other activities (study/travel/parental leave)?

Further information related to this question, such as the distribution between men and women, and employment in the environmental field or in other areas. Similar information for 1993/94 was sought.

The answers may identify a few areas that could be further explored should the Commission or another institution be interested:

Environmental students are finding it increasingly difficult to gain employment. For instance, 27 out of 30 (1992/93) Strasbourg law students found work in environmental law, only 16 out of 30 (1993/94).

The same tends to apply to Eco-Conseil Strasbourg. No answer was forthcoming from the German heads of courses. Could this be an indication of the scepticism found two years previously?

The south is providing new employment opportunities, but this may be a result of the Cohesion Fund applying to parts of Spain, Greece and Portugal, for example. Technical courses and highly specialised courses such as environmental engineering or waste management offer better employment prospects. For instance, 80 per cent of the students of the technical University of Athens found employment; half of those having completed water-related courses and half having completed sewage-related courses.

Courses comprising an element of internship or sandwich courses score better in terms of student employment prospects. In various universities general environmental courses which are not specific enough have been withdrawn. In addition, they seem less attractive to potential employers in a more difficult job market. There is a growing trend to go for further studies at PhD level. A French professor at INSA, near Lyon, warns that unless the students envisage an academic career, they may just be postponing the problem. This was confirmed by companies who said they prefer to employ young graduates with lower diplomas and lower salary expectations than those with the highest possible degree who do not have minimal professional experience.

## CONCLUDING REMARKS

The entire list of recommendations addressed to students, teachers and employers in the last part of the study will not be repeated in this chapter. However, mention of a few significant points will be made below:

Students should be encouraged to specialise in the environmental field at the postgraduate level only after a sound undergraduate scientific, technical or engineering grounding. Employers do not appreciate general environmental undergraduate studies as much as some academics do.

Students should work out a career strategy as early as possible and consequently choose their course options and internship or sandwich course accordingly.

Students should consult the national and international professional press to keep in touch with environmental job opportunities in the European Union and elsewhere.

Teachers should strive to adapt their curricula to meet employers' needs. New environmental courses should meet employment needs rather than following teachers' favourite research topics.

Teachers should perform a first destination of employment survey every year or request that the careers guidance office or another competent body regularly does so.

Teachers should promote co-operation between enterprise and universities. Time and resources should be allocated to them for this (open-door policy, on-site visits, internships, sandwich courses, seminars, continuing education, etc.). Their career advancement should be enhanced rather than suffer from that commitment.

Prospective employers should respond favourably to teachers' desire for co-operation. They should take time to define their future employment needs and make suggestions accordingly.

Employers should keep better informed of course contents and avoid prejudices regarding less known new qualifications and new competencies especially coming from lesser known teaching institutions.

Employers should also think of recruiting young environmental graduates, including women, and not just promote their own executives to positions of environmental responsibility after a short introductory environmental training. Employers should therefore consider a human resources investment as a long-term rather than a short-term fix for the 'greening' of their operation.

Finally, as the Commissioner for Environment and Nuclear Safety, Ms Ritt Bjerregaard, declared at the conference on 'Environmental Risks and Rewards for Business' in Copenhagen: 'The whole area of environmental protection and sustainable development raises a lot of challenges and opportunities for industry – the only thing to remember is to THINK GREEN.'

# 13

# ENVIRONMENTAL EMPLOYMENT

## The right training for the right jobs

*Michelle Dobré and Thierry Lavoux*

## INTRODUCTION

Institut Français de l'Environnement (IFEN) is a public administration created in 1991 to provide scientifically established environmental data at both national and international levels. IFEN is the focal point of the European Environmental Agency as well as the statistics service of the French Ministry of the Environment.

Taking care of the environment is an important economic activity in every industrialised country. In France environmental protection has been seen in recent years as potentially labour intensive. Consequently, figures have shown that 35,000 environmental jobs might be created in the waste and water sectors within five years. However, the accepted figure of 418,000 jobs in the environmental field may be an overestimate as it relies on a very broad definition of environmental activities.

For these reasons, IFEN is engaged in this topic to contribute in the medium term to a better understanding of the situation *vis à vis* environmental training courses, employment and professional aspects of the environment.

## ENVIRONMENTAL PROTECTION JOBS: A DEFINITION

The required employers' qualifications in the field of environmental protection are not easy to define, although new initial training or educational systems are developed every year. There are two main difficulties when trying to define environmental protection employment. On the one hand, the definition of environment is not yet universally established. This will affect the status of environmental protection in relation to economic activity. The accepted definition will also orientate the inventory of initial or professional training systems; the question is therefore raised: should we include established training systems or should we adopt a more restricted definition? The absence of a satisfactory institutional or official definition at local, national or even international level hinders the change from a national to a local scale, as well as impeding comparison between studies or inquiries. On the other hand, the existing job nomenclatures or activity sector lists do not permit the field of environmental protection to be identified in a systematic manner. This situation means that for each inquiry a definition has to be proposed to describe accurately its reference framework as well as to justify the adopted methodological choices to reveal the existing jobs.

Therefore, the number of 418,000 jobs in the environment in 1992 (+ 0.9 per cent compared to 1991) calculated by the Bipe (*Bureau d'information et de prévisions économique* [economic information and forecast office]) and published by the Ministry of the Environment represents the complete number of jobs, either direct or indirect, in the activity sectors associated with the environment. The analysis grid of the technical sectors of environment, by the *Association Française des Ingénieurs Ecologues* (AFIE) [French society of ecologist engineers], is taken as a comparison between the initial training profiles and the executive job proposals.

---

The results of the AFIE study are highlighted by an inquiry conducted at the IFEN's request in 1993 by the BVA survey institute.

Positive replies to the question 'Today, in your company or your town or local council, are there jobs whose function and responsibilities are directly associated with environmental protection?' were received as follows: 54 per cent of the major industrial groups; 60 per cent of the local councils; 8 per cent of the small and medium-sized firms.

---

**AFIE classification of the technical sectors of environmental protection**

---

E 100: Prevention and reduction of pollution, nuisances and hazards (air, water, wastes, technological risks, energy).

E 200: Protection of nature, control of ecological balance, of natural environments and resources (flora, fauna, land and water ecosystems, natural hazards, underground, agriculture).

E 300: Man's protection, labour and environmental hygiene (labour hygiene, health, safety).

---

E 400: Qualitative planning of land and the living environment (infra-structures, city planning, land planning, rural works, mining and quarries, natural parks).

E 500: Society-oriented management of the environment (generalist approach, law, regulations, professional training, communication).

Three other criteria enable the AFIE to classify job proposals: the activity sectors (private, public, local authorities, government-controlled firms and utilities, etc.), functions in the organisation and geographic origin of the proposals.

## 224 INITIAL TRAINING OR EDUCATIONAL SYSTEMS IDENTIFIED

Although it is not exhaustive, the AFIE inventory covers the essential initial training or educational systems in the environment, starting from the French *Baccalauréat* (A Level + two years' college education) giving direct access to the employment market. Its originality lies in the application of criteria which permit an *environment index* to be assigned to these training or educational systems. This index refers to the degree of specialisation established for each diploma. As they are oriented towards direct access to professional careers, these technicians' training courses could be more specialised. In fact, this is not the case: at two years' college education level, the first year is often quite general, whereas the second year is more specific (practically 50 per cent of the courses are dedicated to the environment). The five years' college or higher engineering school levels represent the highest specialisation (index 5, which is the existing maximum, for 30 per cent of students). Among 224 identi-fied systems, a majority ranks at five years' college level (55 per cent), followed by four- and two-year levels equally distributed (18 per cent each).

## ENVIRONMENT DIPLOMAS: A MAJORITY OF UNIVERSITY OR COLLEGE TRAINING OR EDUCATIONAL SYSTEMS AT FIVE YEARS' LEVEL

According to the AFIE survey, 6,064 students graduate each year among the 224 identified training or educational systems; half of them graduate at five years' college level, including 968 engineers from higher engineering schools, and a third graduate from universities. The latter are essentially trained in two

Table 13.1 Student distribution based on technical sectors according to levels of training

| | Bac + 2 Technician BTSA, DUT, DEUST | Bac + 3 BA BSc | Bac + 4 MA MSc engineer | Bac + 5 Engineer DEA, DESS | Bac + 6 Masters | Bac + 6 Doctorate | Total Student numbers |
|---|---|---|---|---|---|---|---|
| E 100 Pollution and environmental nuisance | 682 | 81 | 165 | 687 | 74 | – | 1,689 28% |
| E 200 Protection of nature | 228 | 4 | 468 | 863 | – | – | 1,563 26% |
| E 300 Hygiene and protection | 248 | – | 45 | 303 | 20 | – | 616 10% |
| E 400 Town and country planning | 100 | – | 333 | 791 | 70 | – | 1,254 21% |
| E 500 Society-orientated management of the environment | 25 | – | – | 311 | 105 | – | 441 7% |
| Two or three sectors | 40 | – | 118 | 193 | 55 | 55 | 461 8% |
| Total student numbers | 1,323 22% | 85 1% | 1,129 19% | 3,148 52% | 324 5% | 55 1% | 6,064 100% |

Source: IFEN, AFIE

*Table 13.2* Distribution of the 224 educational systems according to related qualifications and environment indexes

|  | Index 1 20% Specialised training | Index 2 40% Specialised training | Index 3 60% Specialised training | Index 4 80% Specialised training | Index 5 100% Specialised training | Total % |
|---|---|---|---|---|---|---|
| Bac + 2 | 10 | 45 | 10 | 28 | 8 | 100 |
| Bac + 4 | 8 | 13 | 37 | 16 | 26 | 100 |
| Bac + 5 | 13 | 22 | 18 | 18 | 30 | 100 |
| Bac + 6 | 27 | 9 | 9 | 27 | 27 | 100 |

*Source*: IFEN, AFIE
*Note*: Percentages being rounded, the total is 100 ± 1

fields: E 200 (nature protection, management of ecological balance, environments and resources), involving management inventories, physical records or measurements, etc. – for example, the French *DEA* degree (post-master) in *continental aquatic systems ecology* – on the one hand, and, on the other, E 400 (qualitative planning of territories and life environment), oriented towards environmental evaluation, impact study conduct – for example, the French *DESS* (the specialised post-master degree) in *designing of eco-development projects.*

## ENGINEERS FOR THE INDUSTRIAL ENVIRONMENT

The 968 engineers represent one third of the students at five years' college education level in the field of environmental protection. A majority of them specialise in *prevention and reduction of pollution and hazards in the industrial environment* (E 100) and will generally be in charge of industrial risk studies, contracting industrial environmental engineering, technical design of systems or processes for nuisance elimination, etc. Finally, the 324 students at Masters degree level (six years' college education) are usually directed more towards *society-orientated management of the environment* (E 500), i.e. a generalist approach, training, communication or environmental law.

## SOURCES OF ENVIRONMENTAL JOB ADVERTISING

Of these, 54 per cent are in the public sector and government-controlled firms or utilities. According to the inventory of executive job advertisements (specialised or general press, Minitel, professional networks, 501 job proposals in total), the public sector represents 44 per cent of job advertisements,

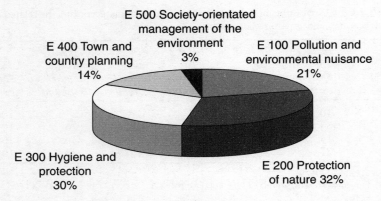

*Figure 13.1* Student distribution based on technical sectors according to levels of training

*Table 13.3* Channels of external recruitment

| | Large companies | Local authorities | Engineering offices |
|---|---|---|---|
| By specialised technical press | 6 | 35 | 21 |
| By specialised environment press | 6 | 14 | 8 |
| By general press | 26 | 23 | 21 |
| By word of mouth, recommendation by a friend, by a professional relation | 29 | 17 | 34 |
| By a recruitment agency | 29 | 1 | 5 |
| By specialised university courses | 23 | 6 | 32 |
| Other means | 13 | 15 | – |

*Note*: Totals do not add up to 100 as each employer could tick more than one choice

followed by the private sector (39 per cent), government-controlled firms or utilities (10 per cent), and the international sector (7 per cent). In each field, there is a prevalence of job advertisements associated with *pollution and nuisance control* (E 100, 30 per cent) and *society-orientated management of the environment* (E 500, 32 per cent), which corresponds to the implementation of global and sectoral environmental policies (water, wastes) primarily in local authorities. Generally, the advertised posts are relevant to the generalist approach to the environment, with a high level of education required.

## RECRUITMENT

For industrialists, one of the main priorities is internal mobility. The most frequently used channel of recruitment is by *word of mouth* and by introduction and recommendation (29 per cent of recruitment for major groups is done in this way, 43 per cent for small and medium-sized firms, and 55 per cent for consultancies). Local authorities and councils are the only exception: they refer to the professional press (35 per cent). However, 65 per cent of the environment-oriented posts in large companies have been filled by internal recruitment. Recourse to the job market represents only 10 per cent of the total for the major groups. Local authorities and entities such as the engineering offices have carried out more external recruitment (46 per cent and 53 per cent, respectively).

## CONCLUSION: THE UNACHIEVABLE RELATIONSHIP BETWEEN TRAINING AND EMPLOYMENT

To conclude: the qualitative comparison of advertised job profiles and training by the technical sector shows an excess number of students trained in the protection of nature (26 per cent of the total) compared to the number of job advertisements (14 per cent). Conversely, in the case of society-orientated management of the environment, 7 per cent of the students have qualified in this as against 32 per cent of job advertisements. Moreover, even though the number of advertisements published only represents a small part of the total job market, we are far from reaching a balance between the number of qualified students (6,000 yearly) and the number of job vacancies (approximately 200–300 yearly). These jobs usually require a minimum of two years' field experience which graduates straight from university will not have.

---

The 35,000 *nature-oriented jobs* operation was launched in 1994 by the French Ministry of Environment, in all French regions. This incentive system was operational for two years and was designed to implement job-creating projects in the field of environment, with financial support from the government: 100 million French francs were distributed to the regional Prefects for the DIRENs (environment directorates) by virtue of the Act No. 93.953 of 27 July 1993.

---

# 14

# TWO PAN-EUROPEAN INITIATIVES IN COURSE DEVELOPMENT AND NETWORKING

*Nora Cantini and Karim Zein*

## INTRODUCTION

In 1992, a new pan-European Masters degree in Environmental Management was launched by the European Association for Environmental Management Education (EAEME). Formed in 1991, EAEME unites the expertise of fifteen academic institutions located throughout the European Union, each with significant experience in postgraduate environmental education.

The current members of the association are:

- Université Libre de Bruxelles (B);
- Fondation Universitaire Luxembourgeoise (L);
- Ecole Polytechnique Fédérale de Lausanne (CH);
- Université de Genève (CH);
- Universität Kaiserlautern (D);
- Universität Trier (D);
- Universitat Politècnica de Catalunya (E);
- Université de Savoie (F);
- Université de Nancy II (F);
- Imperial College of Science, Technology and Medicine (UK);
- National and Kapodistrian University of Athens (GR);
- Politecnico di Torino (I);
- Università degli Studi di Parma (I);
- Università di Bologna (I);
- Katholieke Universiteit Brabant (NL).

These institutions collaborate through the association to deliver a one-year Masters degree that aims to:

- Provide training in environmental management for public administrators and private sector professionals;
- Develop effective tools for integrating environmental considerations into all areas of policy;
- Reinforce links between such training and research.

The unique approach of the EAEME Masters degree programme is to train participants in the management of interdisciplinary problems of trans-national and pan-European character, placing strong emphasis on languages and cultural exchange. Academic expertise is combined with inputs from practitioners, organisations and institutions active in the environmental management field. A key feature of the Masters course is the mobility of participants and teachers between participating institutions.


## THE EAEME PROGRAMME

The fourteen weeks of the Preparatory and Basic Module take place concurrently in the four following locations: Athens (GR) and Torino (I) in English, Arlon (B) in French, or Trier (D) in German.

The Preparatory Module aims to complement participants' knowledge in the disciplines contributing to environmental management including the natural sciences (for better comprehension of soil science, hydrology, atmospheric science, as well as the functioning of ecosystems and biogeochemical cycles), and the social sciences (to better comprehend concepts of scarcity, allocation and pricing of resources, management strategy in organisations, roles of groups of actors in society, national and EU legal systems).

The Basic Module aims to present environmental management as a continuous process in both the public and private sectors, integrating institutions, operators and methods in a European perspective. The main topics covered include:

- Environmental issues at global, regional and local levels;
- Environmental decision-making, including policy life cycle, negotiation procedures, policy instruments and environmental legislation;
- Tools for environmental management in key sectors: agriculture, energy, industry, transport and tourism;
- Implementation of environmental policy, including instruments and organisations;
- Environmental education and communication.

Participants then change location according to the field of application they wish to pursue. The Application Modules offered are:

- Aspects juridiques et administratifs de la gestion de l'environnement (Brussels, Belgium);
- Management of river basins and related coastal areas (Parma, Italy);
- Environmental management in the business community (Tilburg, The Netherlands);
- Evaluations relatives à l'environnement (Lausanne, Switzerland);
- Environmental decision support systems (Verbania, Italy);
- Monetäre Bewertung von Umweltschäden (Trier, Germany);
- Environmental monitoring and management in urbanised areas (Bologna, Italy).

The programme culminates in individual applied research projects, lasting twenty weeks, promoting the development of effective solutions to current environmental issues.

## ONE EUROPEAN INITIATIVE LEADS TO ANOTHER

During the first year of the EAEME Masters degree programme a wonderful group dynamic developed between the participants – a dynamic that was particularly rich owing to the diversity of their ages, disciplines and work experiences, in areas as varied as applied and natural sciences, architecture, economics, engineering, marketing, forestry, medicine, modern languages, law, and social and political sciences. In this complex, multidisciplinary and evolving field of environmental management, the graduates quickly recognised the crucial importance of networking and exchange to enhance professional activities. To ensure the continuity of this new-found group synergy, and to reinforce and expand the contacts, know-how and expertise generated through this Masters degree, in October 1993 the European Environmental Management Association (EEMA) was established.

Although the original members were graduates of the EAEME Masters degree, it soon became apparent that the same needs were shared by most environmental management professionals. Consequently the association has expanded to integrate all individuals who demonstrate a strong commitment to environmental management in their professional or private life and who share the aims and objectives of EEMA.

## EUROPEAN ENVIRONMENTAL MANAGEMENT ASSOCIATION: PURPOSE AND OBJECTIVES

EEMA is an association and growing network of environmental professionals working to raise awareness of environmental issues and opportunities and to develop the capabilities strategically to address those issues and opportunities through the exchange of information, experiences and contacts.

Specifically, EEMA aims to:

- Maintain and enhance professional contacts and collaboration through its international network;
- Maximise awareness and knowledge of its members by providing access to environmental management information, including key events, major publications, organisations and institutions active in the environmental management field;
- Stimulate exchange between EEMA members and increase their professional potential by establishing contacts with other individuals, associations and organisations;
- Promote EEMA and its members to interested outside parties;
- Raise awareness and develop concern for environmental management issues and opportunities.

### Meeting these objectives

EEMA relies on the commitment, enthusiasm, conviction and initiative of its members. To meet the challenging objectives of the association, task forces collaborating across Europe have been established to focus efforts on the following key services and activities:

- The association produces a tri-annual journal for general distribution, *EEMA Review*, bringing together the contributions of significant personalities in the European environmental field, with a view to encouraging dialogue and stimulating partnerships. Each issue examines a particular topic of current interest in environmental management, for example 'The Multi-Disciplinary Approach', 'New Roles and Responsibilities in Environmental Management', Making it Happen in Environmental Management' and 'Coping with NIMBY';
- A newsletter, *EEMA News*, keeps members updated on the activities of EEMA, and its national chapters, as well as on developments in the Masters programme of EAEME;
- Members are able to access directly a database of member profiles and an ever-expanding mailing list of key players and contacts in European environmental management, and the annual directory provides details and contact information on all EEMA members;
- Close ties are maintained with the EAEME Masters programme's organisers and students, not only by participating in the content of the courses, but also by providing advice on academic and career development, and initiating activities for establishing contacts with research counterparts and potential future employers.

The main thrust of EEMA, however, lies in the activities and initiatives that stimulate personal contacts and interaction. In the cities where there are a significant number of members, independent national chapters have been established that develop the local network. Regular reunions of members and colloquia are organised in these key geographic locations, and ideas, experiences and contacts are then shared with the rest of the association via the central secretariat. These reunions foster initiatives for new activities, partnerships and collaborations. One such initiative has led to the organisation of EEMA's first European conference.

The future success of EEMA and its overall goal of advancing the integration of environmental management in all sectors will lie in the initiatives of its members and their openness to crossing traditional boundaries of organisations, disciplines, sectors and nationalities to new forms of collaboration for 'making it happen'.

# 15

# QUALIFYING FOR THE ENVIRONMENT

*Hilary Course*

## INTRODUCTION

This chapter will examine:

1  UK competence-based qualifications;
2  Mutual recognition of existing qualifications across Europe (the 'Euro-qualification' Programme).[1]

## UK COMPETENCE-BASED QUALIFICATIONS IN THE ENVIRONMENT

For the last two decades, concern has been expressed in the UK about the plethora of UK vocational qualifications. In the UK, progression for individuals within a single industry has often involved repetitious 'time-serving' in education classes, repeating lessons already learnt on a previous course. It has also been difficult for people who have not followed a limited number of accepted routes within each industry to progress and gain promotion through that industry.

With the increasing requirement for more skilled and qualified employees, capable of switching occupational sectors at least two or three times in their working lives, the existing 'system' of vocational qualifications was seen as inadequate (Manpower Services Commission 1981), and a completely new system has been developed under the guidance and auspices of the Employment Department, the National Council for Vocational Qualifications (NCVQ), and the Scottish equivalent, the Scottish Vocational Education Council (SCOTVEC). This new NVQ and SVQ system is currently being implemented (NCVQ 1995a; SVEC 1994).

The development of NVQs and SVQs has involved most UK industries setting up employer-led Lead Bodies to develop a new form of standards and qualifications, defining what constitutes competent performance within their industry (NCVQ 1995b; SVEC 1995). The Environmental Lead Body (the Council for Occupational Standards and Qualifications in Environmental Conservation (COSQUEC)), has developed such standards and has configured them into qualifications in:

- Landscapes and Ecosystems (COSQUEC 1993);
- Archaeology and Field Archaeology (COSQUEC 1994).

The former were accredited as qualifications in May 1993, and the latter in September 1994. Both are available at NVQ and SVQ Levels 2, 3 and $4^2$ (NCVQ 1995b; SVEC 1995). COSQUEC are also currently looking to develop NVQs and SVQs in environmental management. They have maintained an interest in qualifications for Building Conservation which are being developed with other Lead Bodies.

NVQs and SVQs attest what people can do in an occupational context (including voluntary and unpaid occupational contexts). The key and distinctive features of NVQs and SVQs are that they include:

- Technical skills;
- Planning, problem-solving and dealing with unexpected occurrences;
- Working with other people;
- Applying knowledge and understanding which underpins overall competence;
- The ability to transfer the competence from place to place and context to context;
- Independence of any particular method of learning, specifying the standards to which the candidate must perform rather than the manner, duration and location in which the candidate learns to perform to those standards;
- Acceptance of evidence from a range of sources, including performance at work, simulation, evidence of past performance at work, and written and/or verbal questioning. The aim is to remove barriers traditionally imposed in the UK by restrictive and sometimes irrelevant methods of assessment.

Thus the Environment NVQs and SVQs incorporate a holistic approach to competence in the industry.

Learning, training and the development of NVQ and SVQ candidates' knowledge and competence still occur, but recognition for competence is no longer dependent upon limited and prescribed methods of learning. Instead, NVQs and SVQs focus upon assessment criteria; NCVQ and SCOTVEC break this down into performance criteria (PC), range statements, underpinning knowledge and understanding which define measurable outcomes of learning:

what the person can do as a result of learning (NCVQ 1995b; SVEC 1995). This contrasts with most traditional qualification systems in the UK, and in Europe, which are defined in terms of the learning syllabus, and often in terms of the nominal hours of learning anticipated for the 'average' learner, e.g. '20-hour modules'.

In practice, the holistic NVQ and SVQ approach means that each time candidates carry out work specified in the NVQ or SVQ, candidates must fulfil all the performance criteria given for that work. For instance, a person would not be deemed competent in constructing boundaries if on one occasion they satisfied the performance criterion:

PC2 boundaries are constructed in a manner which makes them fit for purpose
(*but this was done in an unsafe manner*)

and on the next occasion they satisfied the second performance criterion:

PC5 operations are carried out in a manner to protect the health and safety of workers and the public
(*but the boundary was not fit for purpose*).

NVQ and SVQ candidates are normally required to demonstrate competence on a number of occasions, and in a specified range of conditions, until sufficient evidence has been generated to imply consistent competence (NCVQ 1995b; SVEC 1995).

The methods, venues and schedules of learning are not specified in any NVQ or SVQ, nor are there any 'entrance requirements'. Instead, quality assurance for the qualifications includes national control over the designation of assessment centres (known as 'Approved Centres') (NCVQ 1993).

COSQUEC is researching and analysing the experiences of users of the Environmental NVQ and SVQ standards and qualifications.

The UK-wide nature of the recent and on-going revision of vocational qualifications, with its emphasis on learning outcomes, is facilitating the identification and mutual recognition of common competencies (known as 'common units') between different industries in the UK (NCVQ 1995b; SVEC 1995). For instance, where a candidate has been certificated as competent in a common management unit in the context of one industry, this certificate will be recognised in many other industries, and the candidate will not be required to undergo further training or assessment in that unit.

It is the focus on outcome, and on the definition of what the candidate can do, rather than on where, how and when they learn, which has removed several key variables which had previously hindered the transferability of credit between UK vocational qualifications. The same mechanism may similarly prove useful within the European context, for defining mutually acceptable qualifications.

## THE EUROQUALIFICATION PROGRAMME

The UK contribution to the Environment sector of the three-year Euro-qualification Programme (Phase 1 ended in 1995) used NVQs and SVQs from the Industry Lead Body for Amenity Horticulture (rather than those from COSQUEC). In contrast to NVQs and SVQs, the primary focus of the Euroqualification Programme was the definition and piloting of training syllabuses. Co-financed by the European Commission, it has been an ambitious programme, the brainchild of thirteen national organisations (Euroquali-fication Programme 1993) involved with training and vocational qualifications for adults. All twelve of the then Member States of the European Community were involved.

Twelve occupational sectors were selected (Euroqualification Programme 1992) for piloting both the concept and the proposed methodology. In the Environment and Local Development sector, seven job roles were selected:

- Solid waste treatment officer;
- Technical officer for solid waste treatment;
- Green spaces management and maintenance officer (Level 2) (closest UK qualification: NVQ and SVQ Amenity Horticulture (nursery – interior soft landscape maintenance), at Level 2);
- Green spaces management and maintenance officer (Level 3) (closest UK qualification identified at the time: NVQ and SVQ Amenity Horticulture (constructing and restoring landscapes), at Level 3);
- Technical officer for waste water treatment;
- Ancient buildings restoration worker;
- Agent/facilitator for local development.

The UK partner organisation for the Environment and Local Development Sector was the Local Government Management Board.

The process adopted by all thirteen national organisations was to identify the relevant national qualifications at specified levels in the twelve occupational sectors, to define what was common between those national qualifications of the countries taking part in each sector, and then to add the following further modules to this common core:

- Additional technical content to satisfy the European, as opposed to the national, context. This focused upon present and future job roles, discarding that which was customary but obsolete;
- Preparing to live and work abroad;
- European knowledge;
- Language;
- An in-company placement abroad.

The 'additional technical content' of all the Euroqualification syllabuses was to include a unit on the environment. Two competence-based units were proposed for this purpose by the Local Government Management Board (LGMB 1993a).

In most sectors, the Euroqualification Programme was piloted twice, with two different groups of trainees. The intention was that, overall, 6,000 trainees should each complete the Euroqualification Programme, plus any additional training and/or assessment necessary in order to be awarded the relevant national qualification. Thus each successful and competent UK environment trainee was to gain a Euroqualification Certificate, plus an SVQ or NVQ. The Euroqualification Certificate was to become a form of common currency, with each participating country aware of exactly how its own qualifications related to that Certificate (LGMB 1993b; LGMB 1993c). The total number of trainees completing the Programme is not yet available.

As might be expected in a programme involving large numbers of trainees, 380 experts, 40 wide-ranging occupations, 300 general and vocational language groups in eight languages, and considerable cultural diversity, there were many human, administrative, practical and logistical challenges. The pilot training and exchanges did not, in all cases, turn out as planned. However, the many positive outcomes included the development of a series of multi-lingual glossaries for the vocational vocabulary of the areas in the Programme.

The identification of common syllabuses, particularly in an industrial sector with as long and diverse a history as the environment, was fraught with cultural and linguistic misunderstandings. These concerned factors ranging from assumptions arising from the nature of the national environment itself to overall attitudes to, and expectations of, the environment, to assumptions of the universality of national educational systems and aspirations, and also of the national context, structure, aims and methods of the vocational role being discussed.

A further challenge was that most European national syllabuses aimed to train people so that they had basic skills and knowledge and were ready to develop competence in the work situation, as opposed to the UK NVQs and SVQs which attest that people already have that work-based competence.

The analysis of feedback from all Euroqualification participants has concluded that the experiment should be continued, and a bid has been placed with the European Union for support for Phase II of the Programme.


## CONCLUSION

The full evaluation of the Euroqualification Programme is expected to have identified many examples of good practice which can usefully be adopted by similar schemes in the future. The Programme has also developed, piloted and refined systems, guidance documents and glossaries likely to have a wider application than the Programme itself.

The traditional methodology of programmes such as the Euroqualification Programme also includes focusing on training syllabuses with a view to developing workforces which can perform to standards appropriate to, and recognised throughout, Europe.

However, where different nations or regions aim to train a workforce so that it can perform a single function to the same standard, it is inevitable that the varying national and regional cultures and histories will influence the content and nature of the training required to achieve the same result. This is particularly clear in the environment sector, where regional geology, landform, climate, weather, flora and fauna significantly affect the type of vocational knowledge and skills likely to be endemic to an area, and hence affect that which needs to be learnt in order to perform vocational work in a European, rather than a local context.

The UK NVQ and SVQ systems (and indeed other competence-based systems) demonstrate that specification of learning method or content is irrelevant to the requirement of industry for a system which recognises people's ability to perform competently within that industry. The UK experience is that focusing on learning outcomes has facilitated recognition of common competencies in widely differing industries. The same may apply to the mutual recognition of vocational qualifications within (and possibly between) occupational sectors, across Europe. Experiments such as the Euroqualification Programme may be facilitated by substituting the usual emphasis on the analysis of the training syllabus, to one on learning outcomes.

There is, however, still a need for recognition of, and allowances for, differences between national qualifications attesting to potential, as opposed to those certifying actual competence.

In summary, when defining vocational qualifications in a national or an international context, a focus on the outcomes of learning, rather than the inputs, can significantly reduce the opportunity for misunderstanding and disagreement, thereby releasing time and energy to define better what trainees would be able to do in order to be recognised as having attained satisfactory standards of performance.

## NOTES

1  The Euroqualification Programme described above is totally unrelated to the UK-based Chamber of Commerce and Industry Examinations Board 'Euroqualifications syllabus'.
2  Each NVQ and SVQ is allocated to one of five levels. Level 3 has been recognised in the European Second Diploma Directive as being equivalent to Diploma level, which is defined as 'qualifications achieved after a post-secondary course of between one and three years and equivalent qualifications achieved through other routes'.

# REFERENCES

COSQUEC (1993), Council for Occupational Standards and Qualifications in Environmental Conservation, *National and Scottish Vocational Qualifications in Environmental Conservation Levels 2, 3 and 4: Landscapes and Ecosystems*, COSQUEC, Staunton, Gloucester.

COSQUEC (1994), Council for Occupational Standards and Qualifications in Environmental Conservation, *National and Scottish Vocational Qualifications in Environmental Conservation Levels 2, 3 and 4: Archaeology and Field Archaeology*, COSQUEC, Staunton, Gloucester.

Euroqualification Programme (August 1992), *Les Metiers (Occupations), File 2*, Euroqualification Programme, Brussels.

Euroqualification Programme (March 1993), *The Professional Experts: Who is Who? (Les Experts Professionnels: Qui est qui?), File 1*, Euroqualification Programme, Brussels.

LGMB (1993a), Local Government Management Board, March 1993, *The Development of an Environmental Training Module at Levels 2 and 3*, Local Government Management Board, Luton.

LGMB (1993b), Local Government Management Board, May 1993, *Vocational Training Units: Technical Officer for the Maintenance and Management of Green Spaces (Level 2)*, Local Government Management Board, Luton.

LGMB (1993c), Local Government Management Board, August 1993, *Vocational Training Units: Technical Officer for the Maintenance and Management of Green Spaces (Level 3)*, Local Government Management Board, Luton.

Manpower Services Commission (MSC) (1981), *A New Training Initiative: Agenda for Action*, HMSO, London.

NCVQ (1993), National Council for Vocational Qualifications, August 1993, *The Awarding Bodies: The Common Accord*, National Council for Vocational Qualifications, London.

NCVQ (1995a), National Council for Vocational Qualifications, January 1995, *NVQ Monitor: (Winter 1994/95)*, National Council for Vocational Qualifications, London.

NCVQ (1995b), National Council for Vocational Qualifications, January 1995, *NVQ Criteria and Guidance*, National Council for Vocational Qualifications, London.

SVEC (1994), Scottish Vocational Education Council, December 1994, *SVQ Update*, Winter 1994/95, Scottish Vocational Education Council, Glasgow.

SVEC (1995), Scottish Vocational Education Council, February 1995, *Scottish Vocational Qualifications Criteria and Guidance*, first edition, Scottish Vocational Education Council, Glasgow.

# 16

# COMPETENCIES IN THE ENVIRONMENT

## The role of further and higher education

*Steven Pullan*

### INTRODUCTION

This chapter outlines the present situation regarding Further Education (FE) and Higher Education (HE) involvement in UK National Vocational Qualifications (NVQs) relating to the environment. This primarily relates to the areas which have been developed by COSQUEC. At the time of writing there are two standards in operation with a further one in development (Turner 1995).

The following account will present a summary of the 'assessment centres' involved in environment NVQs developed by COSQUEC. A brief historic consideration of the role of the FE sector which is closely associated with NVQs in the environmental sector will review the advantages both have in assessing the standards and associated education. Consideration of the role of HE and examples of developments at Newcastle University will demonstrate the potential HE involvement in the NVQ system. An evaluation of the role of knowledge and understanding in assessing competencies will be discussed, with consideration of the wider role of professional involvement in NVQs, especially at the higher levels.

### NVQS IN THE ENVIRONMENT: INVOLVEMENT AND ROLE OF FURTHER EDUCATION

Figure 16.1 shows the most NVQ assessment centres located in the FE sector (82 per cent) for environmental NVQs. The industry organisations are only a small proportion of the total (16 per cent). The industrial organisations tend to be those organisations which have been historically involved in this training – the National Trust, British Trust for Conservation Volunteers

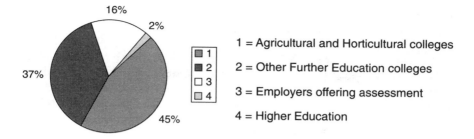

1 = Agricultural and Horticultural colleges

2 = Other Further Education colleges

3 = Employers offering assessment

4 = Higher Education

*Figure 16.1* The range of institutions which are registered as NVQ assessment centres offering the COSQUEC standards (information supplied by COSQUEC)

(BTCV) and the County Wildlife Trusts. The FE sector assessment is split between Agricultural and Horticultural colleges (45 per cent), and other FE colleges (37 per cent).

The advantage of Agricultural and Horticultural colleges is their ability to deliver both the knowledge-based component and the assessment. This is based upon their course format which reflects the traditional requirement of the land-based industries. Most of these colleges have large estates where they have the resources to teach practical skills in the workplace and provide assessment to national standards. Previously this was achieved through the National Proficiency Test Council (NPTC) scheme. This assessment format was the basis for a qualified person being recognised as a 'craftsman' as defined by the Agricultural Wages Board. Achievement at this level was associated with an increased salary, hence a major incentive for industries to increase their skills. The basis of these tests was assessment in the workplace to national standards.

Colleges offer academic qualifications (National Certificates and National Diplomas) which include workplace assessment on part of the education pro-gramme. Any candidate from outside the college could register and be tested in their workplace without being on a formal course. These linked certificates (National Certificates and Diplomas) were awarded by either the National Examination Board in Agriculture, Horticulture and Allied Industries (NABA-HAI) or the British Training and Education Council (BTEC). The workplace assessment and the college academic assessment were integrated, with students having to pass both parts. Often the assessment in the workplace was based on a scale giving scores for competence. This was often linked to such factors as how late the student was in arriving for duties, how helpful and polite s/he was to the stockman, etc. Levels of competence were scaled as: not competent, nearly competent and competent for the award, etc. With the final Certificate/ Diploma the candidate would have achieved a dual qualification. At the Diploma level this was often the full craftsman grade but at the Certificate level units of credit were only towards the craftsman's status.

The availability of NVQs now provides a natural progression to this new form of standards and assessment. In addition, with the changes in the land-based industries and the retraction of agriculture (6 per cent per year for the last twenty years), colleges have diversified into new growth areas, including other aspects of the environment. This change in emphasis has utilised the natural range of skills and assets already present in these colleges, so many of these colleges have become assessment centres for the environmental NVQs (see Figure 16.1).

The type of education linked to NVQs that the Agricultural and Horti-cultural colleges are able to offer is based on their traditional format of lectures and practical classes on the college estates. Other FE colleges without these assets rely on their links with the industry to offer this form of assessment, from the full-blown course which embeds NVQ assessment as part of the package, to assessment only, on the same basis as the Agricultural and Horticulture colleges. All FE colleges in all sectors are using this formula for the range of courses they offer, e.g. the building trade, hairdressing, engi-neering, etc.

## NEWCASTLE UNIVERSITY: AN EXAMPLE OF THE INVOLVEMENT IN NVQS

De Montfort University is the only university currently an assessment centre for environment NVQs. Carried out through Molton College (an Agricultural and Horticultural college), part of De Montfort University, this centre is likely to be the centre for assessment. The majority of HE institutions have no involvement in assessing environmental NVQs.

However, other types of HE involvement in the NVQ process are possible. For example Newcastle University has been involved in environmental NVQs. Courses developed at Newcastle demonstrate how HE can be involved with NVQs without actually assessing candidates directly. The courses fall into the categories of either Adult Liberal Education, or Continuing Professional Development (CPD)/Continuing Professional Education (CPE). Most of these courses are associated with the Centre for Continuing Education at the University. Further development of vocational provision is awaiting the assess-ment of the internal review of the implications of NVQs and Credit Awards and Transfer Scheme (CATS).

Within Newcastle University, the Centre for Continuing Education is now an Accredited Assessment Centre for Management Standards (MCI) at levels 3, 4 and 5, and the Administration Standards at levels 3 and 4. Also offered are Training and Development League Body Assessor Verifier Awards for those involved in NVQ assessments. This is also made available for the School of Education as an optional module for those studying for a PGCE in secondary teaching who will be involved in GNVQ (General National Vocational

Qualification) assessment. The Centre is also accredited to offer NVQ core skills 1–3 and intends to work with other university departments, for example the careers service, to identify and accredit transferable skills to enhancing graduates' employability. The University's Staff Development Unit may implement a scheme to enhance various other standards for its own staff. The areas under consideration are catering, cleaning and portering.

## Environment studies at Newcastle University

Newcastle University offers an Adult Liberal Education Certificate in Countryside Conservation. This takes the form of a flexible course of five taught short courses, with a sixth project assignment for the full Continuing Education Certificate. The syllabus for the course was established by using the NVQ Environment Courses standards to identify the knowledge required, and reformulating the individual component into a coherent series of short courses with assessments. The assignments are intended to help candidates fulfil their evidence of competence requirement while at the same time forming part of a Continuing Education Certificate. Fifty per cent of the marks are from a project of no more than 10,000 words which may take the form of a site management plan, a site survey or a major piece of environmental interpretation.

The objective of the course is to allow students to gain and also be able to demonstrate knowledge about the environmental industry as well as to cover the range. It shows students how evidence can be collected and the sort of evidence required for assessment. The assessments for the Certificate enable candidates to produce evidence directly, to satisfy the range statements of competence for a given level of competence, and to gain direct, or indirect knowledge. The course relates to the highest industry standards although what is acceptable by a candidate's place of work may not be equivalent to the COSQUEC standards. Candidates need to be aware of the range of standards imposed by organisations. When assessment is undertaken assessors need to ensure that a person is 'industry competent' and not 'organisation competent'. The standards are set by the industry so they have to show transferability between organisations. If candidates are only able to work in a particular organisational style then they will not be able to move between employers easily. The education away from the workplace ensures that candidates develop a broader industry awareness. Some assessors have commented that this approach has tightened up their work practices, highlighted areas where they may tend to cut corners, and what should be best practice within the industry.

The course curriculum was originally constructed in conjunction with the training section of the National Trust northern regional office, British Trust for Conservation Volunteers (BTCV) and Urban Fringe Area Management Scheme (UFAMS). Newcastle City Council helped to refine the course content

139

*Table 16.1* Outline of the Certificate in Countryside Conservation at Newcastle University

| Modules | Curriculum subject | Topics covered |
| --- | --- | --- |
| 1 | Conservation industry | Policies and objectives, administration and finance of conservation bodies |
| 2 | Ecological principles and law | History and law: ecology and site selection criteria |
| 3 | Survey the environment | A range of botanical and non-botanical surveys |
| 4 | Habitat management | Site management plans, conservation of habitat types |
| 5 | Interpret the environment | Site interpretation and visitor management |
| 6 | Project | Academic project linked to the workplace |

for the final modules of the potential programme of study. Additional discussion regarding course content was held with representatives of the National Park, Wildlife Trust and regional office of the Royal Society for the Protection of Birds (RSPB).

Table 16.1 shows the outline of the course. After one cycle of the course the curriculum comments from the assessment centres were renewed. Only minor changes of emphasis were needed to the original curriculum in one or two areas.

## Agricultural and Horticultural Standards (NVQ)

Newcastle University has developed NVQs in Agriculture and Horticulture. This demonstrates that universities can provide links with NVQs which are not direct assessment. This is a growth area with an increasing demand for open/distance learning materials. Case study assessments have been associated with specific academic assignments for undergraduates which have then been linked to the NVQ standards (see Appendix 1). Cain, Pullan, Udall and Venus (1995) state: 'One major problem at high level NVQs (levels 4 and 5) is it is physically impossible to manage a range of farms in various areas of the country. Further, the opportunities to demonstrate all the skills required and collect such evidence can be patchy.' They provide advice on the circumstances where resource packs can be used. They place strong emphasis on case studies which have been used to demonstrate competence in situations in which candidates do not have direct access to all the necessary tools/information, or situation opportunities, to enable them to demonstrate competence to the standards. This can be important, particularly when access to private financial information is required. This is often problematic, especially for those employed in farming. Often the farmers are reluctant to release this type of information, but for the candidate to demonstrate full competence they need access to this. Case studies can help students to demonstrate how they would work given the opportunity. This evidence falls under the category of work simulation and role play.

Case studies can also be used to allow assessors to check whether the candidate can transfer skills to a new situation. Assessors can check that evidence generated is not site-specific and candidates' evidence is capable of transferability, this being truly competent to industry standards. This issue has not yet been addressed directly, but rather in the way the standards are written and assessed. Transferability is assumed during the assessment process by the assessor weighting the evidence, using questioning and looking at supplementary evidence, for example academic qualifications, to test knowledge and understanding to judge the transferability. In agriculture and horticulture there is a risk that outside the farm/site an employee would not be competent as they only work to the standard of their employer (this is also partly true of the environmental industry). The situation is complex in that employers themselves may not be competent to the industry standard, and for a particular employer candidates are working to a standard which is acceptable to them. Hence the employer regards the employee as competent. Case studies allow the candidates to demonstrate competence in such situations and to demonstrate knowledge and understanding by way of assignments which have been developed to ensure realistic industry competence.


## THE ROLE OF UNDERPINNING KNOWLEDGE AND UNDERSTANDING IN NVQS

Figure 16.2 is a schematic diagram of the quantity of evidence, represented by the size of the bars, likely to be required to be presented by a candidate. This equates with the amount of work required to confirm competence to achieve the specified standard. The likely forms of this evidence which could be presented by the candidate to demonstrate competence are shown in such ways as to try to highlight the potential links with other qualifications (academic) as well as in addition, assessment of underpinning skills and knowledge is carried out during NVQ assessment, primarily oral questioning.

Mitchell and Bartram (1994) define knowledge and understanding as: 'Knowledge of facts and opinions, theories and principles as well as ways of applying knowledge'. NVQ level 1 (the most basic level) is primarily assessed on evidence of performance with some possible role play/simulation and assessment of the candidate's work by others. It is unlikely the candidate will be asked to demonstrate a large amount of knowledge; questions, if asked, will be at a basic level, e.g. who the supervisor and manager are; relevant Health and Safety areas; and the location of items/information directly relating to the work activity.

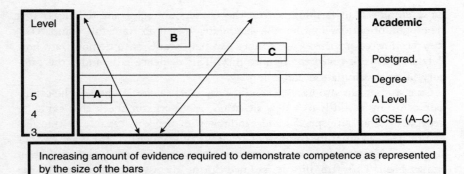

*Figure 16.2* The links between the NVQ levels and academic qualifications

The situation is different for NVQ levels 4 and 5, whereby most of the evidence will be in the form of knowledge and understanding as the candidate is expected to be able to work in a range of complex situations; be responsible for the work of others; and either generate or apply knowledge in new situations (Figure 16.2). The measurement of competence at this level is a complex process and is best demonstrated by considering the range of assessment instruments used by the professions to accept candidates into membership. This is laid down by the profession in their membership criteria. Professional codes of conduct are essentially measures of competence.

## PROFESSIONAL INSTITUTES

Entrance to the professions is primarily based on academic qualifications: first degree and/or postgraduate certificates with work experience within, or additional to, qualifications. The type of evidence accepted generally takes the form of reports and products of professional work. This type of evidence determines whether a person can or cannot perform the task, but requires the candidate to demonstrate 'knowledge' in a complex form in what they produce. Eruat and Cole (1994) constructed a table demonstrating the range of assessments used by professions to assess candidates across a range of professions for membership. The requirements vary from direct observation to written exams. These are the normal forms of assessment used by the professions to assess members' competence for entry to membership. This accords with the learning model of Cavero (1992), who said: 'A major difference between experts and non-experts in any field is that experts have far more procedural knowledge. That is they *know how* [author's italics] to perform their craft'; i.e. they are competent to perform the task, demonstrating the understanding and knowledge required for it. This knowledge and understanding is usually gained during the process of initial and continuing education, but not exclusively. They will apply this knowledge to a range of situations, some of which may be new to them. Hence they have to devise, research or apply knowledge gained elsewhere, but must always be capable of a competent piece of work to the standard defined by the institute's code of conduct. This places a heavy burden by any set of standards on the knowledge and understanding required, and is the reason for the professions relying primarily on academic qualifications to deliver and assess the appropriate knowledge and understanding.

This relationship can be demonstrated by the following examples. Walton (1994) provides examples of how NVQs have been developed in tandem with an academic course in Human Resource Management, and includes Training and Development Lead Body (TDLB) and Management Charter Initiative (MCI) units using a Credit Accumulation Transfer Scheme (CATS) system of points. The assumption is that the two types of evidence were equally valid and hence there was equality of transfer. Challis, Usherwood and Joesbury (1993) developed this further with reference to the role of competencies in the medical profession, generally considered as a very 'high powered' profession. They show that, in those areas where students have to deal with patients and develop interpersonal skills, competence based assessment is the most appropriate. The Engineering Council (1995) outlined the possible range of routes for candidates to gain professional membership, taking into consideration GNVQs as well.

## CORE SKILLS

Thus, knowledge and understanding at various levels are important factors in competence. The greater the level of competence, the greater the amount of knowledge required. The type of knowledge at higher levels is also different. This can be seen by the scale which the NCVQ uses to equate the levels with academic courses (see Figure 16.2). The environment standards at present are available at levels 2, 3 and 4. This suggests that level 2 equates with GCSE level knowledge and level 4 with a degree. CSTAG (1989) was the first major report on environmental education and environment and COSQUEC concluded that those working in the countryside management industry should possess seven areas of 'core' knowledge (Table 16.2).

*Table 16.2* Summary of CSTAG (1989) knowledge base for those employed in the countryside

| | |
|---|---|
| 1 | Policies of the organisation |
| 2 | Management |
| 3 | Environmental issues |
| 4 | The industry players |
| 5 | Current land-use policies and legislation |
| 6 | Farming and forestry |
| 7 | Landscape: geology, ecology, climate |

CSTAG showed that 69 per cent of all staff employed in the countryside industries had postgraduate and/or first degree qualifications and 31 per cent had other recognised certificates and diplomas. The IEEM (1995) places greater emphasis on the last of these core knowledge areas – landscape: geology, ecology, climate. They consider section seven of the core knowledge identified by CSTAG as fundamental to the profession of ecologist and environmental manager. They also add to this 'core', biology, taxonomy and species identification, biotopes, sustainable development and ecological survey. At the higher-level competencies (levels 4 and 5), which equate with professional membership, the IEEM requires candidates to demonstrate considerable knowledge and understanding of this area, and/or to add to new knowledge, or to develop unique ways of applying knowledge. On this basis, knowledge and understanding need to be given a much stronger emphasis in the present NVQs and needs to be assessed directly.

The IEEM (1995) assumes that most candidates will gain an academic award initially (assessment of the knowledge), then complete several years' professional experience (three years). However, there is a mature entry route to IEEM for candidates who have gained over ten years' practical experience and who may not have achieved a recognised academic standard. The IEEM considers that the present NVQs developed by COSQUEC are too broad and that GNVQs are unlikely to be appropriate as they will not provide the 'same level of fundamental knowledge' required by practising ecologists or environmental managers. The IEEM consider the standards of the environment industry require a level of knowledge which is greater than presently expected for NVQ assessment. In essence the industry is driven by knowledge, primarily science and physical geography, but including all the areas highlighted as core by CSTAG and with the addition of transferable skills such as problem-solving, team work, IT, etc. The consequences of this, with the development of environmental standards, have yet to be addressed by COSQUEC, but academic qualifications may become the norm before candidates will be allowed to demonstrate this knowledge (and its application) in the workplace.

The NCVQ has encouraged the formation of the PALS (Plants, Animals and the Landbase Sector) to write common units of competence. It may be generally conceded that conservation and the other land-based sectors have much in common, having an outward expression of similar tasks, but the major difference is in the specific areas of knowledge and understanding relevant to each sector. To illustrate this concept: what is required to become a taxi driver in London is to gain the 'knowledge' and to demonstrate this before applying for a cab licence, but anybody with a car and a standard driving licence can establish themselves as a private hire cab instantly. The competence required for conservation and the skills needed in agriculture, horticulture and forestry may appear at first sight to be similar, but the difference is the extent of ecological science knowledge and understanding required by ecologists and environmentalists.

## DISCUSSION

As shown above, NVQ assessment and its associated education standard is a major activity of all Further Education colleges, including the Agriculture and Horticulture colleges. Increasingly other education institutes outside the land-based sector are offering this standard. This demonstrates that a dual award approach — mixing workplace assessment and formal academic assessment — is the norm and students are keen on the dual qualifications. The two systems should be seen as complementary to each other, each providing the other with direct evidence of a candidate's ability. It could be said to give a more complete picture of a candidate, i.e. they may have the knowledge but can they apply it correctly in accordance with the industry standards in the workplace?

The involvement of the Higher Education sector with environmental qualifications is likely to continue to be that of supplying academic awards at degree and postgraduate level. If professional institutes such as the IEEM accredit courses for membership purposes then it is probable that HE institutions will participate in this. By contrast, it is unlikely that most HE institutions will be directly involved with environmental NVQ standards. However, they may act at the Continuing Education level as suppliers of education linked to NVQs. They are also likely to provide materials which can be used as assessment instruments, as previously mentioned.

From the foregoing account, it is clear that knowledge is important for the environment industry. COSQUEC and NCVQ will have to accept that candidates will gain the knowledge first or enter a course which offers a dual award coupled with workplace learning and assessment. A dual award system can allow for more effective teaching and learning. At the higher levels, HE institutions will only slowly develop the capacity to offer NVQs. This will result in students having to complete several practical years after graduating before being assessed for NVQs and before being recognised as competent. Hence it is likely that professionally validated degrees will be more attractive to HE institutions, as this will accord more closely with the ethos of these types of institutions, whereas NVQs and education associated with NVQs is more representative of the FE ethos. The Newcastle system at the Adult Liberal Education level is complementing and running in parallel to NVQs providing a supplementary qualification. This equates directly with the FE colleges' approach. NVQs will only become part of the mainstream HE provision either if professional bodies incorporate them into their rules of membership, or if candidates have a number of years' work experience where they may wish to gain some units of competence as part of their degree. As the 'environment industry' is largely knowledge-driven, academic qualifications are likely to continue to be the main means for new entrants to the industry, but with an increasing number gaining NVQs after graduation.

The environment is a new area for both NVQs and professional body development (the IEEM was established in 1991). It will take time for the universities in particular to integrate approaches to assessment.

# REFERENCES

Cain, P. J., Pullan, S. G., Udall, C. and Venus, C. A. 1995 'Team farm case studies', Farm Management Unit, University of Newcastle upon Tyne.

Cavero, R. M. 1992 'Professional practice, learning and continuing education: an integrated perspective', *Inter. Journal of Lifelong Education*, Vol. 2, 91–101.

Challis, M., Usherwood, T. and Joesbury, J. 1993 'Assessing specified competencies in medical training', *Competence and Assessment*, No. 22, 6–9.

Countryside Staff Training Advisory Group 1989 'Training for tomorrow's countryside', Countryside Commission, CCP269.

Eruat, M. and Cole, G. 1994 'Assessment of competence in higher level occupations', in *Competence and Assessment*, No. 23, 78–82.

IEEM 1995 'The profession of ecology and ecological management: what I need to know', Institute of Ecology and Environmental Management, 36 Kingfisher Court, Hambridge Road, Newbury, Berks RG14 5SJ.

Mitchell, L. and Bartram, D. 1994 'The place of knowledge and understanding in the development of National Vocational Qualifications and Scottish Vocational Qualifications', *Competence and Assessment*, briefing series No. 10.

The Engineering Council 1995 'Pathways', *Competence and Assessment*, No. 29, 42–8.

Turner, K. 1995 'NVQs in the Environment', paper to the conference on NVQs and Environmental Competence, London Guildhall University (23 October 1995).

Walton, J. 1994 'Vocational qualifications at professional level: bridging the academic/NVQ divide', *Competence and Assessment*, No. 26, 16–20.

## APPENDIX: LINKS BETWEEN A TEAM CASE STUDY AND THE AGRICULTURAL AND HORTICULTURAL NVQS

### Grassland Management Case Study Assessment

You should present an advisory report that a farmer could act upon. The report should include:

assessment of the grassland areas on the farm in terms of potential productivity.

The potential evidence which might be generated by the candidate to the following:

NVQ Unit 87 Plan a grazing programme.

*Performance Criteria*

87.1.2  Grazing programme is designed accurately to meet nutritional requirements and production objectives for the identified livestock.

*Range*

87.1.2  Objectives: maintenance; production.
87.1.3  Modifications: changes in stocking; grass management.
      Monitoring: pasture condition; livestock output; livestock condition.
Some aspects of the element or range will not be sufficient by performance alone. Additional evidence of related knowledge and understanding will therefore be required.

*Underpinning Knowledge*

(Individual case studies do not necessarily match all the performance criteria sought and underpinning knowledge required for assessments)

1  The implications of site on grass production;
2  Influence of seasonal variation on sward production;
3  Physical and financial relationship between nutrient inputs and grassland outputs;
4  Relationship between sward quality and quantity and its influence on livestock production;
5  Variety and species response to nutrient application and defoliation;
6  The effects of weeds on pasture and animal production;

7 Grazing management and livestock health maintenance;
8 Assessment and grassland productivity;
9 Livestock nutritional requirements; the contribution from the pasture, supplementary and transitional feeding arrangements;
10 Grazing systems and their management;
11 Factors affecting stocking rate.

# 17

# CHANGING ENVIRONMENT

## No blueprints for education

*Peter Maarleveld*

Environmental professionals are now recognised employees within both private and public organisations. The job requirements for these professionals are still undergoing rapid change in comparison with other professions. For this reason it is impossible, and also undesirable, to define one or more position profiles. Nevertheless, some general features of the jobs market and environmental professions can be accounted for. It is possible to explore career options either by content or by position. The job requirements for environmental professionals should be viewed in a long-term perspective. Environmental professionals will have the required knowledge and skills, but it should not be underestimated that by possessing positive attitudes towards the environment senior professionals may engender a change in processes and organisations in favour of the environment.

How government, educational institutes, students, professionals and others try to meet the needs of the jobs market will be discussed. In this respect regular exchanges of information, networking, for example between employers and those responsible for education, are more effective tools than regulation. Also quality assessment of environmental education is a significant instrument.

The focus of this chapter is on the labour market for graduates from universities and institutes for higher vocational education. However, the market for those with a secondary vocational education should not be neglected. In a survey of the environmental labour market in The Netherlands (NEI 1989) it was estimated that 25 per cent of the need was fulfilled by persons with secondary vocational education. Following a description of the current labour market and specific careers, suggestions will be given for meeting the needs of knowledge, skills and attitudes of environmental professionals in society.

# LABOUR MARKET

In general the relation between higher education and subsequent career paths is not well understood. To analyse trends in the labour market for environmental professionals is even more difficult. The environmental labour market is dynamic in comparison with other professions, which require graduates of higher education. The changes in the labour market for environmental professions have three major causes.

First, the profession is not yet fully crystallised. More than 50 per cent of the work is and will be done by persons for which the environmental task is only a secondary task (NEI 1989). The proportion of time spent on this secondary task in the private sector is higher than in other sectors, except for consultative firms. It is not likely that the organisation of labour in the private sector in other European countries is very different from the Dutch example. There are reasons to think that these figures have changed considerably in the last five years.

On the supply side three types of environmental professionals can be distinguished:

- Professionals with a traditional disciplinary education and a relatively short additional graduate or postgraduate environmental education;
- Professionals with extensive environmental education within their original discipline;
- Professionals having specialised solely in environmental education.

These three types of educated professionals are competitors in the same labour market. Due to an increasing interest in environmental issues it can be expected that the so-called 'greening of curricula' will be strengthened and extended in the near future. Graduates from all kinds of disciplines, such as economics and business administration, will have in their syllabuses in their specialist disciplines, environmental aspects of their profession. These graduates are not yet considered as 'environmental professionals'. However, they can, with additional training, offer employers the relevant expertise to fulfil the secondary environmental tasks mentioned before.

Second, the knowledge area is very broad and is quickly developing. All academic disciplines are involved except possibly theology and the humanities. To demonstrate the breadth of the area two content classifications are shown in Tables 17.1 and 17.2.

In addition, due to the growing interest in environmental issues in the development of knowledge this area is rapidly increasing by new research findings. New environmental concepts such as industrial metabolism and life cycle analysis are gaining prominence. Most leading economists take into consideration environmental problems.

Third, an environmental professional may have many different positions such as those illustrated in Tables 17.3 and 17.4.

*Table 17.1* A content classification of environmental jobs (1)

| |
|---|
| Hazardous waste management and reduction |
| Solid waste management and recycling |
| Housing and community development |
| Land use and preservation |
| Soil-related issues |
| Water-related issues |
| Air-related issues |
| Fish and wildlife management |
| Fund raising and foundation work |
| Environmental education |

*Table 17.2* A content classification of environmental jobs (2)

| |
|---|
| Pollution prevention and control |
| Disease prevention |
| Environmental planning |

*Table 17.3* A position classification of environmental jobs (1)

| |
|---|
| Policy advisors |
| Executives in policy |
| Business executives |
| Technical and management advisors |
| Researchers |

However, a clear outline of the environmental profession is not expected within the next few years.

## CAREERS

There is little information about career routes and the mobility of environmental professionals. A survey of Dutch graduates of the Wageningen Agricultural University was carried out by Evers and Bos-Boers (1992) of engineers from a four-year environmental sciences curriculum, 'Environmental Hygiene'.

In this survey approximately 500 graduates gave information about changes in their position (response rate of 66 per cent). The programme was established in the early 1970s. Students may specialise in water-, air- or soil-related issues or can choose an environmental management/policy specialisation. After a common basic education of two years, students take courses and carry out research within a wide variety of subjects. Table 17.5 shows the variety of first positions of graduates from 1988 or later.

*Table 17.4* A position classification of environmental jobs (2)

*Environmental science*
　　Research & Development (laboratory technicians; packaging scientists; chemists; biologists; toxicologists)
　　Technical (civil engineering; transportation engineers; environmental health)
*Environmental policy*
　　Regulator (health regulation; environmental regulation; natural resource management regulators)
　　Regulated industry (risk assessment; environmental compliance officers; environmental health officers; environmental impact assessors)
　　Policy analysis (environmental economists; consulting firms; lobbyists; environmental groups)
*Environmental information*
　　Education (elementary, secondary, post-secondary teachers; parks; nature centres; hands-on science museums or centres; outdoor education)
　　Communications (newspapers; mass media; communications for environmental concerns for private industry; information officers for public agencies)
　　Interpretation (parks; nature centres; hands-on centres; exhibition halls; zoological gardens; tourist centres)
*Related professions*
　　Environmental law
　　Biomedical engineering
　　Environmental health

*Source*: Heimlich 1993

*Table 17.5* Division of environmental professionals by their first position (%)

| First position | % |
| --- | --- |
| Engineer | 34 |
| Researcher | 26 |
| Public relations position/advisor | 12 |
| Policy advisor | 10 |
| Project manager/director | 4 |
| Teacher | 4 |
| Expert development aid | 3 |
| Information specialist/journalist | 3 |
| Commercial position | 2 |
| Other (including entrepreneur) | 2 |

About half of the environmental professionals who went on to other employment between 1988 and 1992 found another type of position. Figure 17.1 shows in which directions these changes generally took place. This figure shows only changes which occurred more than twice.

Many of those entering research and engineering positions upon graduation eventually enter management positions, sometimes preceded by another type

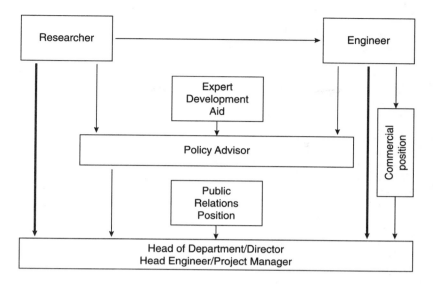

*Figure 17.1* Requirements of graduates given by environmental professionals

of position. About 45 per cent of the professionals who changed from their original positions within this five-year period moved to another sector, as shown in Figure 17.2. Again, only changes which occurred more than twice are shown.

It is worth noting that there is a predominant exchange of professionals between universities and research institutes and also between regional/local government and consultancy firms. However, for the rest it appears there is only a one-way traffic, i.e. from national government to consultancy firms and from these firms to other private enterprises. It is of concern that very few professionals from the private sector return to universities to pass on their experience to students. It can be asked whether this situation is only apparent in The Netherlands or whether it is a common problem experienced elsewhere.

Graduates from environmental studies courses should be interested in 'organisational matters'. This conclusion can be drawn from the opinion of environmental professionals who have a career of five years or longer. In a questionnaire survey the respondents gave their five most important requirements for graduates of environmental curricula. Table 17.6 shows the most commonly ascribed attributes in order of importance (i.e. those cited most frequently from 1 to 18).

Intellectual capabilities are shown to be the most important requirements for graduates. However, particular skills and certain attitudes in combination with professional knowledge are high on the list of desired attributes. These perceptions of professionals correspond well with the requirements of

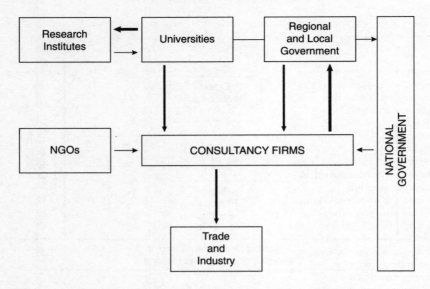

*Figure 17.2* Changes in market sector of environmental professionals

employers for both full-time and part-time professionals (NEI 1989) (see Table 17.7). They usually require:

- Readiness to fulfil environmental work as a secondary task;
- Sufficient attention to the demands of the organisation;
- Good communication skills.

Other demands are equally important, such as experience within the organisation. Employers prefer good environmental training to primary training. However, only 8 per cent of organisations prefer a professional who is a recent graduate and about 30 per cent of the organisations find this undesirable.

*Table 17.6* Requirements of graduates given by environmental professionals

| | | | |
|---|---|---|---|
| 1 | Professional knowledge | 10 | Administrative decision-making insight |
| 2 | Analytical capabilities | 11 | Managerial capabilities |
| 3 | Team player | 12 | Strong commercial attitude |
| 4 | Creative in science | 13 | Didactical capabilities |
| 5 | Organising capacity | 14 | Knowledge of automation |
| 6 | Client orientated | 15 | Business insight |
| 7 | Work under pressure of time | 16 | Societal insight |
| 8 | Carry out research independently | 17 | Diplomatic |
| 9 | Bring about progress | 18 | Command of languages |

*Source*: Evers and Bos-Boers 1992

*Table 17.7* Employer requirements of environmental professionals*

|  | Yes, desirable | No, not desirable | Dependent on position | No opinion |
|---|---|---|---|---|
| Good communication skills | 61 | 4 | 11 | 24 |
| Attention to the demands of the organisation | 60 | 6 | 10 | 24 |
| Readiness to fulfil the environmental work as a secondary task | 60 | 6 | 15 | 18 |
| Sufficient experience in the organisation concerned in another position | 38 | 10 | 32 | 20 |
| Good environmental education | 34 | 15 | 19 | 32 |
| Good education (non-environmental education) | 19 | 26 | 26 | 29 |
| Strong environmental awareness | 30 | 18 | 16 | 36 |
| Environmental experience | 30 | 15 | 28 | 27 |
| Experience (non-environmental) | 6 | 40 | 19 | 35 |
| Younger than 40 years | 30 | 10 | 17 | 43 |
| Older than 40 years | 4 | 23 | 20 | 52 |
| Recently graduated | 8 | 30 | 28 | 34 |
| Other requirements | 1 | 11 | 3 | 83 |

*Source*: NEI 1989
*Note*: * in percentage of the number of organisations, exclusive unknown

*Table 17.8* Filling of the latest vacancy for an environmental professional

| Internal | 65% * |
|---|---|
| add as a secondary task | 39% |
| from other position | 17% |
| same person from start | 9% |
| External | 35% |

*Source*: NEI 1989
*Note*: * of total response (exclusive unknown)

Success in finding an environmental job immediately after graduation is limited. Employers recruit the greater number of environmental professionals from their own personnel and mostly by adding environmental side tasks to the original position (see Table 17.8). Nevertheless, about 85 per cent of the graduates from Wageningen found employment.

PETER MAARLEVELD

# MEETING THE NEEDS OF THE LABOUR MARKET

## Long-term perspective

To achieve a good combination of knowledge, skills and attitudes at graduate level is difficult for both student and those responsible for curricula development. Career and education must be viewed in a long-term perspective. Both before and after graduation students should be aware of their potential capabilities, especially concerning their skills and attitudes. In a review article (Heimlich 1993) about environmental careers in the US, Heimlich noted that, regardless of career choice, basic mathematics as well as science preparation along with skills for applying these concepts were important for success. Translated to the European context a full training in these fields at secondary education level is a very minimum or perhaps insufficient.

The development of desired attitudes is a consequence primarily of upbringing and education in primary and secondary school. However, lecturers and staff in higher education should be able to give students relevant guidance. Educational staff consist of a mix of persons with both academic and professional backgrounds in both the public and private sector as previously indicated.

It is important that clear choices in the design of an environmental science programme are made as it is impossible in education to meet all the needs of knowledge, skills and attitudes (Maarleveld 1994) for all curricula.

The strength of educational institutes, such as universities and polytechnics, is to pass on knowledge and certain skills. These institutes should also provide postgraduate education in specific subject areas. An example of this perspective in education is given for environmental technology (Pöyry, 1991) (see Table 17.9).

However, the knowledge employers need today could be obsolete or irrelevant within a few years. Moreover, employers have different knowledge needs from their staff. Organisations respond differently to demands from outside. A helpful scheme (see Table 17.10) has been developed by the McKinsey Company (Winsemius 1994) which gives four phases in the behaviour of organisations in dealing with environmental issues.

In the first phase shown in Table 17.10 organisations are characterised by purely reactive behaviour. Organisations are looking for end-of-pipe solutions at low costs. They leave the solutions to specialists. Winsemius (1994) considers that the larger Dutch enterprises are in a transition to the second phase. Organisations become receptive to environmental problems and try to invent process integrated solutions. Such organisations are usually dealing with major investments and the responsibility for these shifts to the senior management. The second phase is characterised by the optimisation of existing processes. By contrast the third phase is characterised by a constructive attitude. In search-

*Table 17.9* Levels of environmental technology education

---

*First level*
Basic environmental and ecological courses
*Second level*
Environmental aspects integrated into different courses of technology
   project work
   exercises
   training in industry
*Third level*
Specialising courses
   more profound environmental skills
   special technologies and methods
*Fourth level*
Continuing education
   continuous updating of knowledge
   applying new research results
   special needs of industry
   environmental management
   training trainers

---

*Table 17.10* Response of organisations to environmental issues

| *Answer* | *1* | *2* | *3* | *4* |
|---|---|---|---|---|
| *patterns* | *reactive* | *receptive* | *constructive* | *proactive* |
| integrate | end-of-pipe | process | product | need |
| co-operate | specialists | managers | sector | society |
| generate | minimise | optimise | jump | vision |

*Source*: Winsemius 1994

ing for possible solutions the product itself is involved. The separate managers are no longer responsible. Enterprises co-operate together to tackle the problems. There is co-operation with government and even with environmental organisations, realising that traditional solutions will not help. Yet this is insufficient. A last phase is necessary, a proactive phase. Target groups start to think about the way the need in society can be fulfilled in a sustainable way. It agrees a collective vision for the future and cultural change.

This scheme can help to identify the specific combination of knowledge, skills and attitudes that are required. Knowledge is still the most important need. From phase 1 to phase 4 the requirements for skills and attitudes increase. Those responsible for environmental curricula can analyse a particular economic sector or region in respect of the organisational behaviour expected or required in the future.

In addition students and professionals can utilise this scheme to select possible organisations which fit their capabilities.

PETER MAARLEVELD

## Information and networking

The results of the career survey of environmental engineers (Evers and Bos-Boers 1992) was quoted as information for graduates. There are also examples of active environmental student associations connected with graduate programmes. These associations could have a strong network function and are useful for a number of purposes, for example to find internships. A strong European network between departments of environmental sciences is also recommended, to exchange information and to combine efforts to analyse the needs of environmental professionals.

Productive, regular contacts between environmental departments and professionals/employers was recommended by a Dutch peer review committee which has evaluated higher vocational education in the environmental field (HBO-Raad 1995). The committee concluded that only a minority of these departments has these contacts, as many environmental programmes have only recently developed, so a periodic quality assessment is necessary to guarantee that students are receiving good education.

## CONCLUSIONS

Environmental professionals are now recognised employees within both private and public organisations. The job requirements for these professionals are still rapidly changing in comparison with other sectors. Hence the environmental profession will not be clearly delineated for some years to come. The combination of basic environmental knowledge, skills and attitudes required by an environmental professional depends largely on the response to environmental issues of particular organisations and the position in which a person is employed.

Close and direct links between environmental higher education and the need of environmental professionals in society are not necessarily required at present. Educational institutes and students themselves should gather information about the many career possibilities both in general and in relation to the particular curriculum being followed. Networking between those responsible for education and graduates and employers is recommended, supplemented by regular feedback about educational and professional requirements. In this respect it is also recommended that useful instruments or methods be developed which enable educational institutes to monitor the dynamic environmental labour market in this area.

## REFERENCES

Evers, P. W. and Bos-Boers, M., 1992. *The Position of Engineers from Wageningen: Environmental Hygiene* (in Dutch), Netherlands Institute for Agricultural Engineers, Wageningen Agricultural University, The Netherlands

HBO-Raad, Council for Higher Vocational Education, 1995. *As in a Mirror: a quality picture of environmental studies in higher vocational education* (in Dutch). Report of the Review Committee for Environmental Studies, The Hague, The Netherlands.

Heimlich, J. E., 1993. *Environmental Studies and Environmental Careers*, ERIC Clearinghouse for Science, Mathematics, and Environmental Education, Columbus, Ohio, USA; ERIC/CSMEE Digest, ED 350964.

Maarleveld, P. A., 1994. *Choices in Environmental Education*, Contribution to the Conference *University Training Experts in Practical Environmental Problems*, 10 and 11 June 1994, University of Venice, Italy (forthcoming).

NEI (Netherlands Economic Institute), 1989. *The Need for Environmental Knowledge: A comparison between supply and demand of the labour market for environmental professionals* (in Dutch). Rotterdam, The Netherlands.

Pöyry, S., 1991. *Skills Need in Environmental Technology*, EC Conference *Towards New Models of University – Industry Cooperation: the Example of COMETT*, Amsterdam, The Netherlands.

Winsemius, P. 1994. *Sustainability: Looking for Knowledge* (in Dutch). Report of the Conference *Sustainable Development and Research*, Ministry of the Environment. Publikatiereeks milieustrategie nr. 1994/2.

# 18

# THE EVOLUTION OF
# ENVIRONMENTAL CAREERS

*Bernard Giovannini*

Environmental careers should not only concern natural and technical sciences but should include the socio-economic sciences. Dobré and Lavoux (chapter 13) have pointed out the interesting fact that the only field where job advertisements were more numerous than candidates was in the socio-economic field in France. This chapter will explore how other fields of knowledge can interact together in a dynamic way to achieve sustainable development.

Over twenty years ago my attention was drawn to the potential of energy efficiency. At that time the energy problem was essentially the dependence upon oil and the problem of nuclear energy. It was demonstrated very convincingly to me that energy savings of 70–80 per cent could be achieved by using appropriate technologies. It seemed then that what was required was an approach to governments which explained the basic facts to them and the problem would be solved. Twenty years later some progress has been made but certainly not as much as should have been.

Technical advances and solutions to current environmental problems can only be implemented if there is the political will and support to do so. Figure 18.1 shows diagrammatically the process which is necessary to solve problems and implement appropriate solutions. This process must commence with the identification and definition of a problem, for example the threat to climate; next a technical solution is found which must then be incorporated as a policy option. This process is mainly related to 'hard' sciences where it is easier and usually more straightforward to make progress.

The second part of the equation is effecting policy implementation, which usually meets with many obstacles and problems, and the monitoring of results. This is much more complicated and generally progress is slower. Usually considerable effort goes into the first part, where the technical details of what should be done are calculated, but invariably insufficient attention is paid to the second part of the loop, as shown below.

One example of this policy loop operating is related to energy efficiency and the problem of climate change (see Figure 18.2). Many of the boxes

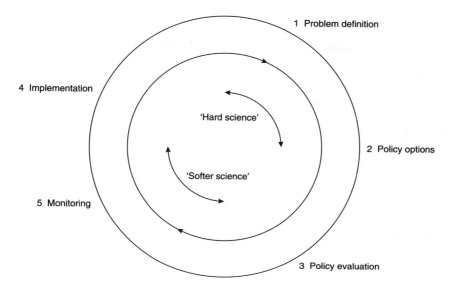

*Figure 18.1* The 'whole policy loop'

in this diagram are specific to this particular example of how things happen.

The process begins with the definition of a certain number of technological options for energy efficiency and then one assesses how these technological options can be implemented in real situations. The economic considerations, i.e. whether the proposed solutions are economically or technically feasible, are studied. It might be assumed that if a solution is found to be technically sound and economically efficient, it should be implemented very quickly. In fact, this is not the case as a number of problems arise which are related to information, communication, special interests, the understanding of the policy makers and of the public, etc. These aspects must then be factored into the loop. Many of the problems at this stage are related to values, as ultimately decisions are influenced by what individuals think is important and what is not important.

The International Academy of the Environment based in Geneva is an institution dedicated to training, research, dialogue and the various dimensions of sustainable development. The Academy specialises in informing decision-makers so as to help them with the second part of the loop.

The IAE provides decision-makers with the basic knowledge and management principles to enable them to take decisions compatible with sustainable development. The Academy aims to target people who are already in employment and who have a high level of responsibility. For such an audience, 'training' is not an appropriate term for what takes place; it is more like a

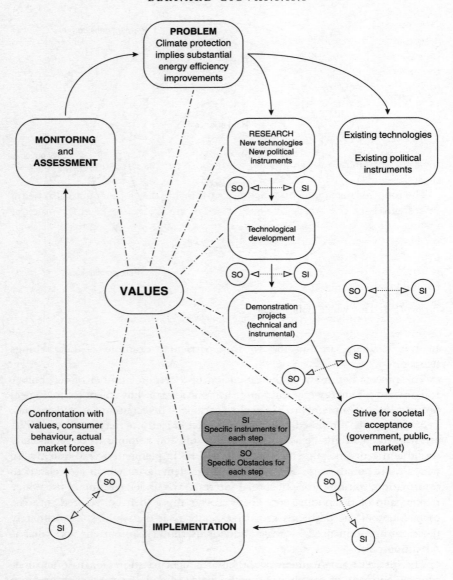

*Figure 18.2* Policy loop: energy efficiency

dialogue where the IAE benefits from their experience and allows the participants to share their experience with others. The essential element of this process is to examine, through collaboration between experts and decision-makers, new solutions that will satisfy the requirements of sustainable development.

A series of seminars has been organised that are called a policy dialogue. The main subjects of the Academy programmes are topical subjects such as biodiversity and biotechnology. This is a programme which examines how to conserve biodiversity while at the same time making it economically viable, especially in developing countries. 'Consumption and Sustainability' is a programme which deals with the changing lifestyles that are necessary for the world to become sustainable.

It is often said that free trade conflicts with the protection of the environment. In relation to the first programme, which deals with policies and tools for sustainable development, it can be seen this need not necessarily be the case.

The tools for management to achieve sustainable development are also being investigated by the Academy, with courses in, for example, environmental impact assessment (this is not a technical course, but investigates the political, social, organisational and participatory requirements necessary for environmental impact assessment to have any effect). Environmental communication is a relevant defence of this activity. Environmental economics and environmental cost management are also important and related to integrated resource management and environmental management in business.

Environmental conflict resolution is an example. This is essentially the second part of the loop, when ideas are formulated about items which demand attention. Action has to be taken to achieve certain goals and often conflicting situations arise as many stakeholders will be affected. A characteristic of environmental conflict is the many actors, with many different levels of power and influence. It can be very complex, touching a vast variety of interests, and it can also have a high level of uncertainty in its scientific aspects.

A number of processes should then be instigated to avoid environmental conflicts. First, it is necessary to learn how to institute collaborative decision-making, not just solving the conflict once it exists, but trying to prevent it with a set of techniques. This means identifying the actors who will be important, communicating with them in time, building up the necessary relationships and networks, and preventing the problem arising before it has become a conflict. It is essential to gain a consensus through negotiation at the earliest opportunity so that a solution can be found.

This is just one example of the kind of activity that needs to be developed so as to be able to undertake the second part of the loop. In conclusion, we need to think of the environment as more like a business and to be more forward-looking in regarding the environment as a kind of future market where the possibilities and potential conflicts have to be foreseen and hopefully solved in advance. These are the kinds of thinking and management capabilities which are, in the case of environmental communications, closer to marketing thinking. This is one of the activities in the environmental field which will develop in the future.

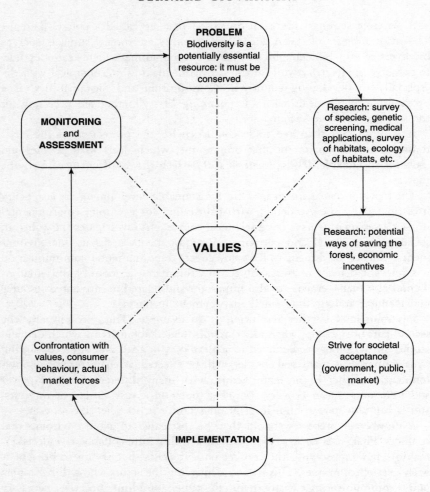

*Figure 18.3* Policy loop: conservation of biodiversity

# 19

# PROFESSIONAL RECOGNITION IN THE ENVIRONMENT ACROSS EUROPE

## First and Second Diplomas Directive

*Alice McLure*

This chapter summarises the background to mutual recognition of education and training systems across Europe and describes briefly some of the initiatives which have been undertaken to provide for academic and professional recognition.

The concept of free movement – whether for the purposes of study, for employment or indeed to live – is fundamental to the Community without frontiers. Facilitation of free movement for the purposes of employment (professional recognition) and/or study (academic recognition) is achieved through *the acceptance of the individual's capability – usually expressed in terms of a qualification or involvement in a course of study and/or experience.*

Barriers to freedom of movement may derive from issues of nationality, rights of entry and residence, and from legal provisions within Member States. Equally they may be due to simple lack of understanding across Member States of each other's education and training systems.

All of this was recognised in the Treaty of Rome and further developed in the EU Treaty. The legal base lies largely within four chapters of Part II, Title III, of the EC Treaty of Rome (1957) covering free movement of workers, establishment, services and goods. This is where the underpinning for the Department for Education and Employment work in implementing Directive 92/51/EEC (Second Diploma or General Systems Directive) can be found. Within this section of the Treaty, Articles 57, 66 and 49 provide for professional recognition. Discrimination based on nationality is outlawed through Articles 48, 52 and 59 of the EC Treaty (1957). Right of entry and residence – based on Articles 49 and 56 of the Treaty – were guaranteed when the Transitional Directives (described later) came into being in the 1960s and 1970s.

Understanding the provision for professional recognition may be helped by a brief description of the relevant articles as set out below.

Article 57 is concerned with the right of establishment of nationals from one Member State in the territory of another and already identifies the need for a system for recognition of qualifications in stating that:

> In order to make it easier for persons to take up and pursue activities as self-employed persons, the Council shall ... issue directives for the mutual recognition of diplomas, certificates and other evidence of formal qualifications.

Article 66, referring to freedom to provide services, simply states that:

> The provisions of Articles 55 to 58 shall apply to the matters covered by this Chapter.

As this includes Article 57, there is again a reference to the need to provide for mutual recognition.

While there is no equivalent provision in the section dealing with freedom of movement for workers, Article 49 states that:

> As soon as this Treaty enters into force, the Council shall ... issue directives or make regulations setting out the measures required to bring about, by progressive stages, freedom of movement for workers.

This is to be achieved:

> by systematically and progressively abolishing those administrative procedures and practices and those qualifying periods in respect of eligibility for available employment, whether resulting from national legislation or from agreements previously concluded between Member States, the maintenance of which would form an obstacle to the liberalisation of the movement of workers.

These three Articles, then, form the joint Treaty base of the general systems Directives on mutual recognition of education and training systems.

Until 1989, progress was slow and limited. It took two forms.

1 There were Directives which required Member States to abolish restrictions on freedom of establishment in respect of particular trades, professions or occupations (the Transitional Directives). Here, the migrant had to demonstrate a specified number of years in a particular profession or occupation rather than proof of qualification or education and training.
2 There were Directives which, in respect of specific professions, required the mutual recognition of given qualifications (the Sectoral Directives).

Largely in the health professions, an attempt was made here actually to harmonise education and training. But it took a very long time!

This piecemeal development of mutual recognition systems was clearly unsatisfactory. The Commission White Paper (1985) on 'Completing the Single Market' therefore considered it 'crucial that the obstacles which still remain to the free movement of the self-employed and employees should be removed by 1992'.

Here then was the recognition of the need to create a robust general system for the recognition of qualifications. In this same paper, the Commission's intent to support programmes between education establishments in different Member States with a view to establishing mobility of students – the genesis of ERASMUS – was noted.

In 1989, the Council adopted the first general Directive on the recognition of qualifications (that is, the first not limited to specific professions) – the First Diploma Directive. Following on from this, second and third general Directives have been adopted and proposed to complete the task which the First Diploma Directive had begun. Responsibility for the Directives in the UK lies with the Department for Trade and Industry and the Department for Education and Employment.

The First Diploma Directive was concerned only with the higher levels of qualification, namely those awarded after professional education and training of at least three years' duration. The other Directives aim to cover the levels of education and training not covered by the First, that is, all other post-secondary education and training courses and equivalents and long or short secondary courses and experience. The Directives are concerned with movement to regulated occupations. It is important also to note that the UK system of NVQs/SVQs attained its first formal recognition in Europe in the Second Directive.

While all this was happening a body of Case Law was building up and principles have now been established for the behaviour of the competent authorities in a Member State when handling an application from a national of another Member State for professional recognition for a regulated occupation. By and large these principles require that the host Member State must examine on an objective basis the qualification on offer and establish the extent to which there is equivalence. There is also, however, allowance for the host Member State to require the migrant to make good any deficiencies identified in the examination of his qualification.

Turning now to the problems caused by lack of understanding among Member States, a number of attempts have been made over the last twenty years to deal with this.

During the 1980s, work was done on comparability of vocational qualifications, but by 1990 it had become clear that this particular route was not the way forward. In December 1992 at the Social Affairs Council a UK

Resolution was adopted whose aim was to meet the Community objective of achieving genuine free movement of workers within the Community. This Resolution recognised that:

1   Individuals need to be able to present their professional or vocational qualifications, and relevant education and work experience clearly and effectively throughout the Community.
2   Employers need access to clear descriptions of qualifications of job applicants and further information on those qualifications if necessary, to establish their relevance to jobs on offer.

Thus the notion of 'transparency' was born, and has been continued in the expectations of some of the strands of the new education and training programmes.

In the Resolution the Commission called for proposals on a number of themes, one of which was the 'individual portfolio'. This idea has been around for a long time as a 'European vocational training passport' and a 'European qualification passport'. In response to the Resolution, Member States have come together in a project to consider the feasibility of the 'portfolio'. The UK's National Council for Vocational Qualifications co-ordinated this project and the report has now been produced. It is likely that future work will be taken forward under the Leonardo programme.[1]

Most recently, the Commission has issued a proposal, which is now in the public domain for consultation, on academic and professional recognition. The outcomes of this exercise should clarify what has happened in the past, identify areas of particular success or failure and indicate possible ways forward.

All of the above demonstrates the need to overcome legislative barriers and obstacles to understanding in enhancing freedom of movement for workers in Europe. Steps towards mutual recognition are both necessary and important in facilitating the process.

## NOTE

1   Leonardo da Vinci is the action programme for the implementation of an EC vocational training policy.

# 20

# CAREER ROUTES OF ENVIRONMENTAL PROFESSIONALS

## UK survey

*Eirene Williams*

## INTRODUCTION

Over recent decades there have been significant changes in attitudes to the natural environment. There is new legislation in Europe for environmental protection, and debate about environmental issues is commonplace in the media. As a result the demand for practical advice and skilled environmental management work in the widest sense has grown, and jobs in this sector are increasing. However proper training and appropriate qualifications in the environmental sector were not until recently recognised in UK, and people with little expertise could set themselves up as environmental advisers. In other professions in the UK this problem is addressed by the establishment and recognition of professional institutes. This paper describes first the career characteristics of practitioners in the existing environmental sector who felt moved to join a new institute, and second, education and training for the next generation of professionals.

## THE INSTITUTE OF ECOLOGY AND ENVIRONMENTAL MANAGEMENT (IEEM) AND ITS INITIAL MEMBERSHIP

As described by Everett (in chapter 21), the IEEM was formed in 1991 after discussions involving the British Ecological Society, the British Association of Nature Conservationists, the Institute of Biology and the Royal Geographical Society. It has rapidly established itself as the foremost forum for setting standards for policy and practice among environmental professionals. It is already accrediting members and addressing their needs and aspirations, as well as advising on and organising programmes for continuing professional development.

Currently, environmental practitioners and decision-makers seem to be a disparate group holding a variety of qualifications and having varied career paths. The Professional Affairs Committee (PAC) of the IEEM was given the task of ascertaining some of the characteristics of IEEM's initial membership. The exact wording of the investigation was 'to establish the past, present and future career track of IEEM members and to identify their conditions and terms of employment'. A questionnaire was designed by the author and sent out to members and prospective members of the IEEM. The results are presented in Figure 20.1 which is a modified version of the original questionnaire. All figures are percentages of the 160 respondents unless otherwise stated. Additional analyses were carried out, in which answers by individuals to questions were cross-referenced. Below are set out factual comments on each individual question, which are followed as appropriate by discussion.

The author acknowledges the assistance of Stephen Steadman in preparing and analysing the IEEM questionnaire.

## Employment sector

The percentages shown in Figure 20.1 are for the only or main job of each respondent: 19 respondents worked in more than one of the sectors listed. The sector distribution shows slightly more respondents worked in local authorities, academia or were self-employed consultants, with relatively few from industry or indeed unemployed.

The most noticeable members of IEEM at this stage of the Institute's development had been the private consultants. However, there were more local authority employees and academics than consultants. It is likely that unemployed ecologists were under-represented (possibly unable to afford the membership fees, or resigned due to lack of a lobby?). Those employed in industry are unlikely to feel either of these constraints but are still poorly represented.

## Job descriptions

The percentages were derived by reading the job titles and descriptions given and assigning them to various generalised categories. Key words appearing repeatedly such as 'project' and 'conservation' were useful in this task. Again consultancy and academic activities predominated, but a wide and miscellaneous range of other job titles and descriptions was revealed.

Question 2 invited a free statement of job title, description, etc., on three lines. There is a plethora of terminology for essentially similar work but the range of work carried out by the membership is equally wide. In many cases it is not possible to get a clear picture of what the respondent actually did.

This could well contribute to the confused public image of the environment profession that many commented on in questions 17 and 18. There seems to be a clear case for tightening up how ecologists and environmental managers describe what they do.

## Salary

The distribution is largely as anticipated. A few respondents pointed out that they worked part time in ecology/environmental management and hence earned less than they otherwise would.

## Satisfaction

The distribution is centralised but wide. Responses to questions 3 and 4 predictably fell into those with lower salaries expressing mainly dissatisfaction while those with higher salaries were more satisfied! General satisfaction with modest salaries was a less extreme response than might have been expected, but tallied with the expectation of the majority to remain in ecology/environmental management for the rest of their careers (expressed in question 16).

## Supervision

This distribution is skewed to the lower end as the majority of respondents did not supervise large teams of staff.

## Responsibilities

Individual respondents tended to have total responsibility for all three areas listed or none. An analysis relating individual answers in question 5 to those in question 6 also showed very significant positive associations. People who supervised a lot of staff had more responsibility in the areas of finance, organisational development and recruitment.

## Hours

The modal class was 41–50 hours.

## Holiday

Almost half the respondents took 21–30 days.

Questions 5 to 8 were analysed separately for private consultants because it might be expected that self-employed people would be different in these respects. The figures showed 54 per cent supervised no staff, implying that

## Section A: Your present employment

**1. In which of the following sectors do you carry out your ecological/environmental work?**

| | |
|---|---|
| Local Authority | 23.3% |
| Statutory body | 15.1% |
| Voluntary body | 13.2% |
| Private consultancy: self-employed | 16.4% |
| Private consultancy: as an employee | 7.5% |
| Industry | 4.4% |
| Academic institute | 18.9% |
| Other | 0.0% |
| Unemployed | 1.3% |

**2. Describe here very briefly what you actually do in your ecological/environmental work including job title, duties and responsibilities.**

| | |
|---|---|
| Consultants/Directors of consultancies | 21% |
| Academics | 17% |
| Conservation specific | 10% |
| Ecologists | 9% |
| Directors of organisations other than consultancies | 7% |
| Environment specific | 6% |
| Officers, in local authorities and of projects | 6% |
| Advisors | 3% |
| Planners | 3% |
| Rangers/Wardens | 3% |
| Recreation/Tourism specific | 3% |

**3. What is your present gross annual income from your ecological/environmental management activities (before tax but excluding overtime or expenses payments)?**

| | |
|---|---|
| Less than £10,000 | 10.1% |
| £10,000–£15,000 | 21.5% |
| £15,000–£20,000 | 32.3% |
| £20,000–£25,000 | 19.6% |
| More than £25,000 | 16.5% |

**4. On a scale of 1–5, how satisfied do you feel that this income reflects your level of responsibility.**

| | | |
|---|---|---|
| Very dissatisfied | 1 | 5.1% |
| | 2 | 27.2% |
| | 3 | 33.5% |
| | 4 | 23.4% |
| Very satisfied | 5 | 10.8% |

**5. How many staff do you supervise?**

| 0 | 1–5 | 6–10 | 11–20 | 20+ |
|---|---|---|---|---|
| 25.8% | 50.3% | 11.3% | 5.7% | 6.9% |

**6. On scales of 1–5, what is the extent of your responsibility for each of the following?**

| | | Financial Management | Organisational Development | Recruitment of Staff |
|---|---|---|---|---|
| Not at all | 1 | 9.6% | 7.1% | 26.6% |
| | 2 | 22.3% | 16.1% | 15.6% |
| | 3 | 17.8% | 22.6% | 20.8% |
| | 4 | 28.0% | 30.3% | 23.4% |
| Totally | 5 | 22.3% | 23.9% | 13.6% |

**7. How many hours do you spend in an average week on your ecological/environmental work?**

| 0–20 | 21–30 | 31–40 | 41–50 | 51+ |
|---|---|---|---|---|
| 6.3% | 13.9% | 25.3% | 37.3% | 17.1% |

**8. How many working days are you able to take each year as paid holiday, excluding public holidays?**

| 0 | 1–10 | 11–20 | 21–30 | 30+ |
|---|---|---|---|---|
| 5.7% | 7.6% | 29.9% | 49.7% | 7.0% |

**9. Which of these types of decision-makers do you have contact with in your professional ecological/environmental capacity? Please also estimate the number of contacts per year next to any boxes you have ticked.**

| | | | |
|---|---|---|---|
| International organisation or foreign gov't | level | 33.1% | 459 |
| UK government: | ministerial level | 16.9% | 126 |
| | senior civil servant level | 50.0% | 726 |
| | member of parliament level | 31.9% | 191 |
| Local government: | chief executive level | 38.1% | 332 |
| | section or district head level | 71.3% | 2578 |
| | project or other co-ordinator level | 72.5% | 4613 |
| Large landowners: | private | 74.4% | 2259 |
| | institutional | 66.9% | 1176 |
| | other | 31.3% | 1284 |

## Section B: Your career development to date

**10. Which of these academic qualifications do you have in subjects relevant to ecology and environmental management?**

| | |
|---|---|
| First degree | 85.6% |
| Masters degree | 39.4% |
| Doctorate | 34.4% |
| Institute exams | 8.1% |
| Other | 11.9% |

**11. Which age bracket are you in?**

| 18–24 | 25–34 | 35–44 | 45–54 | 55+ |
|---|---|---|---|---|
| 3.1% | 41.2% | 39.4% | 11.9% | 4.4% |

**12. In your past and present ecological/environmental work, where have you mainly operated?**

| | |
|---|---|
| Locally | 13.1% |
| Regionally | 27.5% |
| Nationally | 25.6% |
| Internationally | 16.3% |
| A mixture of these | 17.5% |

Home bases:

| | |
|---|---|
| Channel Islands | 0.0% |
| Europe | 2.5% |
| Rest of the world | 1.2% |

Map regional values: 0.6%, 1.9%, 4.4%, 10.6%, 5.0%, 0.0%, 8.7%, 10.0%, 9.4%, 5.0%, 23.1%, 13.1%

**13.** To what extent has each of the following assisted your career?

Voluntary involvement with environmental charities etc.
| | | |
|---|---|---|
| Not at all | 1 | 21.7% |
| | 2 | 20.4% |
| | 3 | 19.1% |
| | 4 | 16.6% |
| A great deal | 5 | 22.3% |

Government training or retraining schemes
| | | |
|---|---|---|
| Not at all | 1 | 71.2% |
| | 2 | 4.8% |
| | 3 | 6.2% |
| | 4 | 10.3% |
| A great deal | 5 | 7.5% |

Professional in-service training
| | | |
|---|---|---|
| Not at all | 1 | 32.2% |
| | 2 | 23.7% |
| | 3 | 21.1% |
| | 4 | 15.1% |
| A great deal | 5 | 7.9% |

Please draw a flow chart outlining your career to date, showing the number of years in each position in brackets as in the example below. Please be sure to show any past or present part-time ecological/environmental work.

Sample career flow chart

Starting point: MSc qualification (age 22)

Assistant Scientific Officer, Welsh Water Authority (Identifying biological specimens) (3)

Temporary summer warden, county wildlife trust (0.5)

Unemployed (0.5)

Habitat surveyor (county wildlife trust, government training scheme) (1)

Field officer (country wildlife trust) (3)

Countryside officer, local authority (1–current)

| Number of jobs | Age bracket 1 | 2 | 3 | 4 | 5 |
|---|---|---|---|---|---|
| 1 | | 2 | 4 | 4 | 1 |
| 2 | 1 | 10 | 6 | 4 | 1 |
| 3 | | 19 | 16 | 8 | 1 |
| 4 | | 17 | 14 | 3 | |
| 5 | | 10 | 7 | 2 | |
| 6 | | 6 | 8 | 1 | 1 |
| 7+ | | 2 | 8 | 1 | 3 |

## Section C: The future

**14.** Are your career prospects limited by any of the following circumstances?
| | |
|---|---|
| None | 44.4% |
| Disability | 1.9% |
| Spouse's job | 15.6% |
| Children | 15.6% |
| Unwillingness to move | 26.3% |
| Other (please specify) | 15.0% |

**15.** How do you perceive your status as an ecologist/environmental manager in relation to that of other professionals?
| | Low 1 | 2 | 3 | 4 | 5 High |
|---|---|---|---|---|---|
| Now | 11.6% | 37.4% | 31.6% | 12.3% | 7.1% |
| In future decades of your career | 2.1% | 4.8% | 33.6% | 34.2% | 25.3% |

**16.** At the end of your career do you think you will still be working in ecology/environmental management?
| | | |
|---|---|---|
| Very unlikely | 1 | 0.0% |
| | 2 | 1.3% |
| | 3 | 12.6% |
| | 4 | 23.3% |
| Very likely | 5 | 62.9% |

Ambitions:
| | |
|---|---|
| Self-employed consultants | 19% |
| Senior management/Directors/Board members | 19% |
| Same as at present | 11% |
| International activities | 5% |
| Early retirement | 3% |
| Writers | 3% |
| Teachers | 2% |
| Fieldworkers | 1% |

Salary expectation: >£35k 1 £30k 9 £25k 6 <£25k 1

**17.** Do you think there are major limitations in the current career structure for ecologists/environmental managers compared with those in other professions such as landscape architecture or engineering?
| | | |
|---|---|---|
| Definitely no | 1 | 3.2% |
| | 2 | 11.0% |
| | 3 | 19.5% |
| | 4 | 33.1% |
| Definitely yes | 5 | 33.1% |

Limitations:
| | |
|---|---|
| Cheap image | 19% |
| No recognised acad./prof. career structure | 16% |
| Top grades managerial only | 15% |
| No chartered status | 11% |
| Bad public image ecology/ists | 9% |
| Employed singly, temporarily | 6% |
| Lack of opportunity | 6% |
| Too willing to volunteer | 5% |
| No unique limitations | 4% |
| No acceptance of skill level | 3% |

**18.** Which of these would you wish to see IEEM addressing as priorities? Number as many as you feel appropriate in order of importance
| | | |
|---|---|---|
| Career structure development | 2.87 | 66.2% |
| Circulation of news about ecological/environmental issues | 3.49 | 64.4% |
| Circulation of news about legal/political issues | 4.28 | 60.0% |
| Circulation of news about methodologies | 3.59 | 63.7% |
| Circulation of news about funding/awards/fees | 4.99 | 51.2% |
| Organising conferences/training programmes | 3.93 | 69.4% |
| Professional endorsement of courses and in-service training | 3.48 | 73.1% |
| Influence the content of academic courses | 4.58 | 58.7% |
| Professional endorsement of methodologies/practices | 3.37 | 64.4% |
| Creation of special interest groups by employment sector | 5.87 | 35.6% |
| Creation of special interest groups by region | 6.69 | 36.9% |

Suggested actions:
| | |
|---|---|
| Increase recognition by employers and public | 28% |
| Enforce code of conduct, demonstrate competence | 20% |
| Institute chartered status, professional exams | 17% |
| Endorse training routes | 11% |
| Create links with other professions | 9% |
| Increase political recognition | 9% |
| Increase publicity, react publically, discuss issues | 9% |
| Promote services of IEEM members, publish fees | 6% |
| Increase membership of IEEM | 4% |
| Sectionalise IEEM | 2% |

*Figure 20.1* Results of the IEEM career route questionnaire

they are solo operators; 67 per cent had total financial responsibility; 57 per cent undertook all organisational development; 50 per cent recruited all staff. Private consultants also worked longer hours than average, with 33 per cent working more than 51 hours as compared with 17 per cent for all respondents combined. The modal class for private consultants' holidays was 11–20 days. Other categories of employment were not separately analysed but some individual variation was obviously due to seniority/age.

## Contacts

Many respondents had contacts with more than one of the types of decision-makers listed. Not shown is the total, 778 contacts irrespective of frequency, made by the respondents with decision-makers. The second figure is the total frequency of contacts at each level. As not all respondents gave frequencies, the total is an underestimate, but is still 13,744! The most frequent contacts were with local government project officer level decision-makers.

Question 9 and its answers are difficult to report on yet the information derived was significant. Widely differing answers were received, possibly due to respondents' interpretations of what was requested, but the total number of contacts, however calculated, remains impressive. This must be a foundation from which to remedy the problem of image and recognition.

## Qualifications

Many respondents had more than one recognised qualification. The majority who possessed a Masters degree and/or a doctorate also had a relevant ecological/environmental first degree.

Qualifications of IEEM members are the province of the Membership Affairs Committee and many respondents expressed the need for stringency in the qualifications accepted for membership in question 18. When comparing the answers to question 10 with the flowcharts in question 13 it is striking how many respondents with a higher degree, especially at Masters level, did not undertake it immediately after their first degree. This may be due to funding considerations or to an interest or need for qualification developed during the intervening periods of work, or unemployment. Whatever the reason it is a feature of career structures at present and may be an integral part of the recognised professional progression that many respondents mentioned under questions 17 and 18. A period of work abroad was also a common feature in the career flowcharts. Government schemes to combat unemployment and voluntary work did figure in a few careers but not as many as the author expected.

## Age

The distribution is somewhat skewed towards the younger age ranges. When the careers of the different age groups were compared, the stable careers of the over 45s contrasted with the hectic lives of the younger majority. The older age groups are not well represented in IEEM yet anyway, and membership drives suggested in question 18 could perhaps be aimed at these bastions of experience.

## Region

More respondents worked nationally or regionally than purely locally, or on an international scale, but all scales were well represented.

## Career

Voluntary work figured highly in some careers but not at all in as many others. The overall distribution of responses was fairly uniform.

UK government training schemes were of no importance in the careers of the majority but the distribution was decidedly bimodal with a significant minority of respondents owing a great deal to them.

In-service training was considered on average as not having contributed a great deal to career development. Comments implied that it should have had positive benefits but it either did not or was not available.

The flowcharts were interesting but not easy to analyse. In order to derive some meaningful information from them, the number of ecological/environmental jobs of at least 6 months' duration was taken into consideration, and cross-referenced to the age of the respondent. Periods of unemployment and higher education were not counted, but periods of voluntary work were, if this was the sole occupation of the respondent. The resulting matrix implies that younger respondents seem to have had relatively more jobs in their shorter working lives than older ones (see also question 11).

## Circumstances

Some respondents had more than one factor affecting them. The percentages are therefore not additive.

## Status

Respondents tended to view their current status as low to medium with respect to other professionals. However the future is expected to bring higher status, as responses were then centred above the median class. Fourteen non-serious replies were ignored in the latter percentage calculation!

## Future

Most respondents were fairly sure that they would still be working in ecology/environmental management at the end of their careers. Those dissatisfied that their salary reflected their level of responsibility were just as likely to think they would end their career in ecology/environmental management as satisfied respondents.

When asked to speculate about the future, self-employed consultancy was the most popular, followed by senior management or board membership in some organisation. The third most frequent ambition was to remain in the same position as at present. International roles attracted some respondents as did early retirement, teaching and writing. A return to fieldwork was the expressed dream of a few.

In the future an encouraging picture of committed IEEM members pursuing their chosen work with increasing status (if not salary) emerged. Ambitions were perhaps rather more modest than expected but this is perhaps due to realism or, indeed, to modesty.

## Limitations

The distribution of responses is skewed towards belief in the existence of major limitations in current career structure. The most frequent theme was the lack of value ascribed to ecological/environmental work by people in general. This was closely followed by an associated concern with the lack of a recognised academic and/or professional progression for ecologists and environmental managers. Third, there was recognition that most senior positions in organisations were managerial or administrative in nature and not usually open to ecologists/environmental managers. The lack of chartered status, and the generally poor public image of the profession, was of almost equal concern. Of slightly less concern was the lack of opportunities, and the willingness of ecologists to work voluntarily, and for short contracts usually in the fieldwork season, and working in isolation. A few respondents felt that the limitations were not significant or not unique to the profession.

## Action

The combined percentage of all respondents who considered that the professional institute, i.e. the IEEM, should take some positive action is shown by each item in the list.

Suggestions of actions to improve the standing of the profession and IEEM members were categorised. The most frequent response was to increase recognition by the public, and by employers in particular, of IEEM and the professional status and work of its members. There followed a large number of statements that IEEM should enforce its code of conduct and demonstrate the competence of its members. The desirability of chartered status and professional exams also featured in many lists. Connected with this and almost as frequent was the suggestion that training routes should be endorsed by IEEM. Next in importance came links with other professions, recognition of IEEM and its concerns by government and in political terms, and the role of IEEM in publicising and reacting to ecological and environmental issues and events through relevant fora. Several respondents also commented on the need to avoid introversion and jargon, etc., among the membership. Some thought that IEEM had a function in promoting the services of its members and in publishing scales of fees. A few stated they wanted to increase IEEM membership *per se* as a priority.

The key role of IEEM in improving the image of ecologists/environmental managers was highlighted in answers to questions 17 and 18, although few people suggested how. Chartered status, enforcement of a code and visible competence were forcefully supported and are straightforward aims for IEEM to pursue. Career structure and development and specific training programmes were perceived as being in urgent need of definition but few detailed criteria were proposed. It was similarly not very clear whether respondents were unwilling, unable or debarred from taking top management positions in organisations because they were ecologists/environmental managers, or what could or should be done about it. Some warned against IEEM becoming too exclusive and others against individuals being too willing to work for a pittance (unlike other professions), for the sake of the environment. It must be decided where, between these, IEEM's route lies. Answers to the two final questions make it clear what respondents want in general, and where their priorities lie. However, a worrying impression was communicated that, by its very existence, IEEM would be able to diagnose and treat all the ills of the profession, while its members happily continue to work as they do at present.

## EDUCATION AND TRAINING FOR CAREERS IN THE ENVIRONMENT

There are currently dozens of university and college courses in the UK specifically tailored to environmental management careers (see Table 20.1). Many of these will be validated as suitable qualifications for membership of IEEM.

Seale-Hayne College, now a Faculty of the University of Plymouth, was one of the first to recognise the demand for such courses. The contents of this section of this chapter are based on experiences at Seale-Hayne, which has offered a Diploma course in Rural Resource Management (RRM) for over twenty years. This was initiated alongside the traditional agricultural courses for which Seale-Hayne was best known, and included some relevant topics from the agricultural curriculum. Recruitment of students and subsequent employ-

*Table 20.1* Numbers of courses in the UK in agricultural and environmental subjects (extracted from the Universities and Colleges Admissions Service (UCAS) *Handbook*, 1994)

|  | BA/BSc | HND |
|---|---|---|
| Agriculture | 14 | 9 |
| Agriculture and Countryside Management | 1 | |
| Agriculture and the Environment | 3 | |
| Environmental Biology | 29 | |
| Countryside Management | 8 | 2 |
| Countryside Planning | 1 | |
| Countryside Recreation | 2 | |
| Conservation of Habitat | 1 | |
| Ecology | 21 | |
| Environmental Economics | 1 | |
| Environmental Science/Studies etc. | 70 | 7 |
| Environmental Analysis | 1 | 1 |
| Environmental Management | 32 | 3 |
| Environmental Monitoring | 4 | 4 |
| Environmental Planning | | 1 |
| Environmental Policy | 4 | |
| Environmental Pollution | 3 | |
| Environmental Protection | 9 | 2 |
| Environmental Quality | 1 | |
| Environmental Resources | 4 | |
| Natural Resources | 4 | |
| Rural Environment | 3 | |
| Rural Resource Management/Development | 9 | 3 |
| Rural Tourism Management | | 1 |
| Wildlife Conservation/Management | 2 | |

ment opportunities have been very satisfactory during the last two decades, despite the emergence of many other similar courses at other institutions. In 1988, a four-year modular BSc course in Rural Resource Management was validated at Seale-Hayne. The modules are shown in Figure 20.2. Later BSc courses in Agriculture and Countryside Management and Rural Estate Management, which incorporate some of the BSc RRM modules, were added. All the Higher National Diploma and Degree courses at Seale-Hayne include an industrial placement of one year. Our experience leads to the following observations on the recruitment, training and employment of people aspiring to careers in the environment.

Applications to RRM courses have increased substantially in recent years. In the mid-1980s, about 30 students a year were recruited to the HND. Currently about 120 students are accepted for the RRM courses annually. Applicants tend to have rather vague aspirations to careers although they generally want a component of outdoor work. If asked to name potential employers, they suggest the National Parks, Nature Reserves, and organisations such as the National Trust,

| S | Stage 1 | | Stage 2 | | Stage 3 | |
|---|---|---|---|---|---|---|
| 1 | **BMS 131**<br><br>Introductory Economics | **BMS 141**<br><br>Political Economy of Food and Rural Resources | **SHF 230**<br><br>Quantitative Methods | **BMS 231**<br><br>Financial Management 2 | **BMS 361**<br><br>Business and Organisation Strategy | **BMS 341**<br><br>Rural Policy Analysis |
| 1 | **RRM 131**<br><br>The Rural Environment: a Physical Perspective | **RRM 141**<br><br>The Components of Change in the Countryside | **RRM 231**<br><br>Landscape History and Protection | **RRM 241**<br><br>Landscape Design and Maintenance | **RRM 331 or RRM 371**<br><br>Diversification and Integrated Land Use **or** Development of Rural UK Economy | **RRM 341 or RRM 361**<br><br>Tourism and the Environment **or** Relations with Nature |
| 1 | **AGR 131**<br><br>Animal Production from Agriculture | **AGR 141**<br><br>Crop Production from Agriculture | **RRM 251**<br><br>Recreation Management | **RRM 261**<br><br>Principles of Woodland and Forestry | **RRM 351**<br><br>Rural Planning | **SHF 341**<br><br>Honours Project A |
| 2 | **BMS 132**<br><br>Financial Management 1 | **SHF 130**<br><br>Information Technology | **BMS 230**<br><br>Human Resource Management | **BMS 242**<br><br>Marketing | **BMS 332**<br><br>Integrating Case Studies (Double Module) | |
| 2 | **RRM 132**<br><br>Biological Basis of the Countryside | **RRM 142**<br><br>Evaluating Change in the Countryside | **RRM 232**<br><br>Tourism and its Management | **RRM 242**<br><br>Habitat and Management | **RRM 332 or RRM 362**<br><br>Pollution in the Rural Environment **or** Representations of Rurality | **RRM 342**<br><br>Applied Woodland and Forestry |
| 2 | **AGR 132**<br><br>Agricultural Technology | **AGR 152**<br><br>Rural and Environmental Engineering | **RRM 252**<br><br>Countryside Leisure | **RRM 262**<br><br>Quantitative Methods in Rural Resource Management | **RRM 352 or RRM 372**<br><br>Planning Problem Environments **or** Environmental Monitoring Techniques | **SHF 332**<br><br>Honours Project B |

*Figure 20.2* BSc Rural Resource Management
*Note*: S = Semester

the Farming and Wildlife Advisory Group, and the Water Authorities. They are not in search of high salaries or material gains, or of a general or academic education. They tend to be philosophically green and idealistic, with little sympathy for mainstream agriculture or the food industry. The 'A' level grades of school leaver entrants (age 18) tend to be mediocre with geography the most common subject studied. Up to 25 per cent of those admitted are mature (over 23), with many in their thirties and forties. The latter seek a career change, and/or formal qualifications to enhance their standing in environmental circles. Many applicants have had substantial relevant work and life experiences, and some have previously had academic failures and/or financial and personal problems. Student groups are therefore generally hard-working, lacking in arrogance and able to discuss and argue issues right from the beginning of the courses.

As can be seen from Figure 20.2, the curriculum of BSc RRM is wide ranging. In Britain most land-use decisions involve liaison between many interested parties, both private and public sector, as well as economic and aesthetic considerations. Therefore the courses aim to make students conversant with all relevant rural issues, as generalists rather than specialists. One third of the timetable is Business Management throughout the BSc courses, with a similar proportion on the HND courses. This ensures that graduates and diplomates are pragmatic about financial, economic, legal and marketing aspects of rural enterprises. The rest of the curriculum comprises modules about land use, such as agriculture, forestry, habitat management, tourism and recreation, as well as related considerations such as landscape, planning control and rural sociology. Methods of delivery and assessment of the courses are deliberately varied, with some traditional lecturing and examinations but also with a wide range of group work, oral presentations, practical sessions, seminars, etc.

Students' general learning and presentational skills are thereby developed and high standards of competence are usually achieved, with the emphasis on versatility and professionalism. A special feature is frequent exposure to practising environmentalists and rural entrepreneurs by means of student visits and visiting speakers. Students are also encouraged to undertake voluntary work, perhaps with a local wildlife trust or youth group, and to obtain training, experience and certification in craft skills such as chain-saw use or first aid, relevant to their future careers or placements. The industrial placement is a key feature of the training programme. In the final year, students have some choice of modules as most have developed particular interests by then, for example in visitor management or the scientific side of habitat management. The Honours Project for BSc students or Special Study for HND students is a further opportunity to develop their individual interests and research skills, as well as producing a document to show potential employers.

Students completing these courses will possess a recognised qualification, recent relevant experience through their placement, and a general capability and self-knowledge. Careers guidance is provided before and after graduation

*Table 20.2* List of current destinations of former RRM students

| | |
|---|---|
| Access Ranger | Freelance Interpretative |
| Acting Director | Artist/Agricultural Contractor |
| Administrative Officer | Furniture Maker |
| Area Park Ranger | Geotechnical Engineer |
| Assistant Conservation Officer | Grain Sampler/Fertiliser and Seed |
| Assistant Countryside Ranger | Salesman |
| Assistant Holiday Co-ordinator | Head Ranger, Forest Enterprises |
| Assistant Land Agent | Herdswoman |
| Assistant Ranger | Horticultural Worker |
| Assistant Scientific Officer | Information Officer x 2 |
| Catchment Planner, NRA | Instructor, Rural Training Centre |
| Chartered Surveyor | Landscape Gardener |
| Community Link Manager | Landscape Gardener and Wildlife |
| Community Woodlands Officer | Consultant |
| Countryside Grants Co-ordination | Musician/Gardener |
| Countryside Management and Teaching | National Park Ranger |
| Countryside Ranger | Nursery Sales Manager |
| Countryside Technician | Parks Ranger |
| Countryside Warden | Partner in Dairy Firm |
| Drainage Engineer | Pig Farmer |
| Education/Recreation Ranger | Project Assistant |
| Environmental Protection Officer | Project Officer |
| Environmentalist | Quarry Operative |
| Executive Field Officer | Radiographer |
| Farm Manager | Recreation/Education Ranger |
| Farmer | Returns Manager, Bookseller |
| Farms Assistant | Rural Practice Surveyor |
| Field Officer, MAFF | Scientific Officer |
| Field Worker | Self-Employed |
| First Officer Boeing 757 | Senior Ranger |
| Foreman, Orchid Grower | Site Engineer |
| Forest Ranger | Staff Nurse |
| Forestry/Woodland Consultant | Student Teacher |
| | Visitor Services Officer |

informally by lecturers and through the library where a collection of careers information is maintained. As with many employment sectors, probably the most significant source of careers information is through informal networks. A recent survey of ex-Seale-Hayne RRM students showed over 60 per cent have found jobs appropriate to their RRM training. A list of their job titles appears in Table 20.2. A number of ex-students have had seasonal and voluntary posts for a year or so, often continuing and improving their relationship with their original placement employer. In this very competitive field, it is important to be known and to have a good reputation, in addition to qualifications and experience. This also applies to those who opt for self-employment. Twenty per cent are employed in non-RRM capacities and 10 per cent are studying for further qualifications, usually increasing their specialisation, for example in forestry or planning. The remainder are unknown.

## CONCLUSION

This chapter describes two related aspects of the environmental career situation in Britain. More specialised careers in, for example, pollution control or leisure management are covered in other Higher Education courses and by other institutes. In this chapter an account of the formation and membership of a new institute is juxtaposed with the history of successful diversification of an agricultural college into environmental courses. This illustrates British infrastructural responses to increasing environmental concern and awareness. It is tempting to speculate about the environmental careers situation in ten or twenty years' time. Probably the recent large expansion in environmental jobs and courses will have slowed. This may be due to economic pressures or to genuine saturation coverage of perceived environmental problems.

Hopefully the IEEM will be a thriving and influential professional body with a large membership of well-qualified, reputable and gainfully employed ecologists and environmental managers. Ecologists and environmental managers should have, by then, surmounted the barrier currently preventing them achieving senior management status in both public and private sectors. The numbers of contacts they already have with decision-makers should ensure their increasing influence. However, dissatisfactions with status and salary, and the predominance of small operators, could continue. Younger IEEM members may well come directly from higher education courses such as BSc RRM, better equipped on graduation to resolve conflicts of interest about land use than was possible for their predecessors. Their careers could be less fragmented and with a more contiguous sequence of promotions and career developments. However, the production of graduates in this whole field may outstrip demand. In this case a qualification in an environmental subject should be seen by students and employers alike as a good general preparation for a range of employment or further specialisation. Many other degrees are viewed mainly as evidence of ability and persistence. The added bonus is that a knowledge of environmental matters is germane to almost every job or station in life.

# 21

# DEVELOPING THE SKILLS FOR ENVIRONMENTAL PROFESSIONALS IN EUROPE

*Sue Everett*

The Institute of Ecology and Environmental Management (IEEM) is a relatively new organisation. It covers a specialist employment area and has members working in a range of sectors, with local authorities, consultancies, NGOs, government, academic institutes and industry being most highly represented. The Institute is primarily concerned with ecology and its applications – working with plant and animal species, wildlife habitats and biodiversity – but broadens out into many other aspects of environmental management.

The Institute aims to raise the profile of the profession to establish, maintain and enhance professional standards, and to promote an ethic of environmental care within the profession and among clients and employers. The Institute was established to raise and maintain standards of professional practice. The major rationale for the establishment of the Institute was that there are many people purporting to practise in this area and there is no regulation of it.

To meet the Institute's overall aims, appropriate training programmes for members have been developed and advice for those wishing to enter the profession is given.

The development of the appropriate skills for environmental professionals requires education and training to build the basic knowledge needed to practise. The acquisition of competence to apply that knowledge (i.e. appropriate skills) is also an essential part of the training required by environmental professionals. Education and training fall into several categories.

Fundamental knowledge is gained at school and at institutes of further and higher education. This starts at an early age but, in terms of professional skills, the basis of this begins between fourteen and eighteen years. Essentially this is a basic understanding of the principles of biology and ecology coupled with general knowledge. Although the emphasis is on developing fundamental knowledge, it is interesting to note that in the UK now even children at school are learning about environmental management techniques.

Institutes of further and higher education (for those over eighteen) offer further development of basic knowledge and also develop some skills, both technical and non-technical.

After this, those in professional practice will be acquiring skills and perhaps also acquiring further fundamental knowledge from a variety of sources, but this development is primarily of workplace and applied skills. In the UK this is called continuing professional development or CPD.

The environmental skill base in Europe is very diverse, with many specialist sectors. There is ecology, waste and energy management, environmental health, soil science, environmental education, environmental management systems, working with industry and so on. This skill base has not yet been fully mapped out, but some professional bodies are now doing this for their areas of expertise, initially at a national level.

Part of the problem is that the environment profession is a relatively young profession, that it is still developing. People outside the profession tend not to know what it does; even parts of the profession itself do not really understand what other areas of the profession are doing. This issue needs to be addressed. In most EU Member States, because elements of the environment profession are not properly established, they are not recognised by other professions; this makes the work of the Institute of Ecology and Environmental Management quite difficult. The IEEM has a confidence building exercise to do and this will affect the development of environmental work in general. If the professions do not exist, how can skills in the necessary specialist areas be developed? Who will drive the training? Training providers and training provision are as diverse as the profession itself. There is formal academic training, full-time, part-time, residential, short course, vocational training, and open and distance learning, etc.

There are short courses, including professional courses and those run by consultancies – essentially to make money. Are they any good? At the other end of the spectrum there are informal workshops which are led by professionals for fellow professionals and interested outsiders. This kind of training is very useful and relevant. It is also cheap. Perhaps we should encourage more of it. The training availability and provision tends to reflect demands from the workplace and the take-up depends on the cost and resources held by those seeking training.

Provision also reflects government policy as this largely controls the amount of money that is made available and regulation: for example the European Eco-Management and Audit Scheme (EMAS) has recently been introduced. Training in these areas did not exist a few years ago, but is now much more widely available in the UK. However, development of skills often requires fairly intensive training and job experience. This can be difficult to attain, particularly for those who are unemployed and seeking to embark on an environmental career; even for those in professional work this presents a problem.

One question we must ask is how environmental skills should be developed across Europe. Ideally we should seek first to map out what the environment profession does, then identify the needs and the skills gaps. This Institute has recently embarked on such an exercise for its specialist area. We have mapped out the fundamental knowledge and skill base held (or desired by) ecologists and environmental managers. This has also been used as a basis for a project to develop a scheme of mutual recognition of ecologists and environmental managers across Europe (together with the Association Française des Ingénieurs Ecologues (AFIE)). Among the fundamental knowledge IEEM members should have are the two key topics of the principles of biodiversity conservation and the principles of sustainable development. This profession may well be unique in defining these as the key areas underpinning its profession.

The IEEM has itemised areas of work, skills and fundamental knowledge which IEEM members possess. The rationale behind this is to provide guidance to both training providers and individuals considering a career in ecology and ecological management. By providing this kind of guidance the IEEM is trying to encourage training providers to include the appropriate skills that are needed to meet the demands of the profession, particularly from government regulation, Local Agenda 21 and the biodiversity convention, etc.

This approach can be mirrored by other specialist sectors so that a much larger menu of knowledge and skills is then held by the environment profession as a whole. One of the problems with the profession currently, and with the environment not being resourced sufficiently, is that those who are not involved in it still do not realise what it is and what it means. The IEEM's menu approach is in need of constant review and revision. The need for specific skills continually changes so that such a document needs to be regularly updated. This system of menus should also help Member States to develop in professional areas that are not currently well developed. It could assist them in identifying major skills gaps. This may also help to direct support from the EC and other institutions to areas where there are deficiencies or underdeveloped skills.

Encouragement should be given to the establishment of organisations and institutes for the environment profession in Member States, for such institutions can help to promote training and develop standards of good professional practice. We are seeing this increasingly now in the UK with the establishment of bodies to accredit individuals who carry out environmental management and eco-audit work.

With respect to resources for training, there is a range of initiatives to promote environmental training through many different institutions. There is the Know How Fund in the UK which helps to fund training for former Eastern Bloc countries. There are funds from the European Commission, the European Bank, the World Bank, the Global Environment Facility and so on. As has been mentioned, this area is very diverse.

# REFERENCES

IEEM (1995) *Proposals for a Mutual Recognition Scheme for Ecologists and Environmental Managers in Europe*, IEEM, UK.

IEEM (1995) Annex A, IEEM, UK.

IEEM (1995) *The Profession of Ecology and Ecological Management: What You Need To Know 3*, IEEM, UK.

# 22

# SKILLS FOR ENVIRONMENTAL PROFESSIONALS

## Towards a European framework

*Martin Cahn*

At present environmental professionals in each country are recognised (or not recognised) by their own regulatory system. The European Federation of Environmental Professionals (EFEP) was established in 1988 and one of its prime objectives is to harmonise these systems and to encourage the establishment of professional associations in those countries where environmental professionals are not organised.

The EC has promoted initiatives aimed at the reciprocal recognition of professions after 1992, and their Directive 89/48 makes it obligatory for 'regulated professions'. They have shown particular concern about the need for qualified staff to carry out environmental impact assessments under the EC Directive 85/337. However, environmental professionals are perhaps the most difficult of all the professional sectors to define; indeed, to be a good environmental professional means working in a multidisciplinary manner.

The Federation is composed of professional associations in nine European countries, together with a small number of individual members. It is a non-profit-making association registered in France under the Law of 1901. It has a Board of Management with two representatives from each country, and in its turn each country is establishing its own national committee of EFEP to bring together professional associations covering the environmental field. It has adopted a common code of ethics, and requires members of each professional association to have suitable tertiary level education and experience in their particular environmental field. However, like the EC itself, subsidiarity is a key principle in the organisation. The Federation does not pretend to take on the role of each national association or committee.

There is a wide variety of national cultures in the EFEP member associations. Table 22.1 gives an idea of the character of the associations in each country.

*Table 22.1* Types of member association of EFEP in different countries

| Country | Types of member association |
|---|---|
| Britain | Five national level professional associations defined by areas of professional expertise. Size from 100–8,000 members |
| France | One national level association of ecological professionals (approximately 600 members) and one small association linked to the graduates of a particular course |
| Finland (applicant) | One national association of environmental professionals |
| Germany | A federation of eight very small associations mainly regionally based* |
| Belgium | One small association linked to a particular course |
| Italy | Large national association for graduates in sciences of the natural environment |
| Spain | One large national association (biology graduates) with an environmental section |
| Switzerland | Large association of ecological professionals* |
| Portugal | One national association for graduates in environmental engineering |
| Luxembourg, Hungary, Poland | Effectively individual members |

*Note*: * These associations are mostly confined to consultants. There are also a couple of small associations restricted to local government (UK and Finland) and three others are dominated by this sector (UK, France and Belgium). All the other associations have professionals in several economic sectors

The diversity is evident – in particular the division between course-based, professional field-based and 'holistic' associations. Course-based associations may develop to become national ones as individual courses become more widespread. This has happened, for instance, with the eco-counsellor courses in Belgium and France and the geo-ecologists in Germany.

The size of member associations is very varied – from less than 100 members to over 8,000. They also have greatly differing financial resources – while the British Institute of Environmental Health Officers has about 40 paid staff, the majority of associations are small and run on a voluntary basis.

Environmental professionals can be defined in two broad categories:

1 Environmentalists dealing with the natural environment, its management and impacts upon it – the Ecology and Environmental Management school;
2 Environmentalists dealing with human impact on the environment and human health through the production of waste and pollution (including the majority of those working in industry).

Each of these fields can be further sub-divided according to the many specialities involved.

*Table 22.2* Some environmental professions recognised by the European Federation of Environmental Professionals

| | | |
|---|---|---|
| Ecologist | Environmental Planner | Ecological Land Manager |
| Geo-ecologist | Energy Policy Officer | Hydrologist |
| Environmental Auditor | Nature Reserve Manager | Environmental Co-ordinator |
| Pollution Control Officer | Waste Control Officer | Environmental Health |
| Soil Scientist | River Water Quality | Officer |
| Environmental | Officer | Environmental Publicist |
| Interpretation Specialist | Landscape Analyst | Environmental Impact |
| | | Specialist |

Initially a 'holistic' recognition scheme for all types of environmental professions was intended but it became evident that this would be impossible without considerable time and money. EFEP had neither of these resources in sufficient quantity but this would not have been an easy task even if it had. The diversity of expertise is too great.

Table 22.2 shows *some* examples of environmental professions which EFEP considers to be part of the range of professions in this area.

Further problems arise when trying to compare the professions between countries. Some professions only exist in certain administrative systems. For instance environmental health officers are a British and Irish phenomena – although positions with the same general role are evident elsewhere, environmental health officers administer British or Irish environmental health legislation which has no exact parallel elsewhere; 'geo-ecologists' are confined to Germany – their function lies between soil scientists and ecologists; environmental engineers in Portugal have a wide range of responsibilities which could not, for example, fit easily in the highly sectoralised British or German systems; eco-counsellors exist in several European counties – they function well in local government systems organised in small communes (there is no exact equivalent in the UK where local authorities are larger and the nearest equivalent is an environmental co-ordinator); in Italy (like Spain and Portugal) degree qualifications follow nationally agreed syllabuses so professions are therefore very standardised, and generally follow very generalised titles, e.g. natural scientists, biologists, environmental scientists, etc. The jobs, however, are nowhere near so standardised!

To try and find a standardised scheme applicable to this varied profession, across Europe, EFEP first looked at establishing a reciprocal recognition scheme based on one professional field – ecological land management – where there is no existing scheme in place. EFEP would not intrude where perfectly adequate arrangements already existed. A simple draft scheme was prepared, but due to lack of resources no progress could be made to apply it.

EFEP sought funds from the EC so that they could play a more active role in gathering information and bringing associations together for a wider ranging scheme. However, the majority of the associations did not have sufficient resources to put to such projects as these associations are generally run on a voluntary basis.

In June 1994 the Commission's Task Force Human Resources, Education Training Youth (now DGXXII) issued a call for an incentive subsidy scheme to encourage projects for developing international mutual recognition of professions not yet regulated, and therefore not covered by the existing directive.

Previous attempts to develop a scheme at Bachelors degree level had foundered through lack of resources, and because of differing levels required for entry to the professional associations. Therefore EFEP considered the possibility of a mutual recognition scheme at postgraduate (Masters degree) level. The level at which different associations recognise their professions differs between countries – for instance the French association recognises at troisième cycle (degree plus two years), the British at Bachelors degree level. The proposal was to get round the problem of different standards by rounding them up rather than down. In effect not all members of some associations would be able to join: a selective register would be created which could be internationally recognised. This has some advantages – it is vital that environmental professionals are taken seriously in the marketplace if their advice is to be respected. Restrictive professional qualifications are one way of ensuring this.

A project was proposed which was largely determined by practical management considerations. EC funds were limited and only covered a maximum of 50 per cent of the costs and so the number of partners had to be limited. The British and French associations are the strongest associations in Europe specialising in the field of ecology and both these associations have a permanent staff. These two associations agreed to participate in a scheme to be co-ordinated by the Federation. The intention was to agree a standard between the two associations to which other European associations could adhere. EFEP would ensure that the scheme would be compatible with professions in other European countries.

It is essential with the current trend towards market-based solutions that well-qualified and recognised staff are employed for projects that will be carried out, in effect, by the polluter under the 'polluter pays' principle. Functions such as environmental assessments, eco-labelling, the bathing waters directive, etc., will generally be carried out by industry itself. However, experience shows that industry does not like employing environmental staff from outside, so the staff they train need to be appropriately qualified, or the consultancies they employ must use reliable, professionally trained staff. To achieve this there needs to be a standard by which to judge such professionals. The mutual recognition project offers a practical means to achieve this.

The project was subsequently overseen by the Institute of Ecology and Environmental Management (IEEM) and the Association Française des Ingénieurs Ecologues (AFIE).

The project was designed to set up common standards for a register of ecologists and environmental managers. To develop and establish common standards, it is necessary to know what skills ecologists and environmental managers need. The first phase of the project prepared a common framework of skills which the two associations used as a common basis for comparison. These skills depend largely on the tasks expected of ecologists in the market-place. The distribution of the members of the two associations among different economic sectors is similar but there are also a number of differences. For instance there is no real equivalent in France to, for example, English Nature – so the public sector professionals fulfil different functions (Conservation Foundation 1996).

Following this, a system needed to be agreed to assess applicants. This makes use of the skills framework agreed for assessing applicants from the multiplicity of environmental courses currently on offer throughout Member States. The extent of the problem can be gauged from the EC study guide to environmentally related courses. The proportion with ecology as a basis varies widely between Member States. It is approximately 40 per cent in Britain with between 10 and 15 per cent in engineering. In Germany it is less than 20 per cent in ecology, with over 40 per cent being engineering courses – often civil engineering. Clearly the definition of environmental courses is based on different cultural and ethical perspectives.

A key question is whether increased funding will produce an increased demand for environmentally qualified staff and, if it does, whether these will move between countries.

To demonstrate how far the recognition of the environment as a profession still has to go, it is worth mentioning that M. Jean Rabuel of the French company SITA at the EFEP conference on 'Environmental Employment in the Open Market' (held in 1990) complained that what he needed was better managers rather than specialist environmental professionals trained in univer-sities who invariably have no detailed knowledge of what was going on in

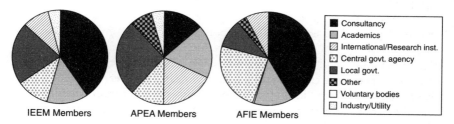

IEEM: Institute of Ecology and Environmental Management (1993)
APEA: Associação Portuguesa de Engenheiros do Ambiente (1990)
AFIE: Association Française des Ingénieurs Ecologues (1992)

*Figure 22.1* Membership of three associations belonging to the European Federation of Environmental Professionals: sector of activity

191

his particular company. He said give him a manager and he would give the person the environmental knowledge they needed. This troubleshooting approach to environmental management is the antithesis of integrated environmental control, and demonstrates that there is a long way to go before environmental professionals are fully integrated in the production process!

The exchange of environmental professionals is a vital element in resolving some of these conflicts. This is not just between industry and other sectors (although this is important), but there is a need to look at wider ranging schemes. EFEP ran an exchange between Britain and France in 1991. Other exchanges are in the pipeline, but these schemes take time and money – outside funding is vital if this is to be more commonplace.

In the long term environmental professionals should be encouraged to train in other European countries, to promote wider movement of professionals. Exchanges under schemes as mentioned, and under the former ERASMUS (now SOCRATES) schemes can include students studying subjects other than languages, business studies and literature for whom the need to travel is beneficial. Languages are vital to mobility, so it is important to encourage biologists, planners and pollution scientists to undertake exchanges as well.

## REFERENCES

AFIE (1992) Membership leaflet.

Carsignol, J. (1990) 'Le marché de l'emploi Cadre Environnement en France', in *Les Emplois-cadre environnement dans l'Europe du grand marché. Proceedings of the Avignon Forum*, EFEP, 21–2.

Conservation Foundation (1996) 'Careers', *Network 21*, No. 5, 20–31, Conservation Foundation, London.

Institute of Ecology and Environmental Management, Membership profile. *Ecology and Environmental Management in Practice*, 6, 9.

Rabuel, J. (1990) 'Les emplois liés à l'Environnement dans le secteur industriel, l'exemple de SITA', in *Les Emplois-cadre environnement dans l'Europe du grande marché. Proceedings of the Avignon Forum*, EFEP, 38–9.

# 23

# REACHING A COMMON LANGUAGE OF SKILLS, QUALIFICATIONS AND PROFESSIONAL DEVELOPMENT

*Martin Cahn*

The goal posed in the title of this chapter presupposes a desire to achieve a common understanding. European legislation on the open market and EC policy clearly looks to harmonising qualifications, but it was clear from the contributions of speakers at the conference 'Careers in the Environment across Europe' that this would not be an easy goal to achieve in practice.

The goal was examined by posing four basic questions:

1   Why do we want to reach a common language of skills?
2   Who are the environmental professionals?
3   How could a common language of skills be achieved if this goal is aimed at?
4   Who pays for the work involved in achieving commonality in the environment profession?

The vast bulk of the discussion centred on question 1.

## WHY DO WE WANT TO REACH A COMMON LANGUAGE OF SKILLS?

The European Federation of Environment Professionals (EFEP) project on mutual recognition has been completed although it is difficult to achieve a common language of skills. There are two possible reasons why movement of environmental professionals between countries should be encouraged and promoted. International movement is currently very limited – only 5 per cent of the total workforce overall in Member States, and less for environmental professionals. Town planners, a regulated profession within the environmental arena, have established an adaptation mechanism under the directive covering the mutual recognition of regulated professions, but there has been no demand to use this since it was established. There is no real evidence, therefore, of the objective of mutual recognition being market-led – the objectives for establishing it are more political.

However, there is a second motivation – the integrity of national standards is enhanced by placing them in a uniform European context. At the national level this will give those with a qualification recognised as a European standard an advantage in the marketplace.

A further justification is that even though the majority of students on international courses return to work in their country of origin, many, particularly those working in consultancy, may remain in the international arena on temporary assignments. An internationally recognised qualification could therefore be a distinct advantage.

The EFEP mutual recognition project was presented as a proposition to meet these limited goals in a specialist area. The EFEP proposals can be criticised as being too exclusive, while the entry route into environmental employment was often taken by people with no formal environmental training or with training that would not reach the standard required by the EFEP proposals. Proposals to classify the full range of environmental professions in one scheme foundered due to their complexity, but specialised schemes risk encouraging sectoralism and environmental professions are multidisciplinary.

There is a wide variety of courses labelled environmental (e.g. in the EU environmental courses guide) – from civil engineering with no real environmental component to specialised courses in ecology.

Qualification and recognition schemes are required for specialised areas such as ecology since in many instances, e.g. public inquiries, it was an advantage to have a system of professional credibility. However, it is more difficult for environmental specialists where different administrative and legal frameworks restrict cross-recognition. For example, courses for environmental health officers and eco-counsellors could never be interchangeable since they depend on particular administrative frameworks.

The motivation behind a common framework is varied. Should it be market-led – behind the demand for environmental jobs which, from current evidence, were simply not available in sufficient quantity? Or should the environmental professional be an advocate, leading public opinion? There is some concern over the latter point about mixing roles between advocacy and professional integrity. However, environmental professionals have always been involved in awareness raising.

In conclusion there is a need for common bases for skills and qualifications in specialist fields (e.g. ecology) as much to give status and certainty within the profession within each country as to promote international movement. These will initially have a technical content and be relatively sectorial.

As for environmental generalists, there is a need to harmonise skills in courses calling themselves environmental and these should be based upon a common core of skills centred on the human sciences. The environmental generalist can come into the profession from a wide variety of backgrounds but essentially must have the skills from the human sciences to complete the policy circle referred to by Bernard Giovannini (chapter 18).

## WHO ARE THE ENVIRONMENTAL PROFESSIONALS?

The EFEP project proposed four grades at which common skills should be recognised, including a non-graduate technical level.

There is a need to identify competencies for specialist fields through agreement between peers, i.e. the professionals themselves, in the form of their associations where such associations exist. For general environmental expertise, however, it is more a matter of ensuring that the training available is able to place diverse backgrounds into a common socio-political framework; this is a problem of harmonisation at the university level.

The translation of the NVQ-type competence-based qualifications into a pan-European standard is difficult since professional training varies so much between countries. The UK scheme is based on German practice but might not translate elsewhere. Work experience, including voluntary work experience, needs also to be recognised in such schemes.

## HOW COULD A COMMON LANGUAGE OF SKILLS BE ACHIEVED?

A dichotomy arises between general environmentalists, where exchanges between trainers can identify a common framework of skills and competencies to be addressed in training, and specialists, where such a language should normally be identified by the professionals themselves. In the first instance it is the educators who will need to act – it is not yet obvious how work experience can be assessed by professional bodies or whether it would help professionals. An initial way forward would be for several university courses from diverse European countries to act together to agree the common socio-political bases of knowledge for such courses.

For specialists, whose professions can be more clearly defined, progress is more likely to be made by agreement between professional associations such as that currently being developed by ecologists.

MARTIN CAHN

# WHO PAYS FOR THE WORK INVOLVED IN ACHIEVING COMMONALITY IN THE ENVIRONMENT PROFESSION?

The establishment of a common language of recognition by universities or trainers falls in the remit of the Socrates programme of DGXXII and this could be developed as part of a process of common curriculum development.

However, there is a major gap in the funding arrangements generally for professional associations. No clear European aid is given to them and they have considerable difficulty in running their operations, let alone carrying out inter-recognition projects. The EFEP mutual recognition project is funded by DGXXII as part of an experimental programme, this having a total budget of only 1 million Ecu. Other programmes such as Force and its successors are primarily industry-led and leave little opportunity for professional institutions to get involved. If progress is to be made on mutual recognition of skills and competencies, then this initial funding will need to be expanded to create a wider scheme and reinforce the professional institutions who will carry out these projects.

# INDEX

197